MEANWHILE

BACK AT THE

RANCH

By RAY FRANKS

Thanks for reading this far — Hope you enjoy — Ray Franks

PR
THE PUBLISHING RANCH
P.O. Box 7068, Amarillo, Texas 79114

I dedicate this book to my best friend, my wife, without whose encouragement it would never have been completed.

ACKNOWLEDGEMENTS

For a project of this scope, acknowledgements are endless. Especially helpful with early information were Kempton and Eloise Fieber, Loy Lee Brown, Don Long, Lou Spry, Mike Cleary and Warren Hasse.

Betty Tow was there when I needed a decision in grammar. My former secretary, Shaine LeGrand, went beyond the call of duty to handle the composition for this book and contributed in so many other ways. In addition to Floy, No. 1 proof-reader, encouragers were many. But none was more meaningful than a special friend, Ralph Gibson, when I needed it most.

No doubt key people have been overlooked. To them, I apologize and I'll send them a free book.

CONTENTS

FOREWORD

When Ray Franks asked me to write a foreword for his book, *Meanwhile, Back At The Ranch*, you could have knocked me over with a feather. I'm just hoping this literary effort will qualify me for a pullet-zer prize. The honor has left me egg-static.

I first crossed paths with Ray in 1978, only four years after I started roosting with the "rich and famous" in the sports world. It was on the sidelines of the first Holiday Bowl football game in my hometown of San Diego, California. Since then, I have used his *National Directory of College Athletics* constantly to help spread my wings in the field of collegiate sports.

Meanwhile, Back At The Ranch, the story of Ray's 50 years in sports, should be interesting to everyone in the field of athletics. During this time, Ray has been winging his way to exotic ports of call worldwide. His three chapters on sports escapades to Russia particularly intrigued me. After all, I was first hatched as the "KGB Chicken," KGB being the call letters of my sponsor radio station in San Diego. And my coat of feathers was red. Honest.

Ray's many writing and publishing contributions to sports puts him at the beak of his career. Just recently he was inducted into the Texas Panhandle Sports Hall of Fame. It is my dream to some day roost in Cooperstown, New York. At the Baseball Hall of Fame, there's a player's wing and a broadcaster's wing. So maybe one day, they'll have a chicken wing!

Best Wishbones,

The Famous San Diego Chicken
TED GIANNOULAS

WHY THIS BOOK?

A ranch in West Texas, one of the last vestiges of cowboy country, is no big deal. The largest and most famous—the XIT—spans three million acres and is encompassed by 6,000 miles of single-strand barbed wire, enough to stretch from New York to California and back.

But a "publishing ranch" is a different story. When I was searching for a name for a small maverick publishing company more than 30 years ago, I said to myself:

"A publishing house in the Southwest should be called a publishing ranch."

Considered hokey by some and a source of curiosity for many others, the name has endured. And so has the business, unique in many ways.

The "ranch" in Amarillo, Texas has been the spawning ground for several important publications and the launching pad for writing assignments to the far corners of the world.

Never in my wildest dream while growing up on a share-cropper farm in Southern Illinois did I think I would ever get to visit the Ginza in Tokyo, the beaches of Rio de Janeiro, the Arctic Circle of Finland, Australia's exciting cities or Red Square in Moscow. And most trips at little, or no expense, to me. Or rub elbows with such luminaries as Billy Conn, Alice Marble, Sam Snead, Sam Huff, Oral Roberts, James Michener, Jesse Owens, Kareem Abdul Jabbar, O.J. Simpson, Cyd Charisse, Newt Gingrich and Roy Rogers.

But this book is about more than 50 exciting years in sports. It's about growing up in the Great Depression, entrepreneurship, the Great American Dream and enjoying life to the limit.

Have I been blessed? You better believe it.

"Most people work all their life at a job they don't particularly enjoy," friend Bill Chandler remarked recently over a bowl of hot Italian soup. "I tell people all the time that you have made a profession out of two things you enjoy most in life, sports and journalism."

And he's so right. But I must confess, this project has been my most difficult challenge. I have started and stopped this book a dozen times, only to be encouraged to continue by my wife or a friend. Writing in the first person about one's experiences is much more gut-wrenching than reporting on others. And to keep it in the right perspective, leaving a legacy for our children, grandchildren and great-grandchildren, has been my goal.

The warts are there too. Two bouts with open-heart surgery are addressed, along with some bad business decisions. How can we recognize the good life without tasting adversity?

While I dabble a little in philosophy, don't get bogged down with sober thoughts. After all, how can you take seriously a book that has a foreword written by a chicken?

Ray Franks

1

LOST IN ZAGORSK . . . WITHOUT A RUBLE

Big snow flakes were falling in slow motion to the slush-covered brick pavement, much like oak leaves wafting to the ground in a West Texas autumn.

I turned first one way and then another. All I could see were strangers, odd-looking people wearing black rabbit fur hats and dishwater-gray babushkas. All of a sudden I felt completely alone in cold and dank Zagorsk, Russia, and I wouldn't see a familiar face for another eight hours.

It was March, 1992, and I had arrived in Moscow only the day previous. I was there to cover the first football game played in the former Soviet Union by an American college. If that event weren't exciting enough, we had landed in this mysterious country halfway around the world just six months after the fall of communism. In essence, we were being afforded front-row seats to one of the most important and most improbable peaceful revolutions in the history of mankind.

The exhibition had been arranged by International Sports Connection, a travel and marketing firm out of Gadsden, Alabama, with extensive contacts in Russia. A non-scholarship NCAA Division III school of 1,200, Western Maryland College was selected to make the long road trip to assist in still another step in the globalization of American-style football.

One of the last countries in Europe to embrace the wildly popular American sport, the Russians were countering with an all-star team that had been playing the game only three years. I had been asked to tag along and chronicle the history-making event for the *National Directory of College Athletics*.

Sunday was our first full day in Russia, and we weren't moving too swiftly. Little wonder. I left Amarillo, Texas, at 10:40 Friday morning, and didn't arrive in Moscow until 5 o'clock Saturday afternoon, spanning 7,000 miles and 10 time zones.

After devouring a breakfast of three fried eggs, toast, fresh fruit and apple juice, the 47 players and accompanying entourage boarded two buses for Zagorsk. I had never heard of the "Z" city and I doubt if many Americans have. It's the birthplace and home of the Russian Orthodox Church. Its big attraction is spectacular onion-dome mosques, those edifices of unusual beauty that are as synonymous with Russia as caviar and vodka.

Getting out of vast Moscow took about an hour. We passed dozens of massive skyscrapers with hundreds of spires and spikes, described by some as Lenin Gothic architecture. Most locals were sleeping in and travel was extremely light. Of course, few people in this impoverished land own cars so traffic is never a serious problem.

The 47-mile trek to Zagorsk required another hour, but it afforded us a rare look at the countryside. It was the first and only time we would see anything that resembled single-family dwellings, and most were shabby wooden shacks. Moscow is all apartments, very-crowded apartments.

In the last days of winter, the fields were crusted over with patches of old snow. The roads were in poor condition, pock-marked with numerous pot holes and ruts. We couldn't keep from noticing the many disabled cars alongside the highway, reflective of the general status of disrepair in a bankrupt land. We saw the same thing at Sheremetyevo Airport, Aeroflot planes missing an engine or tailpiece, or both.

Entering Zagorsk, it looked much like any other small provincial European city. Old buildings, brick-paved streets. Then we saw them. Nearing the walled complex of religious buildings, the beautiful onion-shaped domes stood out like sparkling lights on a Christmas tree. Some were painted dark blue accented with speckles of gold, but most were solid metallic gold that glistened brightly when spanked by an intense sun. We could hardly wait to get inside the huge walls that stood 30 feet high.

"Hey mister, wanta buy picture cards?" yelled a young Russian boy waving a handful of brochures as we stepped down from the bus. We were quickly surrounded by a dozen teenage boys and young men selling souvenir items of all varieties. Capitalism had hit the former Soviet Union in a big way, and I was surprised at the freedom of the new entrepreneurs. After all, communism had bit the dust only six months previous, and something like this was unthinkable when I last visited Russia in 1973.

It was our first taste of the new economic climate in a land that also had a new name, Confederation of Independent States. One teenage boy hustling picture cards stayed close to the big, burly footballers. He was wearing a red, white and blue stocking hat and a letter jacket that read "Georgetown". He, too, probably didn't know what a Hoya was.

After entering the huge arched gate, we encountered dozens of Russians strolling the courtyard, dressed in dark conservative coats and jackets. By contrast, though, the colorful, uniquely-shaped domes lit up the area like a religious Disneyland. First, we visited a monastery built in 1340. "Our country has been involved in many wars, rebellions and bloodshed," apprised our guide, "but not one time has this religious compound ever been touched."

Then we moved into a museum that contained priceless treasures of jeweled crowns, icons and the like. Our last stop before returning to the buses and heading for lunch was a small cathedral that was extremely crowded. And then we found out why. It was dark and quiet inside. We had to nudge, push and shove a little to see what was the big attraction. At the front of the room was a casket, and a long line of warmly-dressed Russians.

"That's Metropolitan Sergy, former patriarch of the Russian Orthodox Church," whispered our guide. "He died in 1944, but our people still idolize him."

These people were more than tourists. They were standing in line to take their turn at kissing the casket of their former leader, the Russian church's answer to the Pope. Then they would light a candle, the only illumination in an otherwise cold, dark room. For 75 years, since the takeover of communism, Russians had literally experienced religious starvation. Now, with a new spiritual freedom, they were drinking it in as fast as they could.

As we looked around the room, we saw elderly women kneeling at chairs and small pews. In a prayerful stance, they were chanting and singing softly in muffled tones, providing a pagan-like ritualistic background for a fallen religious hero. It was strange and eerie, causing me to pause and try to sort out what was really happening.

I stayed too long. After being mesmerized by the strange scene in front of me for about five minutes, I turned to leave. The small group of Americans I had been with was nowhere to be found. I rushed out the front door and scanned the courtyard. There was a maze of black, gray and brown, but still no familiar faces. After walking double time to the parking lot full of buses, I checked one at a time. Still a zero. I looked at my watch and it was 12:30, the appointed time to head out for a nearby restaurant. I couldn't understand it. What had happened? Where was my bus?

For the next three hours, I would get to know that parking lot like the lines on my face. All the time watching the bus area, hoping and praying one of the American vehicles would return, I checked out the vendors. For sale on their small folding tables were balalaikas (Russia's triangular-shaped guitar), fur hats, hand-painted pens, jewelry boxes and Snickers bars. Snickers bars?

I don't know how long the American candy treat has been available in the old Soviet Union, but somebody has done one heck of a selling job. Not only did the individual entrepreneurs on the streets have them, but we saw Snickers in stores alongside bottles of wine and vodka and tins of caviar. I picked up one and looked at the wrapper. Sure enough, it looked just like the ones I could buy in Amarillo, Texas.

An hour passed, and then two. I even started counting the times a colorful blue and white buggy circled the area. Pulled by an old gray mare, it was for hire, exchanging short rides around the block for rubles. Another sneaky capitalistic trick.

I had plenty of time to think. And then the thought crossed my mind that made me shiver from my head to my frost-bitten toes. I was in precisely the same situation we had been warned to avoid: "Alone in Russia."

By 3 o'clock, I was in a near state of panic. It started snowing harder and vendors began packing up their wares. As shadows lengthened over the parking lot, the last visitors headed toward their buses and cars. The entire area was becoming isolated, and I knew I was in really big trouble.

Then, another realization hit me like a sledge-hammer. I didn't have any Russian money on me, not a single ruble.

"No shops will be open on Sunday," our leaders had told us at a morning briefing, "so there's no need to exchange money until Monday. Besides that, we'll get our best deals at banks."

In other words, if I find a bus or train back to Moscow, I have no way of paying for it. Foreign money cannot be used legally except at hard-currency stores. Besides that, all information about our Moscow hotel, the Red Star, was in my camera bag, and yes, it was on the bus.

Like most tourists in this part of the world, I had no knowledge of the funny-looking Cyrilian alphabet and the very complex Russian language. However, as my luck had seemed to hit rock bottom, I remembered something. Earlier, as I kept passing this one vendor near the big arched gate, he would yell out at me in clear English:

"Hey, Mr. America, come buy my book." He had me tagged early, what with the Minolta camera around my neck and a confused look on my face. Fortunately, he was still there when I made a bee-line for his table.

"I'll buy that book you've been trying to sell me and give you a bonus if you can help me get back to Moscow," I told the middle-aged, bearded vendor wearing a full-length black coat and lambskin hat. "I'm lost!"

"Victor" immediately closed his table-top concession, accepted my offer and headed in the direction of the nearest train station.

"It's only a short walk," he said. But long ago I learned when a European tells you "it's only a short walk," it could wind up being several miles. We trudged through slush that was beginning to freeze, up one street and down another. I explained the details of my plight, and he told me a little about himself.

"I teach English in a technical school in Zagorsk," said Victor, who looked scholarly with his full face of hair and carefully-manicured goatee. "There is no class now, and I must sell books, or whatever, on the weekend just to survive. We are very poor here."

As we neared a long, Gothic-style stone building that resembled a train station, I noticed dozens of grim-looking, cigarette-smoking Russians standing around on the platform near the tracks. I made a quick exit to an unkempt restroom that must not have been cleaned since Lenin and his henchmen seized the country 75 years ago. The rank odor was indescribable.

When I returned, Victor had a worried look on his face. Glancing at the tell-tale camera hanging around my neck, he made an observation.

"I don't know if this is a good idea," he shook his head. "Crime is at an all-time high in Russia, and foreigners are easy targets for robbers. The economy is so bad that some people will rob and kill for small amounts of money."

Then he made an offer. "I tell you what," he continued, "spend the night with me in my apartment, and I'll drive you to Moscow tomorrow. Your hotel will be difficult to find, and it's too late to start today."

I glanced again in the direction of the group of drably-dressed Russians over by the tracks waiting for the next train. Was there even one among them who appeared to be trust-worthy? I remembered that these were the same people who were our mortal cold war enemies not long ago. A former leader, Nikita Kruschev, had even gone so far as to tell Richard Nixon: "I will bury your people."

It was a tough decision. His offer was tempting, and on the surface, it sounded like the safer route. But, I didn't know this guy from Yakov Smirnoff, and I was concerned American tour officials would be trying to locate me. While I felt I needed to get back to the hotel as quickly as possible, I knew I was treading on thin ice.

After my new Russian friend bought me a train ticket (remember, I have no rubles), he gave me another chance to change my mind. He posed a series of questions that seemed appropriate. And sobering.

"Where will you get off the train in Moscow? How will you communicate with the Russian cab drivers since most don't speak English? How will you find your hotel? And what will you do all night if you can't find your hotel? And besides that, you have no rubles."

All valid questions. Dusk was upon us and the international puzzle was getting more complicated. There didn't seem to be any easy answers. Just then, a man came by with a box full of balalaikas, and Victor's eyes lit up. He spoke with the passerby for a few moments in Russian, and then turned to me.

"My friend here, Dick, says he's taking this bus to Moscow," pointing to an olive drab vehicle only a few feet away. "He lives there and we both agree you have a better chance of getting back to your hotel safely by going with him."

I handed my train ticket back to Victor and Dick purchased a bus coupon for me. Still no rubles. As the bus started its engine, I gave Victor a hearty handshake, thanked him for his kindness and handed him my business card.

"You're a publisher?" he exclaimed with more than casual interest. As we pulled out of the lot, my new friend was still examining the card. It was the last time I would see Victor, but not the last time I would hear from him.

Already, I felt more comfortable on the bus with my second new Russian acquaintance than I would have on the train alone. As we made the hour-long trip to Moscow, Dick, who also was well schooled in English, began sharing his story. Clean-shaven, looking more Western than Victor and in his mid-30s, he related that he was a geologist just back from Siberia. His name "Dick" didn't sound typically Russian to me, like Vladimir, Yuri or Alexander. But he assured me it was the closest thing to the English equivalent.

"I live in Moscow with my wife and young daughter," he confided. "We would like to have more children, but it is too expensive. It's very difficult to provide for just the three of us. I have no job right now and that's why I sell balalaikas at Zagorsk on weekends. These are very difficult times for our people."

Like Victor, Dick had never heard of the Red Star Hotel. He doubted that Moscow taxi drivers had either. Just six months previous, it was called Ministry of Defense Hotel for Generals and had been used exclusively for the military. That name failed to ring a bell, also. He scratched his head and pondered what to do.

Traffic was getting heavier as we neared Moscow. Daylight was fast disappearing and a bleak day in strange, mysterious surroundings was looking even bleaker. As we entered the city limits, Dick signalled the driver to stop the bus. We hopped off and my second Russian compadre started looking for a cab.

"At one time, we could walk the streets of Moscow at midnight without fear of being bothered," he revealed. "But not anymore. With fewer police and military around, criminals operate more freely and people steal food and money in broad daylight. Some even believe the KGB is linked with organized crime, the Russian Mafia."

After getting into a cab, Dick barked instructions to the driver and then turned to me. "He knows nothing of your hotel, and it will be very difficult to locate," he reasoned. "Cab drivers can't be trusted either; I'm going to stay with you until we find it!" Then he gave me a pat of reassurance on the shoulder. I breathed a little easier.

"What about a phone directory, wouldn't the hotel be listed in it?" I asked.

"What phone directory? We have no phone directories in Russia."

He considered heading for the U.S. Embassy. But would they know any more than the cab drivers? Then I remembered something.

"This morning," I spoke excitedly, "I took a picture from the back balcony of our hotel. It was a scene of Moscow State University. It was a thick, wooded area with snow in the foreground."

Dick looked pleased. "Ah, that's very good information; now we can narrow it down to one part of Moscow. This is a very big city, you know." He spouted more instructions to the cabbie, and for the first time I felt we had a break. A big break!

Although Moscow is a city of eight million spread comfortably over a large geographic area, thirty minutes later we were in the section that was home to the world's largest single-building university. Capable of handling 50,000 students at one time, the striking Gothic cathedral-style structure loomed in the distance like a lighthouse beckoning to a lost sailor. It's the same building that housed 3,500 foreign athletes during the World University Games in 1973, and I had been inside its halls several times.

But we were far from being home free. While we could see the university at a distance and circled it from afar many times, the hotel remained elusive. It seems the Red Star was more secluded from the citizens of Moscow than even we had suspected. The cab would pull over to a curb, Dick would duck into a store and come back empty-handed. We even stopped at another large hotel in the area and inquired. Still no luck.

It seemed hopeless after we scoured the area for nearly an hour. Then fate smiled our way at a most unlikely place. Desperate for information, Dick rolled down his window at a stoplight, where several people were waiting for a bus. In his native language, he asked if anyone knew of our phantom hotel.

A distinguished-looking, elderly man wearing a heavy black coat, gray scarf and brown fur hat stepped forward. With no change in expression, he pointed around the corner. Indeed, we were only two blocks away from the 10-story stone structure that was nestled in a grove of trees, well off the main thoroughfare. As we headed up the driveway to the front entrance, I heaved a giant sigh of relief and thanked God for answered prayers. My watch said 5:30.

I gave my new Russian friend American currency to take care of the cab fare, and an additional amount for his time and kindness. Then I embraced him with an emotional bear hug that must have told him how grateful I was for bailing me out of a stressful and potentially devastating situation.

And one that had taken on international implications. At 8:30, three hours later, Kent Dunston, our group leader, and the football team returned to the hotel after its first practice. He too was emotional, learning for the first time that I was safe.

"Am I glad to see you," said Kent with a big smile on his face. "We've got all the police in Moscow and the surrounding countryside looking for you. You're the object of a massive international manhunt."

Kent and his assistants had missed me upon returning to Moscow from Zagorsk late in the afternoon. The search started then.

"You're very fortunate," asserted Vladimir Gomelski, International Sports Connection's man Friday in Russia. "Only recently, an important Paris art dealer disappeared from his hotel. He hasn't been heard from again."

And then I thought how stupid I had been for carrying that Minolta camera around my neck throughout the entire episode. Talk about waving a red flag. It evoked a well-deserved shudder.

"It was my fault," I told Kent, "I should have stayed closer to my small group in the compound."

"And we should have taken a head count," our bearded leader returned. "I

A young Russian boy wearing a Georgetown University jacket tried to sell us picture postcards upon our arrival in Zagorsk. He too probably doesn't know the meaning of a Hoya.

This picture might have saved my life. Well, at least it was vital to finding my hotel in crime-infested Moscow after being left in Zagorsk. I took this from the back balcony of our hotel on the morning of our visit to Zagorsk. That's Moscow State University in the background guarantee you we'll never start up another bus without knowing if everyone is there."

And why couldn't I find the American buses when I first darted out to the parking area? In restructuring the chain of events, I remembered limiting my search to the main parking lot where the souvenir vendors were set up. We had unloaded at an alternate area about a block away, and I had completely forgotten that fact in my frustration.

The experience had a happy ending though, thanks to a couple of Russian guardian angels named Victor and Dick.

And just who was the scholarly gentleman named Victor? The one who looked as if he had something else to say as we pulled away from Zagorsk for the bus ride back to Moscow.

About a month after returning to the States, I received two letters from "Victor Depebyok", accompanied by a pair of short stories. The middle-aged man who befriended me in Russia's religious capital was hopeful I would publish some of his literary efforts, not realizing our small company dealt exclusively in sports subjects.

The first letter, bearing a Russian postmark, included an article describing labels on cans that he had received in a package from America. He found them fascinating since such things don't come with products in his native country. "Isn't there anything that people don't invent?" he asked.

The second envelope came from a "Dan Ford, Orleans, MA", indicating it might have been handed to Ford to be mailed from an American post office. The second story, translated into English, literally oozed with intrigue and revealed a lot more about this man named Victor.

It was titled, "The Arrest", and the words "a true story" followed. It tells of him attending an International Book Exhibition in 1978 in Moscow. He went with the express purpose of meeting Western journalists at a time when the cold war was at a fever pitch and oppression was still in vogue behind the Iron Curtain. After engaging a correspondent from the Washington Post's Moscow bureau, several phone calls and personal encounters followed. He tells of "a few phone talks with Alexander Sakharov", the well-known Russian dissident, and police warnings advising him to leave Moscow.

Eventually, the KGB moved in, arrested Victor and shipped him to Siberia. The well-written story ends with him stating, "all this anguish happened to an ordinary, unsophisticated Russian citizen just for disagreeing."

2

MARTIN LUTHER FRANKS DAY

How far is it from Zagorsk, Russia, to the bottomlands of Southern Illinois? About 62 years. And before a ranch, there was a farm.

In the winter of 1991 on a cold and blustery evening, I was sitting in the Olive Garden restaurant eating piping hot pasta é fagioli soup and garlic bread sticks with wife Floy and long-time friends Don and Donna Moore.

"Why don't the two of you just go with us to Amarillo College when we're finished and hear Art Linkletter," suggested Donna who reminded that it was a Community Speaker Series appearance and free to all. Because of the nasty weather, she doubted it would be difficult to get a seat.

The venerable television star has always been a favorite of mine, and when he stood solo on the stage for an hour and a half, unfolding his life story, it seemed a lot shorter. He opened with one humorous story after another, completely captivating his audience.

"Growing old ain't for sissies" is one of my favorite Linkletter lines, and he told a funny story about visiting a nursing home. He went from room to room talking with the elderly, attempting to cheer them up. He found one well-seasoned woman he particularly liked. After talking with her for several minutes and feeling he had gained her confidence, the highly-visible TV personality asked: "Do you know who I am?"

She stared at him quizzically for a few seconds, looked him up and down and then advised: "No, I don't believe I do. But if you'll just stop by the front desk, they can probably help you out."

Then he got serious and started telling about his early life.

"As a baby, I was literally left on a doorstep. I was later adopted and raised by a Baptist preacher and his wife," he said. Then during the course of his talk, Linkletter related that he had graduated from high school at age 15, had been especially proficient in typing and majored in English in college.

My wife and I exchanged glances of incredulity. "I can't believe what I'm hearing," I whispered to Floy.

These were carbon copy characteristics of my early years growing up in the Midwest. Unlike Linkletter, though, I was not left on someone's doorstep. Instead, at an early age, I was handed over to my maternal grandparents, with whom I lived until starting to college.

Growing up as a sheltered farmboy in the bottomlands of Southern Illinois during the Great Depression gave no hint of what my life as an adult would hold. It was a far cry from a career in journalism and a life that would open the gates for extensive international travel. However, I genuinely believe the vagaries of this chaotic period in history helped many in my age group develop valuable characteristics of mental toughness, perseverance and aggressiveness. To this day, I still cling dearly to conservative values that were ingrained at an early age, values that have served me well in entrepreneurial endeavors.

While I spent my formulative years in Southern Illinois, that was not the birthplace. My dad was a telegraph operator for Union Pacific Railroad in North Platte, Nebraska, when I first saw the light of day. It was January 15, 1929, a noteworthy date because it more recently has been designated a national holiday.

I was born the same day and same year as civil rights leader Martin Luther King. When his birthday was declared a national holiday a few years back, I kidded my friends that to be really fair, it should be labeled "Martin Luther Franks Day." At least our children have no excuse for forgetting the date of my birth.

Shortly after I was born, my father, Raymond Senior, lost his job. Mom, Dad and I moved back to my maternal grandparents' farm in Southern Illinois, penniless. Times were tough, supplying plenty of ammunition for marital problems in the best of households. The story goes that when Dad was unable to find work after a reasonable length of time, my mother, Marie, booted him out. He walked the seven miles from the farm to his parents' house in Maunie, carrying all his worldly goods with him.

"I found a job for your father in a florist shop after he was laid off by the railroad," Mom, the aggressor, revealed to me many years ago. "He turned it down, though, saying he wasn't about to take any sissy job."

I saw my father only a few times until Mom died at 58, the victim of leukemia. That's the way she wanted it. In the 30s, divorce was a nasty thing and an embarrassment to all concerned. "Friendly break-ups" had yet to be invented.

I have few memories of early visits to see my father and his relatives, but one stands out that has always provided a lot of laughs. I was about four or five when attending a vacation Bible school in a Maunie church. At the outset, our teacher told us: "If you children aren't quiet and don't mind, then I'll have to scold you."

That really got my attention, because I went home and told everyone "that if I didn't mind at Bible school, I was going to get *scalded.*" At this same school, I was given one of those tin telescoping drinking cups to use at breaks. No one had bothered to show me how it worked. Man, it took a lot of sips from that flat cup to satisfy my thirst. Talk about being naive.

Although my mother took jobs in nearby area towns, and worked in Georgia during World War II, I never left the farm. She remarried twice during this time and her third husband, Harold Schmittler, was killed in the Philippines during the war. Mom's life was not a happy one. She left high school to work on the farm as a young girl, and although very attractive, had to settle for low-paying jobs as a waitress and grocery cashier in later years. Some say she just didn't make enough money to feed two during these times.

Embittered by divorce at 25, my father lived alone the next 20 years, and I rarely saw him. A long-time employee of the Louisville and Nashville Railroad, he did remarry at middle age. He moved to Henderson, Kentucky, just across the Ohio River from Evansville, Indiana, where he experienced poor health for many years before passing away in 1994.

While I missed the love and special attention of my parents in those formulative years, I will always be grateful to my grandparents, Tim and Evalee Fieber, for taking care of me until college. I grew up in the shadows of two uncles, Kempton and Tim Junior, who were 10 and five years older, respectively. These were exceedingly tough times and it was the "hand-me-downs" of my uncles that kept me clothed during this period.

Kempton wasn't there long, though. He married his long-time sweetheart, Eloise Green, and then joined the Navy at the outset of World War II. However, Tim Junior, an outstanding athlete, was married while in high school, and brought his wife, Betty, to the farm. They fought and fussed from the day they were married but often made up in a bed not more than 20 feet from mine in an undivided second story area.

Making it even more crowded in those early years, a cousin two years younger, Loy Lee Brown, also moved into the farmhouse. Also a victim of divorce, he left with his mother, Aunt Genevieve, and her new husband after the first year of grade school. Often the objects of Granddad Fieber's kidding, Loy and I grew close, more like brothers, and thoroughly enjoyed each other.

"I bet I can outrace you boys running on just one leg half the time," he baited us one day. We looked at each other, and said, "no way." So he took us outside and said he'd show us. After picking a post to run to, we took off and he easily beat us, running in normal fashion.

"Hey," we protested, "you said you'd run on just one leg." "No," said Granddad, "I said I'd run on just one leg half the time. And everyone steps on only one leg at a time when they are running." The joke was on us and we never lived that one down.

A full-blooded German and small in stature, he was always kidding with us in the old language. He tried to teach us some common phrases and words, but to no avail. German is tough to master, and when I chose a foreign language in college, it was Spanish.

A tenant farmer until 85 who lived to be 94, Granddad Fieber was a hard worker who nearly always wore overalls. As a sharecropper, he bought his own equipment and seed, tilled and harvested the soil and then gave a percentage of the crop proceeds to the Lincoln Ford family in exchange for use of their land and house.

It's a shame he didn't own some of that rich, fertile bottomlands soil in the early 40s. That's when oil was discovered, producing millions for the already wealthy Ford family. And the opportunity was there, at one time. The story goes that son-in-law Alfred Bonn tried to coax my grandfather into co-oping $2,000 to buy mineral rights to the farm he was tilling and living on. Each would invest $1,000, a lot of money in those days.

"Do you think I'm crazy?" replied my grandfather, dismissing the idea as "a waste of good hard-earned money." A huge oil boom swept the area only a short time later, and a favorable reply would have changed the course of the entire Fieber family, for better or for worse.

In those early days, farm work was truly hard work. I well remember my grandfather and uncles going to the field at daybreak and working until total darkness, taking only enough time for a hearty noon meal. At first, horses were the sole source of power, but along came the Farmall tractor with metal wheels that churned up enough dust to choke a cow.

Too young to operate equipment, I had daily chores of gathering wood for the kitchen stove, coal for the living room pot-belly, pumping horse-trough water and gathering eggs. I was a lousy farmer, and at an early age knew I wanted to pursue other challenges in life. I was a day-dreamer, and on the farm with no television, there was ample time for that.

It was tough making ends meet as a sharecropper, especially if hail storms or a lack of moisture came into play. But we ate well. No doubt that succulent, down-home cooking cultivated my taste buds for an insatiable appetite I still enjoy today. And it's the basic stuff I continue to order at restaurants and cafeterias. Navy and pinto beans, boiled potatoes, turnip greens and homemade cobblers. Wow!

We raised a flock of White Leghorn chickens every year, and I can still see my grandmother Evalee, a quiet gentle woman, out there in the yard wringing off their heads with the vengeance of a grizzled executioner. After the headless chickens flopped around for several minutes, they were scalded in hot water, plucked and in the frying pan in short order. Crisp fried chicken with cracklings, complete with a bowl of cream gravy, was a favorite meal on the farm any time. Occasionally, I was known to eat left-over, finger-licking fried chicken for breakfast.

In addition to the commercial grain crops of corn, wheat and soybeans, we always had a big summer garden near the house. It provided us with ample amounts of green onions, radishes, new potatoes, tomatoes, lettuce, green beans and other fresh vegetables until the first frost. And if that weren't enough, my grandmother, a marvelous cook accustomed to preparing heavy and wholesome meals for the field workers, baked the best hot buns in the whole world. Breakfast would hardly be completed before I could hear her in the kitchen kneading and rolling out dough for those high-rising, delectable, melt-in-your-mouth dinner rolls.

No doubt my grandmother learned to cook southern style while growing up in Tennessee. One of eight children, she shared with us many times about being a cousin to one of the outstanding statesmen of our country, Cordell Hull. In fact, Hull, who for 11 years served as Secretary of State under President Franklin Roosevelt, boarded with my great grandmother, Zerilda Parsons, a schoolteacher, when he was an eighth-grader. My uncle Kempton Fieber wrote Hull about this period in his life in 1940, and received a letter confirming the fact.

"I did for awhile board at your grandfather's home while attending a country school," wrote Hull on official government stationery. "I have always known well all of the members of the Parsons family who constituted the elder groups."

Called by some the father of the United Nations, he was awarded the Nobel Peace Prize in 1945. He died 10 years later. I thought I was proud to be related to this great political figure until I later learned he was the

THE SECRETARY OF STATE
WASHINGTON
June 25, 1940.

Dear Mr. Fieber:

Thank you for your letter of June 20, in which
you inform me that you are one of a Parsons family
which once resided in Pickett county, Tennessee.   As
I recall, your great-grandmother was a second or third
cousin to one of my parents.   I did for awhile board
at your grandfather's home while attending a country
school.

I have always known well all of the members of
the Parsons family who constituted the elder groups.

Sincerely yours,

Cordell Hull

Mr. Kempton Parsons Fieber,
    200 S.E. 6th Street,
        Evansville, Indiana.

1940 letter received by uncle Kempton Fieber from Secretary of State Cordell Hull, a distant cousin.

author of the federal income tax law in 1913. Come to think of it, I'm not too thrilled with what the United Nations organization has accomplished in its less than illustrious history. Despite my misgivings, this famous relative is still revered in his home state of Tennessee. Traveling along Interstate 64 through Central Tennessee last summer, we spotted a highway sign pointing the way to "Cordell Hull Dam."

While long, hard work was the order of the day during the week, Saturday was a different story on the farm. The schedule went something like this. We would sleep later than normal (maybe until 7:00), perform the daily chores and take a tub bath. We would get to Carmi, ten miles away, about mid-morning, where my grandmother did the grocery shopping and Granddad hit the seed, feed, hardware and implement stores.

Most of the time, there were enough additional eggs from the chicken house to sell to Reinwald Produce Company. That was grandmother's own spending money and during the fall, I often picked up enough pecans from wild trees to take to town. I remember buying my first pair of high-top boots, decorated with a pocket knife strapped on the side, with pecan money I had earned. That experience helped teach me the value of the dollar, something I've never forgotten as a self-employed businessman who grew up in the Great Depression.

Noon meant going to Wehrle's Confectionary on Main Street and devouring a grilled cheese sandwich and Coke. The menu never varied. A popular spot, Wehrle's had a bakery on one side and on the other a large soda fountain with a huge mirror behind it. Wrought-iron chairs and marble tables filled the floor, along with a jukebox.

Then at one o'clock, Grandmother Fieber and I would be off to the Strand Theater for the western movie of the day. Sometimes it was Gene Autry, Rocky Lane, Hopalong Cassidy or Roy Rogers. It made little difference because the plot was usually the same and the outcome predictable.

Before leaving town, it was customary to stop at Stoco's Dairy on Cherry Street and get a double-dip ice cream cone. Orange pineapple was my favorite, and that never varied.

The end to a perfect Saturday was the evening meal, or "supper", as we called it. After a steady diet of ham, chicken and steak all week, we would gather around the kitchen table and genuinely lust for a fresh bologna sandwich with sliced bread. Add to it a slice of onion, lettuce, tomato and mustard, and man, we had a delicacy fit for a king. And if it had been a good week with the eggs, we'd wash it down with a bottle of Nehi orange pop.

Grandmother Fieber with a flock of her White Leghorn chickens. That's me on the left and cousin Loy Lee Brown at my side. (Below) With Mom when starting to college.

The painting of Dick Pond Elementary School that Floy rendered from a photograph. Looking at it brings back fond memories.

3

ONE-ROOM SCHOOL
AND NO FREE LUNCHES

As I said earlier, there are advantages and disadvantages to spending formulative years in the sheltered and simplistic atmosphere of a midwestern farm. However, I am certain one of those pluses was a one-room school I attended during the early grades.

We lived half a mile from Dick Pond Elementary School, a small, wooden building that overlooked a small body of water by the same name. That pond, the source of a lot of joy during recess and lunch breaks, was a neighborhood skating rink in the winter and a muddy swimming hole in the summer. Many were the times we played a simplified version of ice hockey, using dead tree limbs for sticks and a tin can for the puck.

I remember little before starting to school at age five, but the memories of those six years at Dick Pond are exceptionally vivid, even today. I completed the eight grades in six years, being double promoted twice. Don't get the wrong idea. I wasn't a genius, really about a "B" student. However, it wasn't uncommon in those days to move students up at semester break if they could handle the more advanced material.

Graduating from elementary school at 11 and high school at 15 afforded me no advantage in life. In fact, I would strongly discourage the practice because it provided a number of problems. Being considerably younger than my classmates made it difficult to maintain a normal social life. And of course, in the area of athletics, being younger and smaller gave me no chance to compete at any level.

I genuinely believe the atmosphere of a one-room school made learning easier than it is today. Our teacher was Dallas Ralls, a mild-mannered, bespectacled and sandy-haired man who had the responsibility of instructing all eight grades. Of course, we had only 15 or 16 students in the entire school, making for an excellent student-teacher ratio. Since all classes were conducted in one small room, we had the advantage of absorbing knowledge even when our class wasn't being addressed. Sort of like having a private tutor.

"Today, students, we're going to work on addition with drills, drills, drills," I can recall Mr. Ralls saying. The same would be true with spelling, history, geography and other subjects. In other words, repetition was the key to learning the basics, a practice our three children never received. It was direct instruction and it worked. That style is being revived in some schools today, and wherever it's tried, it is successful. California is one of the leaders in trying to find ways to improve the quality of schools in America.

The high point of each week was Friday afternoon. At that time, students would square off in some kind of educational competition, activity that contributed mightily to the learning process. After lunch, it would be a ciphering match (competition in arithmetic), a spelling bee or a geography contest. It would be one on one, king of the hill format. I can still recall standing up at the blackboard adding long rows of numbers, racing against Salty Finch or some other gladiator next to me.

The competition would start with first-graders and then progress right up through the eighth. As a youngster, I loved the fierce interplay. To this day, I still remember state capitols and can work math equations in quick fashion without the aid of a pencil or calculator. Some present-day educators are trying to take the competitive element out of classrooms, even to the point of not using a grading system. Children would be the losers and socialism the winner.

Unlike today, there were no free lunches at Dick Pond School. We were there for only one reason, and the socialistic agenda that currently devours our way of life was still on the horizon. In the early grades, lunch was carried to school in a brown paper bag, then later in a Hopalong Cassidy lunch box. It usually consisted of a sandwich, pickle and a couple cookies. We drank water from an outside pump near the storm cellar north of the building. Running water, inside toilets and electricity were luxuries of the future, long after I left the farm.

When weather permitted, I walked the half-mile to school. It usually was with neighboring farm kids, and we rarely made the trek without stopping and throwing skip rocks in the small, lazy creek called Jerry Slough.

The vision of that one-room schoolhouse with the big cast-iron bell over the entry way sounding the start of classes each morning is bright in my memories of the farm. Years after consolidation that caused the doors and windows to be boarded up, I returned periodically, "for just another look." On one such visit in the wintertime, I took some pictures and Floy did a great oil painting of the old landmark in a snow setting. It's a piece of art I still treasure, especially since the building was torn down many years ago. Only the concrete storm cellar remains, mute testimony of that special period on the farm.

"Fire, fire," yelled a student one spring day when classes were in session. He was pointing toward our house. Sure enough, it was the old two-story, wooden house that my grandparents had lived in for years. Mr. Ralls and all us students dashed out the front door and ran as fast as we could to the blazing fire. Neighbors soon were there, too, but to no avail.

Fire-fighting equipment was not available in the Wabash bottomlands, and it burned like a heap of kindling. All our clothes, personal items, furniture—everything was gone. It was an empty feeling. However, the Ford family quickly replaced the old house with a two-story concrete block structure on the same spot, a home I remember more vividly than the one that burned.

Because we lived only a short distance from the Wabash River, floods were a nemesis also. In 1937, the year of the Great Flood, I remember water penetrating the bottom floor of our house, causing most of us to move in with Aunt Ada Fieber, an old maid who lived in nearby Grayville. Granddad and my uncles stayed behind and lived on the second floor until the water receded. On more than one occasion, I remember leaving and entering the house by the second floor window and making the trip to higher ground by rowboat. The only benefits I recall from this devastation were the colossal fish that were caught in nets. Some of the buffalo and catfish would weigh 50 pounds or more.

My interest in sports began at an early age. I've been a fan ever since I learned to read. Know the origin of the word "fan"? It's short for "fanatic", which is described in the dictionary "as a person with an extreme and uncritical enthusiasm or zeal." Yep, that's me.

Growing up on a farm, there was plenty of time for day-dreaming and not many choices for recreation. So I started reading the sports pages of the *Evansville* (Indiana) *Courier* from top to bottom. Memorized the names of every major league baseball player, knew their batting averages and pitching records. Just throw out a name and I could tell you more than you wanted to know about the guy.

Sixty years later, my perusal of the daily sports page isn't complete without checking the major league boxscores. However, I have found current-day sportscasters giving me more statistical information than I really care about. The fact that Kenny Lofton was the first runner to steal two bases in the first inning of game one in a World Series is a bit much.

Only thing wrong, on the farm we were 24 hours behind the rest of the world. Our "daily" newspaper was a day old when our rural carrier made his drop just before noon. That's probably why I don't get too excited about fax machines and other forms of instant communication. I grew up in a world that was slow and easy, and that's not all bad.

"There comes the mailman," my Grandmother Fieber would announce, and that would produce an air of excitement around the house.

Dashing down to the mail box, grabbing the *Courier* and checking the scores of my favorite teams was a daily ritual I relished. In those days, there was loyalty among fans, players and owners, an ingredient sadly lacking in this generation of free agency, daily deals and greed. My favorite team was the Detroit Tigers, and uncles Kempton and Tim Junior followed the Cleveland Indians and New York Yankees, respectively. We had our friendly kidding and kibitzing.

Guys like Joe DiMaggio, Bob Feller and Hank Greenberg grabbed headlines on the sports pages, and I followed their every move. While I never collected bubble gum cards, cousin Loy Brown and I molded clay figures into images of our favorite heroes and played mock games with these creations. It was making the most with what we had, coming long before fantasy leagues and Nintendo electronic games.

Another sport had a profound impression on my interest in sports during those days on the farm. Joe Louis ruled the boxing roost from 1937 to 1949 and I followed his career with the same intensity that I dedicated to baseball.

His "prize fights" also doubled as social events, which were few and far between in rural America. Almost every time the Brown Bomber scheduled a fight, we dusted off the ice cream freezer and invited neighboring families over. We shared the thrill of the fight sitting around our battery-powered Crosley radio eating bowls of home-made vanilla ice cream. I well remember Joe's fights with the German champ, Max Schmeling, and later matches with Billy Conn.

When I was a fledgling sportswriter on the *Evansville* (Indiana) *Press*, I had the opportunity to interview Conn two years after his last fight with Louis. And shortly before Louis died, I had a chance to meet him but muffed the opportunity. It was a college athletic directors convention in Las Vegas and Joe, who had his toughest skirmishes with the IRS after retirement, was working as official greeter at Caesars Palace. I spotted him in the lobby one morning. But instead of stopping and shaking his hand, I chickened out.

It was one of the few times in my 50 years in sports that I was overwhelmed by a bigger-than-life athletic personality. The memorable boxing matches, magnified by the imagination of a young, wide-eyed farm boy, made an indelible impression, and no doubt helped whet my appetite for a career in sports. The fact that Louis trained for many of his fights at nearby French Lick, Indiana, added to his appeal.

In addition to the boxing/ice cream socials, there was another event that brought farm families together. Hog killings. Several families would gather in the wee hours of the morning, prepare huge vats of boiling water and start the butchering process. Earl and Eli Sanders, George Doty, Charles Finch and Arthur Hickling were among those who shared in this periodical procedure to keep meat on the table all year long. It took the good part of a day to finish the job, and I remember the wives cooking a banquet-like noon meal while the children romped all day playing tag and hide-and-go-seek.

This era was long before refrigeration had reached the farm communities, making preservation of meat more difficult than today. Granddad Fieber was in charge of smoking and salting down the fresh meat, and I can still visualize those big hams hanging by wires from the ceiling of the smokehouse. The smell was pungent and absolutely appetizing. Sausage was ground from special parts, seasoned and then stuffed into casings, or hog guts, before being canned in Mason quart jars.

One of the fondest and sweetest memories of early life on the farm involved watermelons. It also provided me with my first experience as a real-live entrepreneur. We planted about 40 acres of this delectable product each year, and while I was a little too young to be working the horse teams and tractors, I got my share of summer labor in the melon patch.

Let me explain my job. Watermelons are planted in wide rows so cultivators can get in there and knock out the weeds. Because they grow on long, winding vines, they must be turned several times for the field to be properly cultivated. That was my job, turning the vines.

"I'll find you a good stick, son," Granddad Fieber would say. He'd come back with a dead tree branch and then do some whittling on it to make it an operational tool. It must be pointed out that 40 acres is a lot of watermelons and they grow best in sandy soil. Man, was it hot and steamy in the middle of summer walking up one row and down another flipping those vines. And sometimes I got a surprise . . . like finding a big bull snake hiding beneath a vine to escape the searing sun.

But it was all worth it when they ripened. Harvest time was an exciting time. Cutters, brandishing sharp pocket knives would start the process, selecting the melons they deemed to be ripe. Others would then carry them to a row and wagons would take them to waiting trucks. Loose hay was used to stack the melons for the long ride to market.

My favorite kind was a green and white striped round melon called "Early Kansas." It was unusually sweet and my Granddad's best seller. I still consider watermelon one of my favorite foods and have been known to polish off half of one before coming up for air. But they're still not quite as good as the days on the farm when we would bust them in the patch, eat only the heart and leave the rest to the birds.

Almost as enjoyable as eating melons was selling them. The enterprising juices were flowing at an early age when I hawked watermelons and cantaloupes from the front yard. I built a crude wooden stand and sat out there hours at a time. There was little traffic on the dirt road in front of our house, and when I would see a trail of dust signalling the presence of an oncoming vehicle, my heart would start pounding. As pay for my work in the fields, I was allowed to keep all the money from the sale of cantaloupes. Between the occasional passing of cars, I had enormous spans of time to read the latest Superman and Archie comic books.

In early summer before watermelon season, I often visited my cousin, Loy Brown, in Evansville. It was on these occasions that I also had opportunities to practice capitalistic ventures with my cousin. He lived on Plaza Drive in a fast-growing suburban neighborhood and we delivered fresh-squeezed lemonade to construction workers. Aunt Genevieve bought the first sack of lemons and sugar, and from then on, we were self reliant, making a nice profit on hot steamy days. What made this operation more profitable than the typical front-yard lemonade stand was the fact we were willing to deliver, long before the pizza industry got smart.

And then we put together complete carnivals in Loy's backyard, attracting all the neighborhood kids with change in their pockets. We had ball throwing stands, "go-fishing" booths and other games of chance. One boy got so carried away he went home and took money from his parents' bedroom and lost every cent of it. We caught a tongue-lashing for that.

4

SUCKER BORN EVERY MINUTE

In high school, there was an entrepreneurial experience a bit more ingenious than the watermelon stand and lemonade business.

Riding a daily bus was a necessity for farm students attending Crossville Community High School in the early 1940s. After a long day of study, and ping pong, most of us craved a snack of some sort when boarding that big, yellow bus driven by George Meriwether. For some of us, the ride home would take a good part of an hour.

These were the days of penny candy and I had an idea. The next time I went to town I invested a dollar in 100 DumDum suckers. You know, the round ones that were solid hard candy in flavors of orange, cherry, root beer and grape. They sell for about 50 cents today, if you can find them.

In just a few days, I sold every one of those suckers at two cents each to bus riders, netting 100% profit. With no overhead. After having duplicated that feat several times, I had still another idea. My mother was working for Wesselman's Market in Evansville and was able to buy boxes of suckers at wholesale prices. This increased my profit even more, and I was learning the ropes of free enterprise.

"I believe I remember paying a nickel for two suckers," good friend Don Long told me not long ago. "But you know, we didn't mind paying that for them because you were providing a good service."

Supply and demand. Even though this was small potatoes, the experience taught me a good lesson that has served me well on down the line.

"Only one out of every 10 new entrepreneurs succeeds," I read someplace in a business magazine. Which, to me, says you'd better study the market and see if you have a product that is wanted or needed. There are other ingredients involved in the success or failure of a business, but that's the first question that should be addressed.

Let me cite a good example. Several years ago, Tommy Bryant, former sports editor of the Amarillo newspapers, and another friend, Jim Holmes, came to me with an idea for a new monthly magazine. They were calling it *Amateur Coach*, and it was to be aimed at all the volunteer coaches in the country. Little league, Babe Ruth league, legion ball and the like.

I didn't encourage them. "These coaches spend little money on equipment and supplies, and your advertising revenue will be limited," I evaluated.

They proceeded anyway. It was a good-looking product, complete with excellent instructional articles. However, after half a dozen issues, it disappeared from the scene, the victim of an inadequate advertising base. A good idea, but not a good business venture.

Having your own business is the American dream many attempt in this great country of free enterprise. It sets us apart from those countries that rely on socialism, communism and other collective ways of life. Just look at all the people who set up card tables at flea markets and antique malls. They are practicing entrepreneurship, even though on an elementary level.

High school was much more than DumDum suckers and the school bus. It was there where I received my first introduction to the typewriter. And I loved it. My buddy, Don Long, and I both found it exciting, and that's probably why we excelled at it. We could hardly wait for typing class each day and the smiling face of Leona Munzenmaier, our teacher.

Forget computers and word processors, I still use my ancient but trusty IBM Executive typewriter when wanting to compose. It would be difficult to put words and thoughts together at any other set of keys after all these years. I understand James Michener, one of the country's most successful and prolific writers, still uses an old typewriter for putting down his masterpieces.

The atmosphere and equipment are important factors when it comes to composing. People who write for a living know what I mean. And still, it doesn't come easily at times. Funny thing about typing. I've developed crippling gouty arthritis in my fingers over the years, but I can still type. I have a theory that since the affliction has progressed slowly I have been able to adjust to the changes by typing almost daily. Now gripping the shaft of a golf club is another story.

Here's another point. Composing is a heck of a lot different from just copying something. I can operate my IBM typewriter as fast as I can think, maybe faster. Friends tell me about the speed of word processors and I say: "So what?"

While I had an insatiable appetite for sports, my activity as a gladiator was limited in high school. Being several years younger than my classmates and smaller in stature made a difference. My uncle Tim Junior was one of Crossville's all-time great athletes and Coach Bill Sanders allowed me to hang around and play with the scrubs in basketball.

But my real talent, if any, came in that great sport of ping pong. I'd never played it until high school, but took to it like a duck to water. Funny thing, my typing buddy, Don Long, also became addicted, and we were among the best in school. Dead even competitors in still another arena. Often, we had to eat lunch in a hurry—or not at all—during "king of the hill" competition at the noon break. Still another quirk, Don and I wound up with precisely the same four-year grade point average upon graduation, somewhere in the low 90s.

Many students are satisfied with a diploma after four years of high school. I got much more. It was in the fall of my senior year, when I was asked to be sports editor of a new school newspaper, the *Tigerette*. I had always done well in English and adored sports, so why not? I found the new challenge exciting, challenging and fulfilling.

The masthead of one of those old papers lists the editor as Ed Armstrong, another fellow bus jockey and good friend. The experience no doubt had an indelible effect on Ed, also. Before recent retirement, he enjoyed an illustrious career with the *Springfield* (Illinois) *Journal*, eventually becoming editor. Not since high school days had I spent any quality time with Ed until our graduating class celebrated its 50th anniversary recently.

When I packed my bags and headed across the Wabash River to college, there was little doubt that a career in journalism would be in my future.

5

OFF THE FARM AND OFF TO COLLEGE

Day and night, black and white. If you can think of other 180-degree contrasts, then you'll accurately describe the next transition in my life.

After completing high school at 15, I chose nearby Evansville College in Indiana for further study, becoming the first in either the Fieber or Franks families to go beyond the 12th grade. Most were farmers and chose to stay with the land. I honestly did not enjoy farming and was looking for an escape hatch, as much as anything.

It was only 30 miles away and my mother was working there as a checker at Wesselman's Market. Besides that, I received a $100 a year scholarship from the Ford Foundation, the people who owned my grandparents' farm. No chump change in those days.

But here's the picture. For the first 15 years, I lived the simple life of a Southern Illinois farmboy, going to bed with the chickens and getting up with the chickens. Taking a trip to Carmi, a town of about 7,000, on Saturdays had been the extent of my worldly experiences.

When moving to Evansville in the summer of 1944, I found a bustling city of 140,000 knee-deep in war-related activities. Factories worked three shifts, right around the clock. Republic Corporation had a plant on the outskirts of town that built P-47 Thunderbolts for the Army Air Force. Appearing to be at least a mile long, it was the biggest building I'd ever seen in my life. It still is. I marvel as I pass by it today, now owned by Whirlpool Corporation and the site of refrigerator manufacturing.

Then down on the Ohio River, a shipyard was building LST landing barges as fast as they could. The 24-hour activity literally meant the city didn't sleep. Movie houses, restaurants, night clubs and other entertainment centers had a hey-day as people were seeking R and R from the rigors of World War II. Talk about another world.

The life-style was an eye-opener for a naive 15-year-old as he joined his mother in a tiny one-bedroom apartment on Rotherwood Avenue. I slept on the front room couch that converted into a lumpy bed and we shared a bathroom with another renter, a single woman. But I didn't complain about the bathroom set-up. It was my first time to enjoy the luxury of indoor plumbing and running hot and cold water.

"Don't forget to latch the other door", Mom warned, "when you use the bathroom". Yes, I did forget once, and an embarrassing confrontation ensued.

Making ends meet was extremely difficult in the beginning, and I accepted the job as stoker of the coal furnace for our apartment building. That occupied my early mornings and late nights. Then I found a job at nearby Kuester's Hardware, hardly knowing a bolt from a nut or a screw from a nail. After floundering at the outset, I did learn a lot though and before I left that job was capable of cutting and threading custom pieces of pipe with the confidence of a pro.

Taking a full load in college and holding down two part-time jobs, I rarely saw Mom. However, Sunday was our day together from the beginning. A wonderful cook who rarely had time for it, she would get up on Sunday morning and start a sumptuous meal of fried chicken, mashed potatoes and gravy, green beans, salad and strawberry shortcake. Then we would get on a bus and go downtown for a movie at Loew's Theater. The marquee changed each week and it didn't matter what was showing, we went. While it was a day reserved for special time with mother, I have to admit I completely strayed away from the Lord during these times. There didn't seem to be time for things like that. Later, I realized I had my priorities all wrong.

It was at this time in history when a strip between the Evansville city limits and the Ohio River was called "no man's land." Roadhouses breeding public gambling, prostitution and about anything else you wanted lined Highway 41, and the area was often labeled "Little Las Vegas." Gambling was illegal in this area, which actually was in the state of Kentucky, but officials looked the other way and seldom caused any trouble. Henderson, bordering the Ohio River to the east, even had slot machines in gas stations, drug stores and restaurants.

But the one place most people remember was a plush, two-story stucco night club called "The Trocadero". Owned by Clarence Wood, this combination dance hall and gambling casino flourished from 1938 to 1951. The bottom floor included a big hardwood dance floor with Tommy Dorsey,

Glen Miller and all the top big bands of the era coming in. It was glitzy, including a beautiful mahogany bar. Even slot machines finished in mahogany lined one wall. People traveled from all over the country to frequent this elegant night club.

A red-carpeted stairway led to the second floor that was the site of crap games, roulette and other types of gambling. The basement was reserved for high-stakes games and all employees wore ties. Later an antique mall, the Trocadero burned to the ground only a couple years ago, a fitting climax to a chapter of illicit history in the Evansville area.

"The law ignored the gambling houses because they were being paid off," confessed a 74-year-old retired deputy who remembers that period very well. "I'll tell you how blatant it was . . . there was a special parking place at the Troc marked for the sheriff."

Even though I was under-age, I have to admit frequenting the place a few times with older college classmates. Of course, age wasn't a big deal because about everything going on was illegal anyway. Still, I kept waiting for someone to tap me on the shoulder and show me the way to the door.

Another major event took place at this juncture of my life. After leaving the farm, I was determined to change my name. I was given my father's label at birth, and relatives and schoolmates called me "Junior". It was a name I always detested. It always reminded me of a junior partner in a law firm, someone at the bottom looking up. A subordinate.

In high school, records indicated I was "Raymond Maxted Franks Jr.", but classmates called me "Frankie", a play on my last name. I liked that. I preferred anything over "Junior". When I moved across the Wabash River to Indiana, I adopted "Ray", which suited me better and fit nicely in newspaper bylines.

What I didn't learn until later though, many people would thoughtlessly refer to me as "Frank" when calling me on a first-name basis. And it seems the older I get, friends fall into that trap more and more. But the corker of all wrong name-calling occurred when I was sports information director at West Texas State University in the 50s. I was there eight and a half years but the athletic director rarely called me by my right name.

"Frank, uh I mean Ray," would be the salutation more often than not when he called my office. That was the case right up to the time I resigned in 1963. And guess what, his first name was "Frank", Frank Kimbrough.

It's really funny when good friends—I mean really good friends—greet me with "Hi, Frank, uh I mean Ray." It got so bad a few years back that I took a cue from a then popular beer commercial and would respond:

"You can call me Ray, you can call me Jay, you can call me RJ, but don't call me Frank." It was offered in good fun, of course.

It wasn't long before I had a chance to use my new name in print. When I entered Evansville College (it's now University of Evansville) in the fall of 1944, most college-age men were away defending their country. I had hardly closed the door on my first visit to the college newspaper office when I had my arm twisted to be sports editor. It was a lock since there were no other male students on the staff of the *Crescent*, a weekly tabloid.

It was a great opportunity for a fledgling journalist. Officed in the basement of the Administration Building, I wrote a weekly column labeled "The Sports Ray", quickly taking advantage of the new name. Then when basketball season opened, I covered the Purple Aces in the nearby 3,000-seat Armory.

Evansville was a school of about 2,000 students and didn't have the luxury of a sports information director. When Coach Emerson Henke asked me to send press releases to the media, little did I know that it would open doors for my big break. Shy at first, I got to know some of the sports writers of the local dailies, and in the spring of '45 made my aggressive move.

I put on my best clothes, gathered up writing samples and ascended the long staircase to the editorial offices of the *Evansville Press*. A member of the Scripps-Howard chain, the *Press* was the city's evening paper with a plant at Second and Vine, only a stone's throw from the beautiful Ohio River.

I promptly spotted Dick Anderson, the sports editor whose picture always appeared in his column. He was a balding, heavy-set man who looked like a character out of Damon Runyan's world. With my knees knocking and heart pounding, I made my way to his desk.

In his words, a later column, he described the visit:

> *It has been almost eight years now since a cherub-faced young man walked up to my desk, introduced himself, and said: "I want to be a sports writer."*
>
> *I asked him to sit down. He did and his feet just did touch the floor from the vantage point of one of our better pieces of furniture. He jarred me a little when he told me that he was going to college at Evansville College and wanted to work in a schedule of sports writing in his off hours.*
>
> *I had him pegged maybe as a sophomore in high school. But he assured me that he had finished up his work at Crossville, Ill., High and*

was all set for a full bloomed adventure into life. Such was his approach that we found a place for the young man and he pitched in with both hands, eager ones, and managed to carry a full load at Evansville College along with his sports writing adventures.

Having just turned 16 when I was hired at the *Press*, I did a lot of growing up the next five years. In retrospect, this was one of the most exhilarating periods in my life, thanks to the job at the paper. It served as a great training laboratory for a career in journalism. Actually, it was much more valuable than the college education itself.

The editorial office literally oozed with excitement. The steady rat-a-tat-tat of United Press teletype machines echoed around the large room, punctuated only by the staccato sounds of typewriters manned by staff writers. In the middle was a horseshoe-shaped desk. Positioned at slots around it were City Editor Jim Margedant, Tri-State Editor Edna Folz and Managing Editor Carl Ritt, a grizzled newspaper veteran who kept a bottle of bourbon in his desk. More often than not, he celebrated putting another paper to bed with a toast from the bottom drawer.

Small banks of oak desks dotted the remainder of the well-lighted second story room where various departments created stories to be funneled to the main copy desk. Favorite writers and role models for a young, wide-eyed journalist were Bish Thompson and Ed Klingler, who had facing desks near the copy editor. Reading and following Bish helped me develop skills in feature writing. He possessed a wonderful sense of humor that laced his stories, and here's a good example of what I mean. One Christmas season he retained the greeting cards his family received. The following December, he crossed out the signatures, substituted his name and returned the same cards to the original owners.

"Keep your sentences short and easy to read," was the advice of the more serious Klingler, the paper's No. 1 news reporter and another early mentor. Usually assigned the top local stories, Klingler once told me: "Remember, you're writing for people of all ages and from all backgrounds. Don't exclude anyone from your readership. Don't get cute and use words that people have to look up in the dictionary. Never try to impress readers with five-dollars words . . . you're attempting to communicate."

Because of that lesson learned nearly 50 years ago, I have had a difficult time reading Bill Buckley and other journalists who seem to be writing for their own edification. The late Lewis Grizzard was more my type.

The sports department was located over in the corner near the office of Editor Frank Ford and close to the head of the stairs. There was Dick

Anderson, the veteran sports editor who mostly wrote a daily column and covered big events such as the Indy 500, the Kentucky Derby and sometimes the World Series. He had a special affection for horse racing and covered the month-long season at Dade Park, a track on the strip between Evansville and Henderson, Kentucky. His son, Chick, was in radio and wound up as the race announcer at Churchill Downs. Chick was good at his profession and held that job until one year on national television he called the wrong winner of the Kentucky Derby.

Because of a heart problem, Dick rode the freight elevator to his second-story desk every day. An efficient exponent of two-finger hunt and peck typing, he kept an unlit cigarette in his mouth constantly, a grim reminder of his health condition. A crusty sort who rarely dropped his guard, he had a practice of drinking a coke and then tossing the empty bottle in the nearest waste basket. The "clink" could be heard all over the room. After I had left the *Press* in 1950, Dick died of heart complications at middle age. Son Chick also died prematurely, a victim of a heart attack.

There were three desks in the sports department and the third slot was occupied by a quiet, almost-shy veteran who had just returned from World War II. Bill Robertson was a master wordsmith who wrote a column labeled "The Inside Corner". Also serving as copy editor for sports, he was responsible for page layout and putting the section "to bed" in the composing room.

Bill, who never married, drove 20 miles round trip from Boonville daily and became a close friend in those learning years. We often ate lunch together, and on days when I didn't have college classes, we sometimes would slip over to the Grand Theater just a block away. An elegant palace with crystal chandeliers, red carpeting and fancy balconies, the Grand alternated stage shows with movies. Name bands like Ted Weems and Henry Busse would be there along with novelty acts like the Harmonicats, whistler Elmo Tanner and trick dogs. We even saw a young comedian from nearby Vincennes, a guy named Red Skeleton.

6

THAT FIRST BYLINE

In the beginning, I was assigned menial stories at the *Press*, being low man on the totem pole. Events like bowling tournaments and golf meets. Then better assignments came along. After being on the job two months, I noticed that Anderson and Robertson had bylines on the stories they wrote. I was wondering why I didn't. Maybe I have to pay my dues first, I thought. But when asked to cover the Indiana state softball tournament at Enlow Field, I thought this might be my opportunity.

"This is an important sports affair," I mused. "It's magnitude is state-wide."

So when I wrote the story of the championship game, an event that was sure to get an important position on the sports page, I typed my name at the head of the story. I had never done this before and wasn't sure it was proper. But lo and behold in next afternoon's edition of the *Press*, August 27, 1945, there it was:

"Goshen Softball Champs . . Upsets Favored Briggs . . By Ray Franks"

That was a career first, one of monumental proportions for a young writer. Who knows, if I hadn't made the first move, I might have written in anonymity for five years.

When Evansville's four high schools opened football season in the fall, there came a lot of night assignments on the weekends. Because I had attended a small high school without football, I had never witnessed a game until moving to the big city. I had no idea what a double reverse was and thought the Statue of Liberty was a landmark in New York. The first football game I covered between Evansville Memorial and Gary Emerson was only the second gridiron contest I had ever seen. I hope the story didn't show it.

After football season came basketball and even more nighttime work. Quite often I was logging 48 hours a week at the newspaper while trying to carry a full load in college and enjoying the fruits of belonging to a social fraternity. To work in dates, I often would take them to the sports event I was covering. My colleague, Robertson, wrote about this practice in a farewell column when I entered the Air Force:

> *It has never been considered socially acceptable in sports-reporting circles to allow women in the press box. So if Ray felt that feminine companionship was an asset to his journalistic efforts, he merely left the press box and went into the bleachers.*
>
> *While it is probably not true that he invented the practice of sitting beside a comely brunette while reporting a basketball game, he certainly developed the technique to a remarkable degree of success.*

My schedule on a typical day went something like this:

8:00 a.m.	Arrive at *Press* office to write stories, edit copy and answer phones
12:30 p.m.	Take bus to Evansville College
1 - 5 p.m.	Attend classes
7:00 p.m.	Cover local sport events

Sometimes I wouldn't get back to the apartment until 11 or 11:30, jump into bed and start all over again.

I honestly don't remember when or where I studied or ate during that hectic period of my life. There just wasn't enough time in the day, especially when you remember I was doing all my traveling on a city bus. Despite the harem-scarem, roller coaster schedule, I managed a "B" average overall and even worked in a few games of ping pong at the Temporary Student Union. And I loved every minute of it.

The first out-of-town assignment made me feel important, a real traveling correspondent. It was the holiday season of 1945 and Evansville College was playing in a basketball tournament hosted by Indiana State. I took the bus for the 100-mile trip to Terre Haute and checked into a hotel— the Terre Haute House— three nights. It was my first experience to stay overnight in a motel or hotel. And eating meals in the hotel restaurants on an expense account. Wow, this was big-time. In those days, after composing the story on my Royal portable typewriter, it was relayed back to the paper by Western Union. On close deadlines, stories would be called in via telephone.

I well remember one trip I made in 1946 to cover Evansville College's basketball game at University of Louisville. After knocking out my story and packing up the typewriter, I trudged down to the bus depot in a freezing snowstorm, arriving back in Evansville at 4 a.m. Since the bus station was only a block from the newspaper, I just walked over to the office and curled up on my desk until time to go to work four hours later.

The more I wrote the more confidence I was gaining. People learn to write by writing. Working on the *Press* while attending college afforded me a fruitful opportunity, a laboratory experience that was priceless in value. It would serve me well for the balance of my professional career.

But I must admit to one flash of naivete in an early interview feature. I was doing a story on Leon Balkin, a short squat Greek who was Evansville's professional wrestling promoter. Going down the list of routine questions, I asked: "And what college did you attend?"

"The University of Hard Knocks," replied Balkin, who probably had no more than an eighth-grade education. The unsuspecting young reporter listed the information as "U. of Hard Knox" in his story. Fortunately for me, the wry humor was discovered by Bill Robertson when he copy read the feature. I didn't live that one down for a long time.

Oh yes, professional wrestling was getting a lot of attention on our sports page, and I wondered why. Anyone with a semblance of a brain knew it was staged. After covering some of the matches, I would go down to the dressing rooms and find these "mortal enemies" joking with each other and driving off in the same car to the next city.

But still our paper was treating this as a legitimate sport with advance stories several days prior to the Wednesday card. And then complete coverage of the results the next day. Then one day when I went to Balkin's office to pick up a news release, I found the answer. In addition to the release, he handed me a plain sealed envelope to deliver to my sports editor. I later discovered Balkin was paying $20 a week for complete coverage of the wrestling scene, long before payola was discovered in the recording business.

When I was assigned the golf beat on the paper, I had never played the sport. As the old joke goes: "I hardly knew which end of the caddie to hold."

Not too many golf courses in the bottoms of Southern Illinois, nor time to play. It was an easy sport to cover and guess what, I got the bug. After starting with a used set of mixed clubs, including a Reynolds aluminum-head driver, I developed an insatiable appetite for the sport. On some weekends, our foursome would play 54 holes a day or three 18-hole rounds. From

The sports staff of the *Evansville Press* in 1945. That's Dick Anderson, sports editor, sitting, and Bill Robertson on the right. (Below) Boxer Billy Conn (right) was one of the first important people I interviewed. This is a movie poster of a 1941 movie in which he played himself in "The Pittsburgh Kid". Also starring with him was Jean Parker.

sun-up to sun-down. Since I was 18 before starting, I was making up for lost time.

"Get a comfortable grip, keep your head down and follow through," was early advice I remember hearing from Dutch Rittenhouse, the teaching pro at Helfrich Hills. The first challenge was breaking 100. Then 90, and the incessant desire to improve never stopped. Although I was normally a bogey golfer, I managed rounds of 83 and 85 in the Evansville City Tournament my second year of play. Breaking 80 for 18 holes was a lofty goal I never attained before giving up the game a few years ago.

I was spending a lot of time at the golf course, and because Evansville was the hometown of PGA tour professional Bob Hamilton, I was given some out-of-town assignments. The first pro tournament I ever attended or covered was the 30th PGA Championship at Norwood Hills Country Club in St. Louis. That was in May, 1948, only four years after Hamilton had won the 1944 tourney in Portland, Oregon.

My main chore was to cover Hamilton but the match that stood out most of all was a quarter-final duel between veterans Sam Snead and Claude Harmon. For years, the PGA was a match-play affair and Harmon had to go 43 holes (36 was regulation) before defeating Snead. I was one of 7,000 in the gallery who followed the play in near darkness. For a new golfer, still wet behind the ears, it was a genuine thrill to watch and be near these legends.

Then there was the All-American Tournament in Chicago a year later. Engineering magnate George May sponsored the $66,000 classic, which was big money in those days. A real character, May changed shirts every hour while mingling with the gallery. Gallery fee was $1.25 and first prize was $5,000. Current-day pros can make 50 times that much in some tournaments, showing you how far the tour has progressed. While following Evansville's Hamilton, he was always quick to introduce me to his friends, fellow pros Lloyd Mangrum, Vic Ghezzi, Sam Snead, Dr. Cary Middlecoff and the like.

Because the *Press* sponsored a local caddie tournament each summer, I got to accompany the two winners to the National in Columbus, Ohio. It was played on Ohio State University's championship course, affording me another opportunity to travel and cover a golf event that was pure jubilation. One summer, Middlecoff and Mangrum gave an exhibition for the caddies before competition began, and I renewed acquaintances with them. Mangrum, from Chicago, was especially close to Bob Hamilton and came to Evansville frequently for pro-am exhibitions.

Working on a large daily newspaper has always had its privileges, and I might have stayed with it longer if the pay had been better. I think I was making about $15 a week in the mid-40s. Presidents Richard Nixon and Ronald Reagan both have been quoted as saying the same thing, preferring the sportswriter lifestyle to politics.

In his early years, Nixon worked as a sportswriter, and Reagan, just out of college, labored several years with WHO radio in Des Moines, Iowa. He was a sportscaster, being remembered by many for his re-creation of out-of-town baseball games from information on Western Union wires.

Free passes to sports and other entertainment activities were always available. And as a reporter, I had a chance to meet and mingle with high sports officials and celebrities. In addition to many golf pros, the five years at the Press afforded interviews with Alice Marble, all-time tennis great; Andy Varipapa, professional bowling champion and trick-shot artist; wrestler Gorgeous George and baseball great Bob Feller.

But my favorite was Billy Conn, the handsome heavyweight boxer who had two famous bouts with the great Joe Louis. The Pittsburgh Kid came to Evansville in the fall of 1948 to visit millionaire oilman Ray Ryan. His secretary apprised the paper of his presence and my boss sent me over, along with a photographer.

He was friendly and talked freely of his much-touted bouts with Louis. His first match with the Brown Bomber in 1941 was his best effort. In fact, he was leading on points in the 13th round when he made the mistake of moving in for the kayo and got knocked out himself. The experts agreed he could have become the world's champion if he had just stayed away from Louis for two more rounds.

After a stint in the service during World War II, Conn returned to training and lost an eight-round knockout to Louis in 1946, a much weaker effort.

"I certainly would," answered the dark, curly-haired Conn when asked if he would fight Louis a third time. "I'm working out now in Pittsburgh, and expect to return to the ring one of these days." It never happened.

The affable Conn, who wound up making some oil-related investments with Ryan, never fought a bout as an amateur. "You can't learn anything as an amateur boxer, and besides that there's no money in it," he told me.

At the peak of his career, Joe Louis did most of his training at nearby French Lick, a short drive north of Evansville. Dan Scism, sports editor of our competitive morning paper, the *Courier*, told us about golf matches he had with the Brown Bomber.

"Ol' Joe is a pretty good golfer," related Dan, a squat southpaw who won more money on the golf course than he made at the paper. "But he usually overschedules himself and drops big chunks of change. He loses more often than he wins." Gambling and poor management contributed to Joe's financial woes in the twilight years of his life. He went down swinging, owing the IRS millions. A sad ending to a great athletic career.

Working on a metropolitan daily had other perks. The photography department was constantly looking for attractive young women to use for theme pictures or holiday shots. After suggesting an acquaintance or a name I had gotten second hand, I would accompany the photographer and often get a phone number. Such an incident led to my first serious love interest. She was Georgia Graves, an Indiana University cheerleader who was home for the summer break.

Much later, after I was married and living in Texas, our family was watching the popular "$64,000 Question" television quiz show with Hal March. Lo and behold who comes on as a contestant but "Georgia Graves from Evansville, Indiana." A beautiful, olive-skinned girl but not exactly honor roll material, she won a lot of money—at least $8,000 and maybe more—in the category of "history". A short time later, the show was scandalized and busted from the airwaves when it was discovered some contestants were "being coached." I have often wondered.

Even though my primary job at the *Press* was sports, I occasionally was called on to help out in other departments. Such was the case when World War II ended on September 2, 1945. I had been on the staff only a few months when we were all asked to help chronicle this historic event, one I'll never forget. There are maybe half a dozen experiences in one's life that stand out above all others, and V-J Day was one of them. Walking two blocks from the office to Main Street, I rounded the corner to find a late afternoon celebration that looked like New Year's Eve and Mardi Gras all rolled into one.

"It's over, it's over," people were screaming and shouting while embracing and kissing anyone who came along. It was bedlam. Horns were honking and bells were ringing as the throng poured out into the street. Traffic was at a standstill. The end to almost four years of war that took a heavy toll was being celebrated with passion.

Men were climbing lampposts, taking off their shirts and openly drinking firewater in wild jubilation. Men in uniform were especially fortunate as the young women poured out special affection in their direction. It was well into the night before the thousands in downtown Evansville broke up the party and went home. It was my job to interview people randomly and put their comments together for a sidebar story.

I did find time to work on the college newspaper three years, two as sports editor and one as editor. I served the annual as sports editor three years and managed to make most of my fraternity's social functions. Keep in mind I was about three or four years younger than my classmates and that made it difficult in the social swirl. I matured early in many ways, especially when the grizzled veterans returned to college from World War II, creating even more of a disparity in age.

While my schedule was hectic in college, I found time to discover a hobby that would become an important segment of my life. I had never been more than a hundred miles from the farm in Southern Illinois when the chance came to visit New York City in my sophomore year. Five of us who were rehearsing for the college play, "Joan of Lorraine", hopped in Bill Dorne's 1936 Oldsmobile and made the 2,000-mile trip over Easter vacation. At that time, Ingrid Bergman was playing the title role of Joan on Broadway at the Alvin Theater.

"How nice of you to come all the way from Indiana to see the show," said the elegant Swedish actress who had allowed us backstage. In person, she was just as beautiful and gracious as she appears on the screen.

That initial travel adventure, although abbreviated, whetted my appetite for bigger and better things to come. In the late 40s, Evansville College sponsored three summer sociology trips that really stimulated my wanderlust tendencies. Besides that, each trip was good for three hours credit.

The first was a 21-day bus excursion to Mexico City. To a 17-year-old just two years removed from the farm, a trip around the world couldn't have been more imposing. I conjured up all kinds of exotic thoughts as I lay awake at night just dreaming about it. Mom encouraged me and agreed to help with the expenses. The big obstacle was getting excused from my full-time job at the newspaper.

Then I had an idea.

"I'll send back periodic stories of our trip if you'll let me go to Mexico this summer," I asked my boss, sports editor Dick Anderson. He thought for a few moments, then huddled with the people on the news side and came back with a tell-tale smile on his face.

"You're on", he blurted, "and we'll even keep you on salary all three weeks while you're gone." The same arrangement was negotiated for the next two summers.

We wound our way through the South, spending nights in Birmingham, New Orleans, Houston and Laredo before reaching the Mexican border. Then the real adventure began. We clung precariously to the two-lane Pan-

American Highway, negotiating hair-pin curves all the way after reaching Valles in the Sierra Madre Mountains. For the last 295 miles before arriving in Mexico City, it took 14 hours.

"Don't drink the water and try to eat at Sanborn restaurants", warned our guide, Professor Dean Long, as we gathered in Hotel Regis lobby for our first look at this huge Latin metropolis. After having a couple billfolds and a fountain pen lifted while visiting National Cathedral, we moved out into the countryside. There we visited the Pyramid of the Moon and Pyramid of the Sun, climbing the 242 steps up the latter. It's larger than the famous Cheops of Egypt.

Before heading back to the states, we caught a bullfight and saw the famous Joselito of Spain do his stuff. "Ole" was screamed in unison at every pass of the bull, a cry I could hear in my sleep for weeks later. If you've seen one bullfight, you've seen them all.

The second summer adventure took us through Western United States, visiting Yellowstone National Park and the length and breadth of California. This was the big band era and a highlight was spending an evening at the famous Hollywood Palladium, where Frankie Carle and his orchestra were on stage. It was particularly stimulating for my traveling buddy, Corky Long, who worked his way through college playing the saxophone. Living in Southern California today, he sits in regularly with the likes of Glenn Miller's Tribute Orchestra, Jimmy Dorsey's group and the Charlie Barnett band, one of my all-time favorites.

On the way home, we pulled in late one night to Elko, Nevada. We had reservations at the Commercial Hotel but bus driver Pop McCleary had been overlooked.

"Do you have a room, any kind of room?" he asked the desk clerk.

"Well, let's see", mumbled the clerk. "No, we don't have a thing tonight. But since you'll probably have trouble finding a place to sleep at this time of night, I'll let you have our owner's private room. Mr. Crosby, Bing Crosby, isn't in town today."

On trip three, we explored the eastern section of this great country, getting all the way up to Montreal and Quebec City in Canada. On three journeys, we got to see three different areas of America.

With the proliferation of air travel, covering this much territory would be no real feat by today's standards. But back in the 40s, zipping through 32 states and two foreign countries by bus gave a wide-eyed, young teenager a rare sweeping perspective of North America, helping to prepare him for a career that would include adventures to all but one of the inhabitable continents of the world.

7

PARTIAL TO AIR FORCE BLUE

My next journey would be courtesy of the United States government.

It was 1950 and the nations of the world had not learned a lesson from the carnage of World War II. Korea was bristling with action and America, the world's protector, was gearing up for another conflict. Both 21 and unmarried, Corky Long, my college buddy, and I felt the draft breathing down our neck. We knew we were high on the military's priority list.

"Do ya want to join the Army?" I asked Corky one night on a double date.

"The uniforms are terrible," he replied.

"Yeah, I know, I really am partial to Air Force blue."

While that may not be the only motivation for going down to the local recruiting station and joining the Air Force that fall, it had to be a contributing factor. After all, fashionable young men of the 50s had to be wearing chic apparel, even if it's military issue. I had been out of college two years and my budding newspaper career at the *Press* had to be put on hold.

As the passenger train pulled out of Indianapolis and headed south, I wondered what my next big adventure would bring. There was only one certainty at this stage of my life—the next four years would belong to the Air Force. Picking up new recruits along the way, the long, tiring train ride was uneventful until we reached the Texas border. My early impression of Texans had not been favorable and the dozen or so who boarded our train in Texarkana did little to improve that image.

"Texas is the biggest and the best!", bragged one of the new recruits sitting in front of me. "Yahoo, ride 'em cowboy", echoed another. I couldn't wait until we reached Lackland Air Force Base in San Antonio, where basic training was awaiting. Later, my opinion of Texas would mellow and I would become one of the state's biggest boosters.

Flooded with more new volunteers than they could handle, the Air Force was forced to set up additional basic training centers at other bases. I was in San Antonio only long enough to get a GI haircut and a pair of drab green fatigues before being shipped to Sheppard AFB.

"You're going to Wichita Falls for basic training," I was told. I had never heard of Wichita Falls and thought the guy meant Wichita, Kansas.

One of the country's hottest spots in mid-summer, this city of 100,000 northwest of Dallas was still plenty steamy in mid-September. Six weeks of basic training was an eye opener but tolerable and it wasn't long until I was permanent party and assigned to the base weekly newspaper, *The Senator*. My experience on the Evansville daily had helped me stay in a field I enjoyed.

Since the sports editor slot was filled, I was assigned to do an entertainment column and handled some general reporting. The sports editor was a career airman named Paul McBurnett and he did something I'll always remember shortly after surviving basic training. Knowing I was homesick and without a car, McBurnett and his wife took me to Dallas later that fall to see All-American Kyle Rote play his last football game for SMU. The opponent was cross-town rival TCU and when I saw that crowd of 50,000 in the Cotton Bowl, I was impressed. I still have the program from that December 2 game.

Although my stay at Sheppard was brief, I had one close relationship with another newcomer who was assigned to the Public Information Office shortly after I moved in. His name was Don Parker, the son of famous *New York Daily Mirror* sports columnist, Dan Parker. Don was married to a Powers model, Dee, and he was forced to take a second job with the Wichita Falls newspaper to support an apartment for his wife. She was later killed in an automobile accident and the last I heard of Don he was a staffer for *Sports Illustrated*.

America's military buildup was continuing and an old air base at Amarillo, Texas, was being reactivated. When I headed down Highway 287 in my 1940 Dodge convertible in April, 1951, little did I know I would spend the balance of my adult life in this cattle and oil-rich country, truly one of the last outposts of the Old West. Among the first 50 to be assigned to Amarillo AFB, I found it a major improvement over Wichita Falls. Actually, it was more like a "Garden of Eden" compared to the skimpy social life and poor military-civilian relations prevalent at the previous address.

Weekend brawls between airmen and local toughs were not uncommon at Wichita Falls. On the other hand, citizens of Amarillo opened their arms to the military and the economic boost the base represented. And the mood never changed as I spent 42 of my 48 months at the Air Force's training center for jet fighter and bomber mechanics. Amarillo was consistently rated "good duty" by those transferred here from other ports of call.

"The difference between Amarillo and Wichita Falls is like daylight and dark," observed a fellow Hoosier, George Aiken, who also had newspaper experience as a civilian. "I could spend the rest of my tour right here and not be a bit disappointed."

It was a surprise then in 1967 when Amarillo AFB was one of the first bases President Lyndon Johnson shut down when military might was being scaled back. There seemed to be some credibility to the rumors that it happened because the Texas Panhandle, long a bastion of political conservatives, was the only region of the Lone Star state that didn't back LBJ in his 1964 bid for the presidency. Those who knew the vindictive Texas president found the story believable.

Those early days at my new Air Force home were interesting. Since new barracks had to be built, we lived in make-shift quarters that formerly served as classrooms on the flight line. New construction was advancing at a rapid pace and paint was sprucing up old buildings that remained from the World War II facility. Job assignments bore little resemblance to our training and we learned to be flexible. Assigned to Public Information because of my background in journalism, I spent the first several months helping with the base post office. Going to town, picking up bags of mail and then sorting it was a daily chore until our PIO office was ready for occupancy and a staff was assembled.

Although we grumbled often, a trademark of people marking time in the military, it was fulfilling to see a mere shell of a military facility with 50 men develop into an important installation of 30,000. There was still a lot of pride in our services and the USA in those days. Amarillo AFB had its formal opening November 9, eight months after the first troops arrived and precisely the same date our new paper, the *Jet Journal*, came off the press.

"The first issue took some doing since time was running out and money was scarce," said editor Sam Krieble, a master sergeant who had less legitimate professional experience of anyone on the staff. That's the way the military works . . . time in grade is everything. Actually, Sam was a likable career boozer who stayed out of the way and allowed the rest of us to do what we desired.

Our staff was as varied as West Texas weather. With five years experience on a daily newspaper sports department, Corporal Franks got the job as sports editor. Dan Perkes, a native New Yorker who had done some reporting for International News Service, handled entertainment and general writing, and George Aiken, the fellow Hoosier, brought a journalism degree from Indiana University and a couple years writing experience to the staff. Lt. George McBride, a New Jersey native with questionable talents in journalism, was officer-in-charge of the *Jet Journal*, and Capt. Porter "Portly" Oakes, a rotund, big-jowled Texan with background in public relations work, was Public Information Officer.

But the one person who held the office together was the only female in the place, Carrie Larkin. Carrie, whom I still see occasionally around Amarillo, was the bubbly, always smiling office manager-secretary who was the butt of our practical jokes.

One prank stands out above all. One afternoon after Carrie had gone home, we got a pair of heavy brogan work shoes, stuffed them with two sticks, put the legs in a pair of men's fatigues and carefully placed the dummy in one of the two stalls of the ladies restroom. Next day we all watched anxiously when Carrie, the only woman on the floor, made her first trip to the ladies room.

"Help, help", came a piercing scream and Carrie exited the ladies room with the speed of a fighter jet breaking the sound barrier. No doubt we would be accused of sexual harassment in today's world of changing values.

Perkes, a wavy-haired carefree easterner, and I became best pals. We learned to like Tex-Mex Mexican food together at Mike's Spanish Kitchen on 10th Street, we double-dated and later served as "best man" in each other's wedding. After getting married and moving off base, we drove to work together and had a ritual of eating a fried egg sandwich, with tomato and mayonnaise, at the NCO club every morning.

"Two of the same," we would say as we walked in the door. And the waitress knew.

"Those were the good old days," recalled Perkes from his office with the Associated Press in New York's Rockefeller Center. A thorough reporter and quick writer, Dan got his degree from Texas Tech and then launched a 30-plus year with the AP. He worked his way up the ladder. After stops in Lincoln, Nebraska, Oklahoma City and Des Moines, the likable Perkes culminated a successful career as assistant general manager of the wire service's national headquarters in New York. He was director of AP News Features and Wide World Photo.

Opting for a slower pace, Dan moved out of the pressure cooker not long ago and currently works in Public Affairs at New York University's Medical

Center. In the Big Apple to cover the NIT's 50th anniversary basketball tournament a few years back, we had a nice visit with Dan and wife Norma, another long-time friend. They treated us to a sumptuous dinner on the 107th floor of the World Trade Center and we took them to a Broadway show. Imagine our shock when only a short time later we learned that Norma had fallen down a flight of stairs in their suburban home, killing her instantly.

The base paper, a 12-page tabloid printed at Amarillo's streamlined *Globe-News* plant, was an excellent training ground for a young journalist. It constantly won awards for its bold, attractive makeup and outstanding writing content. And having it printed off base meant those of us involved with layout wore civilian clothes every Thursday and spent the day at the daily newspaper plant. That was a treat.

As the Korean war heated up and a greater need for more jet aircraft mechanics arose, Amarillo AFB had as many as 30,000 personnel at one time. It was fast becoming one of the Air Force's most important bases, adding a Strategic Air Command unit and a home for Peck's bad boys, a Retraining Center. With those numbers, base athletics fielded football and basketball teams that played extensive schedules.

Lt. Bill Miller, a star at nearby West Texas State and son of long-time Buffalo coach W.A. "Gus" Miller, tutored the basketball team and played as well. And he was blessed with big-time college talent that produced winning seasons. Among his best were All-American Gale McArthur and Keith Smith, former stars at Oklahoma A&M and students of the legendary Henry Iba. On one occasion, I traveled with the team to Oklahoma City, where the Amjets played A&M's freshman team in a preliminary to the Aggie varsity. It afforded all of us a chance to meet "Mr. Iba" and then some fond reminiscing for Smith and McArthur.

"It's always good to see some of my old players," said the big-as-life Aggie coach. "You boys can still play a good brand of ball."

In addition to travels with the football and basketball squads, golf afforded me some interesting trips on the workhorse of the Air Force, the famous C-47. The twin-engine prop cargo planes, called "gooney birds," were made passenger worthy by placing bucket seats on each side. Those noisy trips to Biloxi, Phoenix and San Antonio were nice diversions from hum-drum military life but the travel wasn't exactly first class.

On the golf excursions, I got to serve double duty. With my brand of "bogey golf," I made the fifth spot on our six-man team in those early years. As sports editor of the base paper, I had first-hand access to storycoverage.

Another good friend, Don Sbarra of Pittsburgh, was our best player. A long hitter who was the big, quiet type, he carried a two handicap.

Boxing was big and attracted huge weekend crowds to the flightline hangars. In Amarillo's stable was one of the country's finest middleweights, Gene Cooper, a native of nearby Pampa. A southpaw knockout artist, he could rarely find anyone to fight him on the local and regional level. However, in 1952 he won the Air Force light middleweight crown in San Antonio and qualified for the Olympic Tryouts in Kansas City.

I accompanied Cooper, his wife Candy and his mother to the tournament and four days of the finest amateur boxing I've ever witnessed. I was covering for the two Amarillo dailies and the *Pampa Daily News*, as well as the *Jet Journal*. The talented Cooper drew New York's great young gladiator, Ernest Anthony, in the opening round. He was edged in a close decision but most thought Cooper could have won if he had fought his usual aggressive style. It was no disgrace though, for Anthony went on to make the U.S. team as an alternate, later accompanying them to Helsinki, Finland. It was the same Ernest Anthony who carved out a great professional career as a light heavyweight.

Judged the outstanding boxer of the meet was a 165-pound slugger who knocked out every opponent in the first round. His name was Floyd Patterson, who put on some pounds and later became heavyweight champion of the world. Also on hand for the big bash were Tony Zale, the great middleweight champion from Gary, Indiana, and TV host Ed Sullivan.

While sports trotted out a host of name athletes at the base in the early 50s, probably the most famous personality on board was in Special Services, the entertainment branch of the Air Force. Jerry Van Dyke was not as well known as big brother Dick but he was making a name for himself.

"I thought he was funnier than Dick," quipped Dan Perkes, who did a number of stories on young Jerry and followed his ascension to "comedian of the year" in international Air Force competition.

Winning that honor gained him a spot on Ed Sullivan's television show and ultimate roles in many TV series, including the present "Coach" sitcom. As editor of the *Jet Journal* the last two years of my service obligation, I visited with the Danville, Illinois, native a couple times and saw him perform in special base shows on many occasions. But it was my buddy, Dan, who got to know him well on his beat as entertainment guru.

One last anecdote about the Air Force. Years later after our children learned my military time centered around something called the "Jet Journal", they asked:

"What kind of plane did you fly, daddy?"

8

PUTT POWELL, MATCHMAKER

As busy as Air Force activities kept me, I still felt unfulfilled. Sports had been in my blood since those early days on the farm, and I was craving more action. By now I knew without a doubt my niche in life would revolve around athletics in some capacity.

One Saturday I went down to the editorial offices of Amarillo's two daily newspapers, the *News* and the *Globe*. I stopped at the desk of sports editor Harry Gilstrap and inquired about a part-time job.

"Could you help us on weekend sports?" asked the stoic, pipe-smoking Gilstrap. "Things go crazy around here on weekends, especially when Friday night football is in season."

I was assigned a desk opposite the late Putt Powell, legendary columnist who labored for the Amarillo papers more than 60 years. Little did I dream that relationship would lead to my next big adventure several months later—marriage.

Putt was one of those unforgettable characters who indeed was a "character". In the first place, his real name was William L. But from early childhood, he had been called "Putt" because of a stuttering problem. Not quite as bad as country singer Mel Tillis, but almost. Not a talented writer, Putt's strong suit was his ability to recall sports history and statistics, especially if they involved his beloved Amarillo High School Sandies. Long the only high school in Amarillo, the Sandies continued to receive favored treatment from Putt even after three more came onto the scene.

"I was always told by my old editor Gene Howe not to be boring," related Putt, and for that reason he often tackled controversial subjects. He was well read all over the state and refused offers to migrate to other papers, choosing to remain loyal to the Sandies and the Texas Panhandle.

While he was a walking encyclopedia of sports information, the Putter was a horrendous speller. One of my fond memories of working near him were those incessant interruptions when he would raise up from his typewriter and ask how to spell the simplest of words. Often I thought to myself, "Is he pulling my leg?" Always appreciative of any help, he would return to writing, until he was unsure of another word.

While I am grateful for that short professional relationship with Putt, I have him to thank for an event of much greater importance, even though accidental. In the summer of 1952, a sports staff member was being given a farewell party by Putt and wife Frances. I was invited to their home. Another good friend of the Powells, Floy Webb, also received an invitation, precisely to meet a single *News-Globe* staffer, John Masterman. They thought Floy and John would make a good match.

This was Saturday night, and as she did most weekends, Floy was singing with a big band—Hugo Loewenstern's Orchestra—until midnight. Almost backing out at the last minute because she had endured gum surgery earlier in the week, Floy came anyway.

"Who in the world is that gorgeous babe?" I asked when I spotted her for the first time. A 5-2, green-eyed Texas beauty with an arresting smile, she was easily the best looking thing at the party and the center of my attention. I don't know what happened to John Masterman, but I was smitten from the start. Our common interest in big bands—especially the likes of Stan Kenton and Les Brown—made conversation easy and the Powells had been successful in matchmaking. I took her home that night and we dated almost nightly before getting married six months later.

Although I had been gone from the Evansville newspaper for more than two years, my old boss, sports editor Dick Anderson, was keeping up with me. The day after our wedding, he ran a three-column picture of my bride in the *Press*. Not on the society page, but on the sports page! And then he had some comments to make in an adjoining column, calling marriage "my third big adventure."

Here's what he wrote:

> *Ray Franks had a limited basketball career at Crossville High being a little on the short side for a player. But he had an insatiable appetite for all things sports, eventually got himself a sports deluxe auto, Dodge I believe, and bought a set of golf clubs which he was able to master with some success.*
>
> *Eventually he finished up his work at Evansville college, where he had served as editor of the Crescent, and without bothering President Lincoln Hale too much. He then became a full time denizen of the Press*

sports department. But Uncle Sam was breathing down his neck so he looked around, sorta liked the U.S. Air Force and set sail on another big adventure. That was two years ago.

Yesterday, in Amarillo, Texas, young Mr. Franks, now Staff Sergeant Franks, was married. And so begins his third big adventure. Sgt. Franks has considerable to do with the Amarillo Air Force Base paper and in his spare moments works for the Amarillo daily paper. He's a young man who has always succeeded in making his spare moments pay off and we wish him luck in the successful completion of this new story.

Had she preferred it over being a homemaker, I believe my wife could have made it big in show business. With a low mellow voice similar to that of Patti Page, she was in big demand with bands and local television in the mid-50s.

A funny thing happened on a trip to Raton, New Mexico. We were eating in a restaurant where a young blind man was playing the piano quite well. Floy went over and asked if she could sing along on a tune. After she had finished, he looked her way and said: "You sound just like Patti Page, what a wonderful sound."

Auditioning for Arthur Godfrey's famous Talent Scout TV show, she soared over two plateaus and wound up in Omaha, Nebraska. It was the last level before appearing on the popular national network show, and Jeanette Davis, Godfrey's red-haired singer, did the screening.

"How about dinner tonight?" Floy was asked the night before competition by a male Godfrey scout who had been following her rise up the audition ladder. When she refused, citing the fact she was married, it probably dashed her chances of clearing the final hurdle. Show business works that way.

When our family started growing—with daughter Debbie and sons Randy and David—Floy gave up the big bands and met every Tuesday with the Sweet Adelines, women's answer to barbershop singing. Now, it's strictly membership in the church choir, where she occasionally is asked to do solos. It's still a great voice, a God-given talent. Today, her rendition of "It Is No Secret What God Can Do" thrills me as much, or more, as her old version of "Sunny Side of the Street" with big bands.

One other comment about Putt Powell. He was a loyalist, through and through. He was loyal to his profession and loyal to his newspaper. Let me cite a good example.

After our marriage, Floy and I often played cards with Putt and Frances and another couple or two on Friday evenings. Every night about 10,

Putt would jump up, excuse himself from the table and drive down to the *News-Globe* building.

"He's got to make sure every "t" is crossed and every "i" dotted," said Frances. Putt would be gone about 30 minutes, checking his column in the early edition of next day's paper. The president could have been there and it wouldn't have made any difference.

9

"FIRE IN THE BELLY"

What's an entrepreneur and what motivates one? That's one of my two favorite words in the English language.

Webster's dictionary defines an entrepreneur as "a person who organizes and manages any enterprise, especially a business, usually with considerable initiative and risk." It's a word that reflects the spirit of the American Dream and the free enterprise system. I believe what people can do for themselves, they should do, and not look to Washington for handouts. Stories of entrepreneurial success in the business world are my favorites.

Syndicated columnist Don Taylor, who writes a weekly piece called "Minding Your Own Business," says an entrepreneur must have an intense desire to succeed. "They want to win. They work long, hard hours and maintain a high level of energy throughout the long days."

In other words, these animals must have "fire in the belly". And about the long hours, I like the comment: "To have your own business, you must be willing to work at least half a day—either the first 12 hours or the last."

The extremely astute Taylor, whose column is the first thing I read in Sunday's paper, adds that "restlessness" is another common trait of successful enterprisers. "They are frequently bored with repetitive tasks. They constantly seek new challenges. They love competition and seek activities that stimulate personal growth and development."

I'm not sure the lemonade business, watermelon stand or DumDum sucker enterprise qualified as genuine entrepreneurism, but after leaving the farm I can't ever remember being content with having only one job. While taking a full load in college, I worked a 40-hour week, or more, on a daily newspaper. Then when duty in the military called, I tackled another challenge on a Texas daily part-time.

Now that I was married and having trouble existing on a staff sergeant's salary, I not only continued to moonlight at the *News-Globe*, but took my first big shot at true entrepreneurship. Yes, there was risk involved when I decided to launch my first publication, a regional football magazine named *Panhandle Pigskin Preview*.

Always an admirer of Street and Smith's national *College Football* magazine that centered on advance peeks of the upcoming season, along with schedules and past year's results, I reasoned that such a publication would succeed on a regional level. Remembering those Friday night sessions at the newspaper and the Panhandle's insatiable appetite for anything football was like yelling "sic 'em" to a coon dog. I was pumped up and ready to accept the challenge, without a cent in our savings account.

"I don't have any money but I believe I have a great idea," I told Sam Goodner, who had a small print shop on West Seventh Street. Sam looked over the young airman who wore civvies when he was moonlighting at the Amarillo paper, scratched his head and agreed.

We made a deal. He would print 3,000 copies of the 42-page football magazine and wait for his first payment until copies were sold and advertising collected. In printing, that's not the way it works, back then or today. It's customary for the printer to get a substantial down payment from the publisher, especially if he or she is a new customer or a military type who could be shipped out on short notice. So Sam was taking a chance, a big risk.

Next, I secured the services of a small local advertising agency that agreed to sell space for 25 percent of the gross. The rest was all downhill. Working at the paper, I had access to athletic directors and coaching contacts at the high schools and colleges in the area, and flooded them with questionnaires. Don't forget, this was long before the Dallas Cowboys entered the picture and took a huge chunk of fan interest.

In our small, two-bedroom apartment on Duncan Drive, I composed stories on the Royal portable typewriter retained from college days. On our kitchen table, pages were laid out into the wee hours of the night. Well-known area sportswriters Putt Powell and Harry Gilstrap of the Amarillo papers and Art Gatts of Lubbock were paid to do special pieces, adding instant credibility to the magazine. At $125 a page, advertising sold well, and then came the challenge of distribution.

"I have a magazine that should sell on your routes in the Panhandle," I explained to Sam Marmaduke, a balding, slight man with big glasses. His company was West Texas News Agency, located in an unpretentious wooden building out on West Sixth Street.

This was the same Sam Marmaduke who took a small print regional distribution company and developed it into one of the giants of the

50 CENTS

PANHANDLE PIGSKIN
Preview

THIRD ANNUAL

1955

BOB WAY
Golden Sandie

Featuring

- Phillips' State Championship Blackhawks
- Is Amarillo on its Way Back to the Top?

My first challenge as a publisher was a regional football magazine titled *Panhandle Pigskin Preview*. I was still in the Air Force at the time and it got my entrepreneurial juices flowing.

entertainment industry.   With sound business practices and a desire to succeed, likable Sam expanded into records, videos and the hot items of the period.   The business later became Western Merchandisers with Hastings stores serving as its retail outlets.   So big did Sam become he was elected president of the prestigious CMA (Country Music Association), even making an appearance on national TV.   Remaining active in the business until his death in 1993, Sam knew the meaning of entrepreneurship.

A testimony to Sam's importance in the recording industry, superstar Garth Brooks flew over from Oklahoma and slipped into a back pew of a local church at Marmaduke's funeral.   He later reappeared in Amarillo for the dedication of a large distribution complex named after the Texas businessman.

The Sam Marmaduke I approached in 1953 was still a small businessman, and he looked at my magazine with genuine interest.   "I can't see any reason why they won't sell," he said with a grin, knowing full well he was pumping up a new publisher who was walking on egg shells and needed encouragement.   "Bring me a thousand and let's give them a whirl."

Sell they did on newsstands within a hundred-mile radius of Amarillo. And Sam had to order more.   *Panhandle Pigskin Preview* sold for 35 cents. He took 40 percent, 20 for his company and 20 for the participating outlet. We all made money.

Then, Floy and I had another idea—sell the magazines at opening football games in the area.   Dee Walker, athletic director of Amarillo Public Schools, wouldn't allow it but medium-sized schools like Phillips, Childress and Abernathy took a look at the publication and said "come on down."

After picking up carpenter aprons at the nearest lumber yard and rolls of change from the bank, we loaded up our station wagon with relatives and friends and headed down the highway.   Athletic officials allowed us to announce the sale of the magazine at half-time, and then we fanned out among the spectators.   The reception was excellent and brothers-in-law Dean, Clifford and Danny Webb and father-in-law Loyd were top sellers.   But it was a friend, Curly Newkirk, who always outsold all of us.   He was a master hawker, pushing the magazines in front of fans and taking their money at the same time.   Kind of like the famous peanut and hot-dog hustlers at major league baseball games.   It's a real talent.

My first publishing venture made money on that maiden voyage, about a thousand dollars.   But more importantly, its success signalled that maybe, just maybe, I might have the stuff out of which entrepreneurs are made.

So what's my second favorite word in the English language?   It's another "e" word, "enthusiasm".

In his book, *To Dream Again*, Robert Dale told the story of Winnie the Pooh and Piglet. As they walked together one afternoon, Piglet asked:

"When you wake up in the morning, Pooh, what's the first thing you say to yourself?"

"What's for breakfast," answers Pooh. "And what do you say, Piglet?"

"I wonder what exciting thing is going to happen today."

That's one of the best descriptions of enthusiasm I've ever heard. It's a word that literally oozes with action and excitement. And well it should.

Enthusiasm stems from the Greek word "enthos", which means "with God". Pretty good pedigree for a word that I used for years as the basis for a devotional to each new college Sunday School department at Paramount Baptist Church. No doubt boring to my wife, the students didn't know it was an annual thing.

Ralph Waldo Emerson once made the statement that "nothing great has ever been accomplished without enthusiasm."

Here's another description: "Enthusiasm is that certain something that makes us great, that pulls us out of the mediocre and commonplace and builds us into power. It glows and shines and lights up our faces. It makes us sing and makes others sing with us. With enthusiasm and confidence, anything can be accomplished."

My favorite: "If we have it, we should thank God for it. If we don't, then we should get down on our knees and pray for it."

10

PAYING MY DUES AS AN SID

The Air Force was unsuccessful in getting me to re-enlist. No surprise there. The pace was too slow, the waste repugnant and not much incentive for an entrepreneur. Besides that, I had a job in the civilian world weeks before being discharged in the fall of 1954.

There was an opening at nearby West Texas State College for a sports information director and instructor in journalism. Two jobs, one salary. After Amarillo Sports Editor Harry Gilstrap had put in a good word for me, I assumed that position on September 11, one day after shedding my Air Force blues and exactly one week before the school's first football game.

Located 17 miles south of Amarillo on a divided freeway, West Texas State was a medium-sized college of 5,000 with strong departments in agriculture, business and education. In athletics, it was a member of the Border Conference with such schools as Texas Tech, Arizona State, U. of Arizona and Texas Western (now U. of Texas at El Paso). Already a major player in Division I NCAA basketball, West Texas, like most others its size, was struggling financially while trying to maintain a first class football program.

I quickly found out why mine was a split job. By having part-time duties in the journalism department, teaching a couple classes and sponsoring the weekly newspaper, my entire salary was charged to academics. That freed up personnel money for athletics. And while that didn't bother me, I was a lousy instructor who saw most of my enthusiasm for the job drifting toward sports information.

For eight and a half years, it provided still another kind of journalistic adventure that would help prepare me for a publishing career in college sports a little later. At a small college, you do it all. I wrote advance stories for the media, prepared and edited brochures, spoke to local civic clubs and traveled with the football and basketball teams. While the pay was slim, it was a fun job and our growing family survived.

In my first year on campus, I was treated to an exceptional sports experience. Coach W.A. "Gus" Miller had one of the best basketball teams in his long and illustrious career. On the last weekend of Border Conference play, West Texas tied Texas Tech for the championship. A coin flip was conducted by the commissioner immediately after the Saturday night games.

"Heads," said West Texas athletic director Frank Kimbrough. And heads it was. We were boarding a TWA plane for San Francisco the next morning on our way to play the great U. of San Francisco Dons in the first round of the NCAA Tournament.

Everything happened so fast that we literally took the hotel reservations of Texas Tech, who was positive it would be representing the Border Conference in post-season play. In fact, the Red Raiders had bags packed and planned to go on to the West Coast after its Saturday night game in El Paso. But Texas Western pulled the upset and threw the race in turmoil.

"Enjoying your room and having a great time in San Francisco," wrote Amarillo sportswriter Putt Powell on a picture postcard to Joe Kelly, Lubbock sports editor. I shared a room with Putt, who never wasted an opportunity to rub salt in the wounds of his counterpart from the South Plains.

It was a marvelous experience even though legendary Don stars Bill Russell and K.C. Jones led an onslaught that resulted in a 20-point victory before a packed house at the Cow Palace. In all fairness to West Texas though, Coach Phil Woolpert's team won every single game that year, including the national championship, by lop-sided margins. In a classic one-on-one matchup with Jones, the Buffaloes' James Scott outscored the Don All-American and was later named to San Francisco's all opponent team. It was 6-9 Russell who was the difference as he dominated the game like no other player I had ever seen. Of course, it was no fluke as the great leaper went on to star for years in the NBA.

Just before half-time with the score still close, there was an incident that had everyone in attendance concerned. As Russell went up high for one of his trademark rebounds, West Texas' Ray Burrus, a 6-6 solidly-built center, moved under him. Pow! Russell hit the floor with a thud and lay prone and motionless for maybe two or three minutes. The crowd went deafening quiet before he stirred and got back on his feet. We caught a few obscenities and clenched fists as we passed the crowd on the way to the dressing room at intermission.

We didn't win the game but Coach Miller, a dry-humored Texan, easily

As sports information director at West Texas State, I got to accompany the basketball team to the NCAA Playoffs against Bill Russell and U. of San Francisco in 1955. That's Putt Powell next to me and Coach Gus Miller to his right.

came out on top at the pre-game luncheon heavily covered by the San Francisco press.

"We're honored to be playing the No. 1 ranked team in the nation," said Gus. "Heck, we've played the top-ranked team in the country before . . . but we've also lost to them before."

In those days, the Buffaloes were the best known Texas college team in national circles, playing many major powers and making an occasional visit to Madison Square Garden. Wearing cowboy boots and ten-gallon hats, at one time they were billed as "the tallest team in America."

Football didn't enjoy that luxury in the mid-50s. Coached by Frank Kimbrough, a brother of Jarrin' John Kimbrough of Texas A&M fame, the Buffs were respectable but struggled each year to attain and maintain Division I status. A flicker of national attention was generated in 1956, though, when the Buffaloes won seven and lost three, and then whipped giant-killer Southern Mississippi, 20-13, in the Tangerine Bowl at Orlando, Florida.

And the timing couldn't have been better. Saddled with a tiny on-campus stadium for many years, West Texas struck out to attract the football fans of the Panhandle area by building a new showplace just north of the campus and 15 miles south of Amarillo, a city of 150,000. First built to seat 20,000 in a bowl-like setting, long range plans called for eventual expansion to 40,000. During the fund-raising, I was assigned to a Polk Street building in Amarillo and assisted in the final stages of that project.

Kimbrough retired from coaching a year after his Tangerine Bowl triumph and assistant Clark Jarnagin took over. A big likable fuzzball, Jarnagin went 1-9 the first year in 1958 and repeated it in 1959, the year new Buffalo Bowl opened. In his first game as a head coach at Roanoke, Virginia, Jarnagin saw Virginia Tech take the opening kickoff and run it back for a touchdown. That proved to be an ominous play. It was all downhill after that.

These were tough times and I remember having trouble accepting some of these setbacks as the school's new sports information director. It was my job to accompany the football and basketball teams on road trips, taking care of the needs of the press and radio. During a road game at Hardin-Simmons University in Abilene, I was feeling pretty good about a 27-6 lead the Buffs enjoyed going into the fourth quarter. However, Sammy Baugh, the great ex-TCU quarterback, was coaching the Cowboys and had them throwing the ball all over the field. In other words, they were capable of scoring in a hurry and often.

And they did. Each time they forced West Texas to kick, back they would come with a quick touchdown. One, two and three, and each time my stomach kept churning a little more. In the final minute, Hardin-Simmons scored a fourth TD to win the game and I couldn't handle it. Up came everything I had eaten that day, leaving a tell-tale souvenir in George Hine's pressbox. After that episode, I tried to control my emotions a little better.

Another pressbox story I'll always remember occurred at home at a football game. Opening the pressbox a couple hours before the game, I noticed some yellow jackets buzzing around the big glass window. The radio voice of the Buffaloes for many years and good friend Warren Hasse suggested I find some way to get rid of them.

"Don't worry about them, Hasse," I assured. "At this time of the year, they're harmless and will just go away some place and die."

Hasse went on to his booth and did the game. After it was over and he retreated to the main pressbox, guess who had a wet handkerchief wrapped around his neck and big red sting marks? Yes, during the course of the game, I got pasted good by one of those "harmless" yellow jackets, and Warren has never let me forget it.

Incidentally, Warren Hasse is still the best play-by-play announcer I've ever heard. Period. In the late 40s, he migrated from Wisconsin to Pampa in the Texas Panhandle, taking the job as sports editor of the daily paper. He then bought radio station KPDN and settled in as a businessman-announcer, doing West Texas football and basketball for more than 30 years.

Thorough, well-prepared and energetic, Warren could have made it big-time in sports announcing had he so chosen. Possibly major league baseball, as did Dick Risenhoover, another former broadcaster of WT athletics and a good friend. The color assistant to Hasse for a number of seasons, Dick went on to become the Texas Rangers' first play-by-play announcer before dying of cancer on opening day of the 1978 season.

"It's always a joy to come to Amarillo and renew my friendship with your great announcer, Warren Hasse," Coach Dick Versace would say when he brought Bradley University to town. Hasse still keeps close contact with the former Chicago Bulls coach and many other notable personalities he's met along the way.

As I said earlier, it was difficult making budget in those early years at West Texas. Air travel was becoming popular in college sports but we were still using buses and automobiles on even the long 900-mile round trips to El Paso and Las Cruces.

On one such journey, I was riding in Coach Kimbrough's car along with assistant coaches Hatcher Brown and Clark Jarnagin, both practical jokers of the first order. I had closed my eyes and settled into a nice siesta. Suddenly, I was awakened by these gut-wrenching screams, the squeal of brakes and the sight of a huge truck right in front of us.

"What is it?" I yelled, half-asleep and petrified with fear. The coaches were rollicking with laughter and reaping the rewards of a good prank. It was a set-up for anyone who dozed. Kimbrough had pulled up close to the back of the truck, tapped his brakes and everyone screamed in unison. I wasn't the first, or the last.

By 1960, West Texas football was in a real quandary. It had a new beautiful football stadium and back-to-back 1-9 seasons. Jarnagin was fired and a roly-poly whirlwind named Joe Kerbel was hired to save the program. And he did.

Eccentric, unorthodox, energetic, obsessed, football genius. Joe Kerbel was all those things. I worked with him for three years and I've never met anyone like him. He was one of a kind, a Texas original. Little known outside the Lone Star state, where he enjoyed remarkable success at Breckenridge and Amarillo High Schools, the former Marine captain brought a highly-disciplined and entertaining brand of football to West Texas State. His split-T, pro-type offense scored frequently and filled the stands.

At his first practice the first season, he told announcer Warren Hasse: "Nobody's got any better equipment than our kids. It's the same as the Green Bay Packers and the Dallas Cowboys. I ask my kids to give me their best, so the least I can do is give them the best in return. We're going to travel first class, stay in nice hotels and eat well. This operation is going to be first class. When they realize that, they'll want to perform like a first class football team."

Forced to play with the hand that was dealt him, Kerbel won only three games the first year. But then it was 6-4 the following season and in 1962, my last year at West Texas State, the Kerbel plan reaped a bountiful harvest. Led by Pistol Pete Pedro, a jitterbug who led the nation in scoring, and Jerry Logan, later a star for the Baltimore Colts, the Buffs won nine and lost two. But more importantly, they started attracting a lot of attention.

Not only did fans fill Buffalo Bowl at home games, but *Sports Illustrated* sent senior writer Bob Creamer to see the much-awaited duel between Pedro and New Mexico State's outstanding back, Preacher Pilot. Then at the end of the season, the big plum was the host spot in El Paso's Sun Bowl, where we defeated Ohio University, 15-14. Working the game was my last assignment at West Texas State before turning my full attention to directory publishing. While the Sun Bowl win was an appropriate ending, the entire 1962 season was a real hoot.

First, there was the sweet 30-27 victory over rival Texas Tech before 41,500 in Lubbock and then the impressive 49-0 massacre of Texas Western, coached by Bum Phillips. But the most memorable game was the 15-14 win over now Pac-10 member Arizona State University at Tempe, an event in which I became a major participant. In fact, the game and its aftermath became a brouhaha of major proportions.

It happened like this. In West Texas State's first four wins, the 5-8, 150-pound running phenomenon Pedro was setting all kinds of records until he was injured in the Arlington State game. It was the one just previous to Arizona State.

"Pedro will play Saturday," Coach Kerbel told me just before I departed for Tempe the following Wednesday to do interviews and advance publicity for the game. In fact, he had re-entered the Arlington game after sustaining a first half injury and zipped off a 55-yard run. Arizona State assistant Dick Mansperger, a good friend who formerly coached at WT and later was personnel director of the Dallas Cowboys, scouted the game and knew Pedro had been injured.

When the game started, Pedro wasn't in the starting lineup. Half-time and still no Pistol Pete. In the third quarter, Arizona State, with a 14-7 lead, was on the Buffaloes' one-yard line and about ready to salt away the win. However, Jerry Logan, later an All-Pro defensive back in the NFL, intercepted a flat pass near the end zone and ran it back 99 yards for a turn-around touchdown. Kerbel inserted a trick, isolated end, two-point play to take the lead, 15-14.

The Sun Devil fans were stunned, unable to believe their eyes. Still no Pedro. Underdog West Texas controlled the ball the final quarter and hung on for the upset win, one of the biggest in the school's history. And they did it without Pedro, who had not responded to treatment as expected.

But the game was only part of the story, not the bombastic portion. The excitable, intense Kerbel always demanded that his substitute players stand on the sidelines, not sit. At Tempe, where the stadium is built on a solid rock formation, the first rows are ground level. This is the same structure that has been enlarged to 75,156 seats, and just last season hosted the two most important football games of the year. It was the site of the Fiesta Bowl matchup between Nebraska and Florida for the college title, and less than a month later, served as backdrop for Super Bowl XXX.

Arizona State fans couldn't see over the WT players and started yelling. Then they threw ice, paper wads and anything else they could find. Obscenities soon followed.

"Go blow it out," the excited and agitated Kerbel screamed to the fans, refusing to yield to their demands. From the pressbox, we could see the mini-war being waged as animated Joe divided his time yelling at the irate fans and barking instructions to his team. It was a sight to behold.

At half-time, as coaches and players went to the dressing rooms, Kerbel and equally volatile Arizona State coach Frank Kush nearly came to blows. When the second half started, police tried to stop fans from pelting Buffalo players in the back. They also attempted to convince Kerbel to seat his players. Neither side relinquished.

Flushed with excitement and a staggering victory at game's end, the roly-poly Kerbel turned toward the fans behind him and shot them one half of a "V" for victory sign. That wasn't the end of the episode, only the beginning of a much-publicized fiasco. Angry fans called Arizona State officials, protesting the actions of Kerbel. The ASU president was in contact with WT prexy, Dr. James Cornette. And the Arizona press was upset with me.

Headlines in succeeding issues of the *Arizona Republic* and *Phoenix Gazette* blared: "Publicist cons fans, gridders," and "Gotta rate this as A-1 Snow Job". They claimed that fans were cheated because Pedro didn't play. Which is a strange twist. In all my years in athletics I have found the one thing the media resents most is just the opposite. Reporting all week that a player is hurt, then the guy shows up on game day fit as a fiddle.

But typical of what we experienced in this episode was the scathing column of *Arizona Republic* sports editor Frank Gianelli three days after the game. Here's the way it started:

BUNCO DETAIL
Phoenix Police Dept.
Phoenix, Ariz.

Gentlemen: I'd like to report a swindle.
Please be on lookout for Ray Franks, mild-mannered, convincing speaker. Wears glasses and an unassuming air. Occupation: publicist for West Texas State football team and individual player, Pistol Pete Pedro, in particular. Guilty of bamboozling Phoenix press

and Arizona State University football team last week. This man is dangerous.

And that's the way I feel about being snookered into believing a whole Pistol Pete Pedro would be in the West Texas State lineup Saturday against our Arizona State Sun Devils.

Hooked . . . ?

You bet; hook, line, sinker and the line right up to the rod and the reel. I'm afraid to spit for fear I'll find a couple of Franks' fingers in my teeth, too.

If he'd been selling resort lots in the Antarctic, I'd have bought.

Just as I believed his reply to the question, "Is Pete Pedro physically sound? Will he be able to go full steam against Arizona State . . . ?

"You bet. He's 100 per cent okay and eager to make up for last year when he was injured and only got 12 yards against the Devils."

And then he unstrung a glowing list of praise about Pete, the nation's leading rusher, and we used the grist to build stories publicizing the game.

As the advance man for the game, I was told to keep the news on Pedro upbeat. After returning home the winning gladiator, Kerbel made the following explanation to the Associated Press:

"We had every hope Pedro could play. We ran him all over Phoenix for treatment. If Arizona State officials can tell me when someone will play and when he can't, I'll hire them here, not as directors of promotion, but as orthopedic surgeons.

"Pete made the final decision himself. I am not going to play an injured man to please a promotion director or anybody else. I wouldn't have taken Pete with us if I didn't think he could play. If the fans were disappointed because Pete didn't play, think how disappointed I was."

At the end of Gianelli's column condemning my actions, he made the following observations: "So West Texas won the game. So maybe this sounds like sour grapes."

Amen!

Called "an amazing person, an excellent coach and tremendous motivator" by the great Dallas Cowboy coach Tom Landry, Joe not only won football games but prepared young men for life. In his 11 years at little West Texas State, his high-octane program produced 60 players for the professional ranks, an unbelievable accomplishment. His two most memorable were Eugene "Mercury" Morris, who later starred for Don

Shula and the Miami Dolphins, and Duane Thomas, the temperamental running back who also made headlines for the Dallas Cowboys. In books written after retirement, both Morris and Thomas have called Kerbel "the best coach I've ever had."

Kerbel, who walked a thin line between being fanatical and obsessed in his approach to football, stayed at West Texas eight more years after I left. Although he was winning games and had been successful in getting West Texas membership in the Missouri Valley Conference, he was fired after the 1970 season. Always the unconventional breed, Joe often sparred with school administration, who eventually did him in. He went into the insurance business in Dallas, but died two years later at 51. Cause of death: Heart attack and possibly football heartbreak.

A man of intense, boundless energy, he is gone but two decades later Kerbel stories remain.

His automobile driving technique is one of them. I never saw him in anything but a Cadillac, fast Cadillacs. When Joe was on the road recruiting, making speeches or going to ball games, he had only two speeds—fast and faster.

He always had assistants with him in the car. Their duties were to provide company and conversation and serve as look-outs for Highway Patrol officers. They were even instructed to bring along binoculars to better spot patrol cars lurking behind billboards and trees. After a Hardin-Simmons game in Abilene, I made the mistake of riding back to Canyon with Kerbel and three assistant coaches. He kept the speedometer between 90 and 100 constantly, all the time looking away from the road talking and gesturing with his hands. That was my first and last auto trip with Kerbel.

Another practice of Kerbel's was to tell assistants not to come back from a recruiting trip until they had signed players. Jack "Sleepy" Harris, who compiled a book on his former head coach titled, *"A Passion For Victory"*, attests to that fact.

"I would be in California scouring the junior colleges with nothing more specific than find us a big, fast running back' or a quarterback who can win for us.' Even though I would be running out of money and be homesick for my family, I didn't dare go home until I had someone lined up."

And Harris says there was no place to hide from his demanding boss, who spent a big portion of his waking hours on the phone.

"Once while in California, I had left the motel room to go use a washateria down the block. While sitting there, reading a newspaper and enjoying the fact I was the only person in the place, the pay phone mountedon a nearby wall rings. I made the mistake of answering it, and heard this booming voice: Sleepy, it's Joe. Boy, I had a helluva time finding you.'"

Another Kerbel story was related by Lou Spry, who followed me as SID at West Texas State. One day at practice, Kerbel wasn't happy the way Mercury Morris was running a particular play.

"I want you to hit the cheek of the right guard's butt," he told the fleet halfback who was considered a quick learner. To onlookers, Morris appeared to be doing exactly what Kerbel wanted when he ran it three straight times.

After the fourth effort, and still unsatisfied, Kerbel told Mercury to bend over and grab his ankles. Then he proceeded to haul off and kick his star player three times in full view of the team.

"Now run it again," the angry coach blared.

When Morris executed it this time, no different than before, the rotund Kerbel smiled, a la Jackie Gleason, and said: "Now that's more like it. I don't know why I have to kick your butt to get you to run it right".

After Kerbel was forced out of the picture, West Texas State athletics started a declining spiral that has supplied me with one of the biggest disappointments in 50 years of sports. While West Texas officials have opted to drop down to Division II and regional competition in the Lone Star Conference, former opponents have taken the high road.

There are Arizona and Arizona State in the lofty Pac-10 Conference and Texas Tech in the new Big Twelve, another powerhouse. Former Missouri Valley opponents such as Louisville, Tulsa, Memphis State and New Mexico State often are found in the top 25 of national basketball rankings. Shoot, we formerly played home and home football games with the Hokies of Virginia Tech, when they were also known as the Gobblers. An area as large as the Texas Panhandle deserves an NCAA Division I sports program. Besides that, I spent nearly nine years of my life helping West Texas attain and maintain that status.

When Bud Wilkinson was coaching at Oklahoma, the college president made a statement I have always remembered. "It may not be right," he said, "but the athletic department represents the front porch of our university."

11

A NEW VENTURE

Even though the dual job at West Texas State was leaving little idle time, my entrepreneurial juices were boiling in 1955. I was still publishing the regional football magazine, *Panhandle Pigskin Preview*, but the extra income was limited.

I was searching for something more challenging and more productive. Just maybe the fact that we had bought a small three-bedroom brick house that provided me with my first "office" had something to do with it. That first workroom was a six-by-six foot storage area at the back of our single-car garage. It contained a crude desk built out of scrap lumber, a Royal portable typewriter and a two-drawer cardboard filing cabinet purchased in a garage sale. The room was big enough to turn around in, and that was about it.

Boy, was it hot in there during the summer and cold in the winter. To say nothing of all the noise that came from the washer and dryer located just a few feet from my cubicle. While I thoroughly enjoyed the job at West Texas State, I knew it would be just a matter of time before I would be a full-fledged publisher and a full-time entrepreneur.

The idea for a new publication came on a January afternoon while sitting around the sports department of the *Amarillo News-Globe*. Veteran writer Putt Powell was talking.

"Who's that new football coach at El Paso High?" he asked of no one in particular. He pointed to a copy of McNitt's *Blue Book of College Athletics* laying nearby, and remarked: "You know, we need something like that for high school sports in Texas. It would be invaluable to coaches, sportswriters and school officials."

That casual observation on a bleak, wintry afternoon was the inspiration for the birth of *Texas Sports Guide*, a directory listing all pertinent information on state high school and college athletic departments. It would include such information as school colors, nicknames, phone numbers and names of all athletic personnel.

"At long last sports enthusiasts will have available a complete encyclopedia of information on the high school program in Texas," said Dr. Rhea Williams, State Athletic Director of the University Athletic League at that time.   He jumped on our bandwagon immediately, and that was important.

Also giving us a huge boost was L.W. McConachie, Executive Director of the Texas High School Coaches Association. After hearing our proposal, he advised us to get the directory off the press in time for the annual Coaching School in San Antonio. It was scheduled for late July, 1955.

"Get them on down here in time for the start of the show and we'll put you in registration line," offered the business-like but congenial McConachie. "You'll be able to show your new books to 3,000 coaches."

Priced at $4, a fair tag for a voluminous amount of valuable information, the books moved slowly that first year. "We had to stop and explain exactly what the directory was all about to every coach," remembers wife Floy. "It was like pulling teeth; we were discouraged and tired at the end of each day."

And while I thought it was priced fairly, we had to drop it down to $2.95 the next year. What we didn't know that first time out was most coaches had to pay for the books out of their own pocket. Once the books became known, athletic departments would put them in the annual budget. Sales skyrocketed and the new venture was on its way.

"Learning from your own mistakes is an important part of private enterprise," is a remark that well suited our situation. We knew we had a quality product that fit the mold of "supply and demand", and it started showing a profit the second year. Circulation jumped at a healthy rate each year and before long, we were printing and selling 5,000 copies of that directory we couldn't give away the first time out.

Getting that first edition assembled, printed and available for consumption was no easy task. Being the consummate day-dreamer, I have to keep reminding myself that it's the "doers" who are successful in life. The Patent Office in Washington is full of great ideas that collect nothing but dust.

Limited time and finances were the main stumbling blocks. Questionnaire cards were used to obtain the basic information from every high school and college in Texas, and when some didn't respond to two mailings, phone calls were made. Stamped and self-addressed postcards were utilized to encourage cooperation. It was a monumental research project, made more difficult because athletic officials knew nothing of our operation. We were an unknown entity with a box number mailing address.

I scoured *Athletic Journal* and *Scholastic Coach* magazines to compile a mailing list for potential advertisers, information that was recorded on 3x5 index cards. Only 16 advertisers came aboard that first year, even though rates were extremely reasonable—$100 for a page and $60 for a half-page. Like Texas school officials, they too were being asked to step out on faith.

The thrill of the first advertising contract coming in the mail is a sweet memory that still remains. It was from Weldon, Williams and Lick, a giant ticket company that spans an entire block in Fort Smith, Arkansas. They took the back cover and continued to advertise in all my publications for years. That's real loyalty.

The 154-page directory was composed mainly of agate reference material and the challenge of a huge and expensive print job sent me shopping. I had to find a company big enough to effectively handle the project and competitive enough to afford. Dejavu Sam Goodner!

"I have a problem and I'm wondering if you can help me out," I told Dick Keys, manager of the printing division at Russell's in Amarillo. When I was wearing my sports information director's hat at West Texas, Dick turned out some attractive brochures for our office.

"If you can give me extra time," figured the jolly Keys with the ever-present cigarette hanging from his mouth, "we can set your school information as filler type." His linotype operators did just that, working my project in and around the more pressing jobs, at a considerable saving in money. Dick, who always referred to me as "Fay Ranks", is another of those people I can look back to and say "thanks for encouragement when it was needed most."

A much bigger project than *Panhandle Pigskin Preview*, the process of proof-reading and laying out pages continued around the kitchen table as we burned the midnight oil. But it was a labor of love and birth was being given to a publication that would become the "bible of Texas high school sports." Once the word got out about the new high school directory in Texas, similar reference books started popping up all over the country. Sam Ketchman started one in Michigan, Clell Wade in Missouri, Ken Olson in Illinois and Roald Sorensen and Louis Christian in North Carolina.

The group of neophyte publishers started congregating at the National Sporting Goods Association convention in cold Chicago every January. Invariably at day's end, we would wind up at Miller's Pub and Restaurant, across from the Palmer House Hotel. There we would devour a juicy ribeye steak and engage in choice conversation. The NSGA show afforded marvelous opportunities for securing new advertising, and we all benefited from the note-swapping. The state directories were hot new publications that had us all agog.

It was at one of these conventions in the grand ballroom of the Palmer House that I heard the best speech of my life. With 5,000 businessmen waiting on his every word, Norman Vincent Peale communicated like no other banquet speaker I've heard or seen. He entertained, he preached and he instructed for an hour with his "power of positive thinking," and the inspired throng erupted into a standing ovation when he finished.

For years, I had been an admirer of this elderly clergyman with the silver tongue and good common sense. Dr. Peale used a story to illustrate the importance of positive thinking to get ahead in life. A young man was standing in a long line of prospects interviewing for a job he desperately wanted.

"As the line moved at a snail's pace, this young man had an idea," related the glib storyteller. "He broke ranks and walked briskly to the person doing the interviewing."

"I'm the one who's 23rd in line," stated the young man, "and it's going to take a while for me to get up here. I would be perfect for this job, so please don't make a decision until you talk to me."

"That," said Dr. Peale, "is what positive thinking is all about."

It was about this time, the fall of 1958 to be exact, that I made a life-changing decision. I accepted Jesus Christ as my personal Lord and Saviour, and took my position as spiritual head of my family, which now included a daughter, Debbie, and a son, Randy.

In my early childhood days on the farm in Illinois, we attended Phillipstown Methodist Church. While I still recall the marvelous teaching of Mrs. Collins in Sunday School, and the many picnics on the ground, I never got serious about spiritual things. I honestly don't remember anyone talking to me about it.

Later, I didn't have time for church, I thought, and went to Texas still feeling a void in my life. With marriage and a family, my responsibilities increased. We were visiting several congregations when First Baptist Church launched a mission in Southwest Amarillo, where a housing boom was taking place.

Meeting in a schoolhouse only a few blocks from our home and across the street from the future home of Paramount Baptist Church, the new mission attracted our attention. Our family visited a couple times before I felt a strong tug one Sunday to walk the aisle and tell Pastor Chester O'Brien, "I was turning my life over to the Lord." That decision enabled me to plug in to a generator of unlimited power that has guided me through the good times and the bad times. The timing seemed perfect. A new church, a new life; it was the best decision I ever made.

As the Texas directory became more profitable and time consuming, and since I was still laboring full-time at West Texas State, I sold the *Panhandle Pigskin Preview* magazine in 1959 after seven editions. Spare time was hard to find. Insurance man Frank Hodnik, who also coached football at Price College High School, purchased it and the nice profit was put aside for future developments.

With the state high school directories proliferating at a rapid pace, I felt compelled to grab more territory, like the claim-jumpers in the California gold rush of 1849. And it was California where I moved for the second directory venture, in 1960, five years after Texas had been cultivated. And three years later, when I cut my ties with West Texas State and leaped full-time into publishing, six more books covering 10 western states were added. In all, I now had eight separate directories spanning 12 states. I was beginning to feel like a cattle baron expanding his vast ranching boundaries.

A year later, we invaded the South. Eight more guides reaching from Florida to Louisiana were launched. However, after two years, I realized the operation was being spread too thin and sold these properties to my artist friend and his wife, Glenn and Gladys Zulauf. Besides that, the western books were producing most of the profit, especially Texas.

With this aggressive expansion of what was still basically a one-man publishing business, I began running out of space. The garage storage room sufficed for a couple years and later the basement under a den add-on soon became inadequate also.

It was time to get out of the house and find an office building.

12

THE PUBLISHING RANCH

What's the fascination of a ranch? Is it the appeal of the open range? Is it cowboys, cattle, horses, Roy Rogers, Hopalong Cassidy or just the lure of an enduring way of life? Whatever it is, it's western.

President Lyndon Johnson, a Texan, once said: "I want a big, big ranch . . . and all the land adjoining it."

But the best illustration of a love affair with ranching involves my late friend, Ron Trafton. It's a wonderful story, a George Plimpton-style fantasy lived out to the hilt.

It was 1977 and his family printing company had a big share of the business in Amarillo, including our *National Directory of College Athletics*.

"I'm going to buy a ranch," Ron told wife Betty one day, "and fulfill a life-long dream of being a cowboy."

Betty thought he was nuts. But she remembered that this 285-pound hulk of a man had always wanted to get back close to nature after spending childhood summers on his aunt's farm in Oklahoma. "For years," said Betty, "he talked of the rustic, outdoor life." Besides that, he was strong-willed and not easily dissuaded.

They bought a 987-acre ranch near Wellington and started raising a menagerie of animals, including horses, cows, goats, turkeys and chickens. Besides that, they harvested a truck farm that filled three freezers with fresh vegetables. But that wasn't really what he wanted, and when the trips back to the print shop became more frequent, the property was put up for sale.

Shortly after buying two sections west of Amarillo, Ron was told by a banker that the 72,000-acre Masten Ranch near the New Mexico border was up for lease. "Now that's a ranch," mused Trafton.

When he learned the massive spread was owned by Abilene Christian University and 87 lease applications had been submitted, he made it 88.

Always the super salesman, Ron appeared before the board of trustees and convinced them he was the man for the job. Knowing nothing about cattle and probably the least qualified of the bunch, he told them "he could make money."

But his problems were only starting. When he took his wife and moved to the ranch, there were no ranchhands. They had all quit.

"Ron was as low as I've ever seen him," said Betty. "He was ready to turn around and head back to Amarillo."

With help, however, he rounded up a new group of cowboys and started learning how to ride, rope and herd cattle himself. "And what made this even more remarkable," related his wife, "Ron was scared to death of horses and cows."

Which might explain why he sustained six major accidents working as a wrangler. The worst included a dislocated shoulder, seven broken ribs and a punctured lung. At one stage, the big Texan slept at night in a lounge chair for six weeks, so excruciating was the pain with his cracked ribs.

After 17 months on the ranch and to some degree mastering the art of becoming a cowboy, his fantasy came to an abrupt end. While walking across the ranch one July morning with printing plant foreman Gary Cleaver, he collapsed and died of a heart attack. Ron and Gary had just caught a mess of fish, which was to be the main fare of Ron's 50th birthday party that night.

"He lived exactly the way he wanted to live and died exactly the way he wanted to die," surmised Betty. "With his boots on."

When it came time to find a name for the publishing business in 1960, I started searching for something that was appropriate but different. Something with a gimmick. And then it came to me.

"A publishing house in the Southwest area of the United States ought to be a publishing ranch,'" I reasoned. "Yes, Ray Franks Publishing Ranch has a nice ring." Besides that, Amarillo, Texas, is one of the last outposts of the Old West and the center of many huge ranching empires.

Little did I know just how much attention this unusual name would gain, or how much fun we'd have with it. And what a paradox. Here's a guy creating a business with a Western image who has never worn a cowboy hat or a pair of cowboy boots. I still haven't. Actually, I adore jeans and western attire but my flat feet require fitted inlays, aids not compatible with snug-fitting boots.

In 1991, when *NCAA News* did a story on the sale of the Directory portion of the business, a front page headline blazoned: "College Sports' Best-Known Rancher to Retire". The opening paragraphs went like this:

Ask those outside college athletics what "Ray Franks Publishing Ranch" produces, and you'd likely get answers that include everything from beef cattle to salad dressing.

To athletic administrators and coaches, however, the name means one thing—the National Directory of College Athletics. At least, that's the way it's been since 1968, when Ray Franks, the Ranch's Ben Cartwright, began publishing the men's edition of the directory.

Comments about the unique business name were many and varied. We received a letter from Knowles Dougherty of the Cross Country Journal in Wright City, MO. "From the name of your company, I assume that you do (or did) some agriculture on the side," he wrote. "Our complete name is Sunrise Valley Farm and Press. So perhaps we have more in common than we first realized."

A representative of CNN (Cable News Network) in Atlanta called one day to see if we had a "real ranch". He had bought a copy of the Directory and his curiosity had gotten the best of him. Then one year we received forms from the Randall-Potter County Taxing Appraisal office asking us to list our farm machinery and livestock.

William Woods College in Fulton, MO, had fun with the name one year when they sent us a check that read "Pay to the order of: Ray Franks Dude Ranch." And while some may declare the name hokey, it never failed to be an attention-getter.

And to answer the guy from CNN, "No, it isn't a real ranch." In fact, it wasn't even a building for five years. Merely a title to keep several publications in one stable.

However, when it came time to construct a 3,200-square foot office building in 1965, we had the draftsman give it a rustic look. Shingles were added to the exterior, reflecting the flavor of a western ranchhouse. Well, if you have a good imagination.

To keep expenses down, it was decided to sub-contract the building myself, which turned out to be a real learning experience. I knew nothing about building, but went to see a friend at W.C. Roberts Lumber, Dean Barnett. "Pick out about three reputable companies in the key areas, like carpenters, plumbers and electricians," said Dean, "and get competitive bids."

Since it was off-season for the directories, I opted to do some of the finish work myself. Like painting the drywalls and stapling the acoustical tile to the ceiling. It was fun, fulfilling and saved a lot of money. The two-

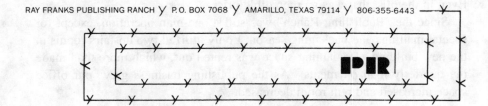

RAY FRANKS PUBLISHING RANCH ⅄ P.O. BOX 7068 ⅄ AMARILLO, TEXAS 79114 ⅄ 806-355-6443

Ray Franks PUBLISHING RANCH

AREA CODE 806 ■ FL 5-6417 ■ P. O. BOX 8016 ■ AMARILLO. TEXAS 79109

While it may not be stocked with cattle and horses, the Publishing Ranch is for real. The top letterhead with the barbed wire fence was created by artist Ken Parker and won a special award. The one below, penned by Glenn Zulauf and including a sketch of the building, was used on earlier envelopes and letterheads.

story southwest Amarillo building came in at $16,000, or $5 a square foot. Even in the 60s, that was an incredible price.

Since the "Publishing Ranch" was still a one-man operation, except for special mailings and packaging season, I only utilized two upstairs rooms in the new building. Remaining space was rented out, which more than made my quarterly loan payments. As the publishing business grew, our office space increased and rent room decreased.

The three logos we've used at the Ranch reveal an interesting evolvement of styles. At the outset, a plain image was utilized, combining script and heavy P.T. Barnum type, and reflecting a rustic look. After we made the transition from the house to the new office building, artist Glenn Zulauf, my friend from the Air Force days, jazzed it up. He made a pen and ink sketch of the spanking new building and added it to the existing type. It was warm and folksy.

Then, when we entered the national advertising arena with the college directory, I felt strongly that another image was needed. Something more unique and attention-getting for our stationery and envelopes. As Will Rogers once said: "You never get a second chance to make a first impression."

I called Ken Parker at McCormick Advertising, Amarillo's top agency, and made an appointment. He was McCormick's head artist and a veteran in his field. My only suggestion was that he try to implement the letters "PR" in the logo to create a double entendre (publishing ranch and public relations).

His first draft was a winner, one that I readily accepted. Shown elsewhere in this chapter, the new brand incorporates a bold modernistic "PR" surrounded by a rustic barbed-wire fence box. On our original letterhead, the "PR' was printed in raised gold and the fence appeared in a blind embossing. It was rich, unique and effective.

We weren't the only ones who liked it. Autrey Brothers of Denver, who first printed the letterheads and envelopes, asked for permission to enter the striking material in the Engraved Stationery Manufacturers Association's annual competition. Lo and behold, it took second place among thousands of entries in all of North America in 1967. It won first among all entries coming from the United States.

In thousands upon thousands of mailed pieces coming out of our office the past 30 years, that unmistakable, one-of-a-kind barbed-wire fence logo has become synonymous with college athletics. In a business that is basically mail-order oriented, I have always contended the extra money spent to produce quality letterheads and well-written messages is well worth the cost. Especially when you are dealing with class companies such as Monsanto, Bulova and Coca Cola, and their high-octane advertising agencies.

I had to smile recently when I picked up the local newspaper and read a quote from Dr. Elizabeth Carter, a certified image consultant. She said: "Before we sell any product or service, we sell ourselves through our professional image. First impressions may not always be accurate, but they do last and last."

Now that a ranchhouse has been built and the spread "fenced in", let's find a franchise product, something akin to an Emmitt Smith or a Shaquille O'Neal.

13

THE FRANCHISE IS HERE

Minneapolis was calling, and the voice on the other end started: "I understand you're putting together a new college directory and record book."

It was spring of 1968 and Mike Cleary, executive director of NACDA (National Association of Collegiate Directors of Athletics), was the stranger at the other end of the line.

"I'm going to Albuquerque in a couple weeks for the Olympic basketball tryouts," he said. "How about meeting me there; I'd like to discuss your new college directory."

As a 13-year publisher of high school coaching directories, our company was looking for a way to expand. We saw a need for an accurate and comprehensive college directory, and were laying the groundwork for the first edition to be published in the fall. Actually, the original college directory, *McNitts Blue Book*, had done a good job in the beginning. I used it all the years I was an SID at West Texas State. But when it changed hands in the 60s, the new owners got sloppy.

It had deteriorated badly in quality and accuracy, and was guilty of running pictures of athletic personnel who had been dead a couple years. Because we had developed a good national advertising base with the state directories and had considerable experience in that field, we felt we were in a solid position to challenge. It proved to be an accurate assumption.

I met Mike two weeks later at the Pit on the University of New Mexico campus, and we talked preliminaries while watching the basketball action. That night, in a Western Skies Motel room on Central Avenue, we signed an agreement whereby the National Directory would become the official publication of NACDA, and in return we would give the organization $1 off the sale of each book. Mike recalls the original agreement being penned on a brown paper bag or a scrap piece of paper. I honestly don't remember.

But let's back up a minute. It took a series of coincidences that would have made Ripley blink twice to bring about our initial contact, and Lou Spry was the man in the middle. Now the Associate Executive Director of the NCAA (National Collegiate Athletic Association), Spry followed me as SID at West Texas State a year after I resigned the post. He remained there two years before moving on to the NCAA in Kansas City.

When we began the record-gathering process for the new college book, it was natural we would contact Spry. At that time, I spilled our plans for the new venture.

"I couldn't believe my ears," says Spry, "when I attended the Final Four basketball tournament at the Sports Arena in Los Angeles a couple weeks later." Lou ran into Mike Cleary and heard him elicit some sketchy plans for "a more concise and accurate college coaching directory."

"Here were two guys in separate parts of the country with virtually the same idea," remembers Spry. "It was unbelievable."

After Spry apprised Cleary of our plans, the head of the brand new athletic directors organization made the call to our office. The rest is history.

But there's another strange twist to this chain of events. Cleary spent some time with NCAA before becoming the first and only executive director of NACDA. When he was preparing to leave Kansas City, Mike recommended Spry to be his replacement. Officials at NCAA heeded Cleary's advice and Spry has climbed to the No. 2 position in the prestigious collegiate regulatory organization.

The new alliance was a good deal for both parties. Although I never doubted for one minute we would be successful with our new publication, the relationship with NACDA gave us instant credibility with the most influential group in college sports. After all, it's the athletic directors who control the purse strings, and also the ones who buy directories. No question, the marriage helped accelerate our ascension to the No. 1 spot in college publications in short time.

In return, we gave this new organization an accurate, first-class publication of which they could be proud. "The accessibility and wealth of basic information in your directory has made the handling of our duties at ECAC more efficient and more effective," wrote Scotty Whitelaw, upon his retirement as commissioner of the Eastern College Athletic Conference, the country's largest and most diversified. "You should feel good about your role as its editor and publisher."

Besides the prestige of a quality reference book, we gave NACDA an extra annual income that wasn't small potatoes. During the 23 years we produced the directories, a total of $192,662 was contributed to the association's treasury.

It took a couple years to get the attention of college athletics and break old buying habits. In that first year, 1968, we printed 5,000 copies of the *National Directory of College Athletics*. We sold about half of them, and mailed complimentary samples with the left-overs the following spring.

We kept looking for new ways to improve our product. In the fourth season, we added a plastic spiral binding that I believe was the single most important improvement in the evolution of the directory. It helped put us over the hump and left the competition in our dust.

"Your new binding is wonderful," wrote athletic directors. "Not only does it add to the durability of the book, but it allows it to lay flat at any page. Our secretaries especially appreciate that factor."

Like oak trees, circulation grew slowly but steadily. We soon surpassed the Blue Book both in sales and advertising. In that first edition, surprisingly, we had 66 advertisers. Four of them—Bulova, Champion Knitwear, Robbins Floors and Weldon, Williams & Lick—were aboard in every one of the 23 editions we published. Now that's loyalty.

"Advertising pays most of the bills, doesn't it?" I've been asked many times. It may be surprising to most, and maybe our rates were on the low side, but that's not the case in directory publishing. In our peak years, advertising constituted only about 15% of total revenue with directory sales making up the balance. Actually, in directory publishing, where a premium price usually accompanies the product, advertising isn't needed at all to show a nice profit.

We made a lot of good friends in the advertising end of the business and possibly the best-known is Sam Huff, the college and pro football Hall of Famer. Handsome Sam, who wears a disarming smile as easily as he put on a football helmet, was a bulldog at linebacker when he played at West Virginia University and for the New York Giants and Washington Redskins in the pros. He carried that same tenacity with him when he joined Marriott Hotels.

Vice-president in charge of sports marketing at the outset, Sam grabbed a big chunk of the football team market with his personal approach and persuasive demeanor. Floy and I got to know Sam well through the years, and after the first couple editions, he always reserved page five in the directories.

"I don't spend another dime of advertising money anyplace else," he once told me at a NACDA convention. "Your books are great and we require every

At right is a reproduction of the first edition of the "franchise". (Below) Wife Floy and I are with Sam Huff, long-time advertiser in the Directory and a Hall of Fame inductee at both the college and professional levels.

Marriott Hotel to buy copies." I know that to be a fact because his secretary, Del Nylec, requested hundreds of order blanks at the beginning of each season. They even paid the postage for sending out the brochures and never asked for a discount on the many orders that came from Marriott properties all over the country.

Through our longtime friendship with Sam, we have discovered another side to that guarded, linebacker exterior. A broadcaster of Redskin games in the fall, he flashes a warmth and compassion that few people know when he engages in countless hours of volunteer work with underprivileged boys in the D.C. area. I didn't learn that from Sam, but from a mutual friend.

I pretty much handled the procuring of advertising in the directories, and it was an exciting challenge each spring. Anyone who had a service or product for college athletics was a prospect. About the first of April, we would start the letter-writing process to advertising directors and other contact people all over the country. Most of the correspondence would be to people I'd never met, which made the challenge all that more interesting. Let me cite an example.

After discovering that Clair Sims was the contact person at Coca-Cola in Atlanta, I dutifully wrote personalized letters to her for several years. The company was advertising in national coaching magazines and I felt they should be in our publications.

"It's too bad you only write once a year as I always enjoy a chuckle when reading your letters," she wrote one year. "I really am sorry that I cannot do more than purchase your directories. As you can imagine, I receive many requests from publishers of college related magazines which I am unable to support because of budget limitations."

I wasn't discouraged. Next year, I wrote her again, and guess what? She reserved a full page in four colors, and has been ever since. Finding the right contact at the big corporations, no easy feat, and perseverance can work wonders.

About 90% of our circulation went back to the colleges, whose athletic directors, coaches and other officials use the books every day of the year. Hoping not to sound irreverent, we labeled the directories "the Bible of college athletics". And they truly have become just that.

"The University of Arizona continues to find your publication invaluable," remarked Maxine Tenbrink, Administrative Assistant to the Athletic Director. "I can vouch for the fact that, by the end of the year, just about all our copies are totally dog-eared."

Colleges order from one to 150 of these books annually. Yes, Mike Lude, former AD at University of Washington, did requisition 150 directories each spring when he returned the completed questionnaire. For the life of me, I can't imagine how one college can use that many books, but who am I to question that decision. Consistently, University of Nebraska sent in orders for 100 annually. Go Huskies, go Huskers!

My radio friend and sometimes columnist Warren Hasse had this interesting comment about the circulation: "It's a best seller every year. And why shouldn't it be. It's filled with as many cowboys, Indians and wild mustangs as any Zane Grey or Louis L'Amour western, a colorful travelogue to rival *National Geographic* and more bust shot photos than *Playboy Magazine*."

And while the bulk of the circulation is among college people, many directories are utilized by the media, sporting goods companies and professional sports. But the most gratifying mail of all always comes from guidance counselors who use the books to help high school seniors further their education.

"I can honestly say your reference book enabled one of our athletes to get a college scholarship," wrote a guidance counselor from Grant Community High School in Fox Lake, Illinois. "This young man will always be indebted to your company for this invaluable guide."

Even presidents are prospects. It was fall, 1976, when we got a call from Charles McCall, Director of the Research Office at the White House.

"President Ford is planning to attend the Texas-Oklahoma football game in Dallas, and he wants a copy of your fine Directory."

When paying for the book a couple weeks later, McCall sent a note: "Thanks so much for the copy of the *National Directory of College Athletics*. It is a useful addition to the library." Before entering politics, Gerald Ford was an outstanding football player at University of Michigan.

In nearly 25 years of having a front row seat to college athletics, there have been a lot of memorable stories. But, I would have to label the biggest of all the emergence of women's athletics on an intercollegiate level. It has totally changed the face of college sports. Instead of one Final Four in basketball, there are now two; instead of one athletic budget to finance, there are two; and instead of only one *National Directory of College Athletics*, there are two.

It was a slow process. In 1972, college leaders formed the AIAW (Association for Intercollegiate Athletics for Women), and national tournaments were staged in seven sports. Only 200 colleges were members that first year, and it prompted Jo Anne Thorpe of Southern Illinois University at Carbondale to comment:

In its 66th year, the NCAA has discovered that its efforts to coordinate the nation's schoolboy sports may have overlooked someone who does not wish to be overlooked—the schoolgirl.

That same year, 1972, women's athletics got its biggest shot in the arm. Congress passed Title IX legislation that called for gender equity in intercollegiate athletics. While it was a great victory for women's sports, out at the Ranch we had to make a tough decision.

Were we going to add women's information to a predominantly men's directory, or initiate a new publication? We went to college athletic administrators, both women and men, talked to advertisers and did a lot of soul-searching in the wee hours of the night.

"The women want their own publication," reported Dr. Karol Ann Kahrs, then Director of Women's Athletics at U. of Illinois, who had been asked by our office to check around and get some feedback.

"It gives more stature to the women's program and a sense of identity," others volunteered. There are pros and cons to the argument, because some overlap is necessary in two directories. But maybe the deciding vote involved the fact that an already huge men's book of 400 pages would be clumsy and difficult to use if hundreds of additional pages were added.

While one directory would be more suitable for administrators, it made no sense for coaches, who comprised the majority of our subscribers. "It would be like combining Ladies Home Journal and Popular Mechanics into one magazine," said one observer. "Men coaches have no interest in women's information and vice versa."

When all was said and done, a second directory seemed like the way to go, and apparently it was a good choice. The inaugural edition was published in the fall of 1973, five years after the start of the men's book. However, not everyone was happy with our ultimate decision. One belligerent men's athletic director came to our NACDA Convention booth yearly and complained about having two directories. In fact, on one occasion, he became so hostile, he reduced my wife to tears. The following winter he died of a heart attack.

In all fairness, I must confess that the comments of Clell Wade, a fellow publisher of state high school directories, helped in the decision-making process. "Women's sports is big stuff," he remarked at a sporting goods convention, "and I'm thinking of starting a women's college directory next year." I asked him to wait and give us a chance to add a logical running mate to our men's book. He did, and I will always be grateful for that consideration.

From the beginning, we wanted to make the *National Directories of College Athletics* different from past reference books. It was our goal to make them the ONE book all college officials would keep on their desk all year long. We first included story roundups, upcoming tournament schedules, detailed conference data, advertiser product indexes and short features on outstanding college personalities.

Even advertisers helped us out. In the late 60s, Monsanto's AstroTurf was pioneering the synthetic recreational surface market and spent big bucks with our company. They were taking the college market by storm.

"We want to do something special in your publication," said Pete Kalison, Manager of Advertising and Promotion, from his office in St. Louis. "We'd like to sponsor a complete 16-page section."

For several years, Monsanto did just that, adding a new dimension to the already popular directories. "The Ten Greatest Backs in College Football" was the theme of one special we researched and compiled. A "College Bowl Guide", spinning the story of football bowls, was another. My favorite was "The Ten Greatest Upsets in College Football", complete with a four-color cover by Willard Mullin, America's greatest sports cartoonist, best known for his Bob Hope caricatures in Chrysler advertising. Working with this legendary artist from New York was a genuine thrill and honor, plus making a handsome and provocative supplement to the Directory.

When I first contacted the legendary Mullin at his office in New York, he was less than enthusiastic about doing a cover for an unknown publisher down in Texas. After we talked about the content of the page, he asked about the money. I held my breath.

"I couldn't do something like that for less than $500," he advised. Guess what? Monsanto had given me a maximum allowance of $500 for this piece of art, and we were in business. I got to keep one of the two original pieces of artwork he did for Monsanto. It hangs in my office today, and is treasured as much as some people would relish a Rembrandt.

Because West Texas State had been invited, I decided to cover the 1968 National Invitation Basketball Tournament for a Directory special. It was during this trip that I encountered Howard Cosell for the first and only time in my career. My son Randy and I were in the press room of Madison Square Garden receiving our credentials for the tournament when the swaggering, loud-talking and brash sportscaster entered the area.

"Hello, boys, how's it going today," he bellowed in his signature monotone and raspy voice, at the same time blowing out a big puff of smoke from his cigar. "Have you got any news that's fit to use?" he asked of no one in particular. One of the NIT officials handed him a press release and most of us went on with our business.

Often labeled the "mouth that roared", Cosell was an enigma in the world of journalism. He attempted to project himself bigger than the event he was reporting on the TV screen. And most of the time he succeeded, making his biggest splash on Monday Night ABC Football. I enjoyed him to a point but had a problem with accepting him as a pure journalist. Actually, Cosell entered the communications arena at a late age after only a mediocre career as a lawyer.

In that much imitated staccato voice, Cosell was different and obviously commanded a great following. However, part of his style involved pulling multi-syllable, hundred dollar words out of the dictionary that had many of us saying "huh?" That was part of his gimmick, along with his desire to "tell it like it is". Personally, I never watched or listened to Cosell for just Cosell. It was the event that attracted me to the tube, and I believe that's the way it should be.

These specials, designed to add a heart-beat to a directory heavily loaded with small agate information, weren't going unnoticed. Early in 1971, Chuck Mills, then football coach at Utah State University, called the Publishing Ranch and announced: "We're taking our football team to Japan in December. How about going with us?"

The face of the Directory was never the same.

I purchased my first professional camera, a Minolta SRT-101 35-millimeter beauty, and embarked on my first overseas trip ever. Two years later, an opportunity to accompany the U.S. delegation to the World University Games in Moscow came my way. Then an excursion to Brazil with Eddie Sutton and his Arkansas Razorback basketball team.

The idea was snowballing and pretty soon we were logging as many frequent-flier miles as Bob Hope on his USO tours. Overseas sports travel was proliferating and travel agencies were contacting us with "offers we couldn't refuse." The Ranch became a launching pad for complimentary excursions to the far corners of the world, all the time trying fervently to top the previous year's travelogue.

"Where you going next year?" subscribers would ask while vicariously enjoying the unique college events in exotic ports of call. Along came adventures to Honolulu for the Hula Bowl, West Germany for American football's first visit to Europe, Finland for the Arctic Bowl, Melbourne to chronicle the premier Australia Bowl, Nassau for the Goombay basketball shindig, and two subsequent journeys to Moscow for history-making sports events. These adventures were fast becoming the modern-day versions of the old "road" movies that featured Bing Crosby, Bob Hope and Dorothy Lamour.

Sandwiched between the overseas jaunts have been exciting stateside assignments worthy of note. There are the Holiday, Cotton, All-American and Gator bowls; 50th anniversaries of the NIT, NCAA and NAIA basketball tournaments; the NCAA Track Meet; and the College World Series of Baseball. Heck, we even got invited to spend a day with Oral Roberts, the evangelist, to take a look at his university's basketball program.

In addition to a good portion of America, these "business trips" have afforded my wife and I an opportunity to reach all the world's inhabitable continents except Africa. And there's been another bonus. A writer at heart after cutting my journalistic teeth on a daily newspaper, I have used these adventures as an excuse to get back to the typewriter. My late-attained hobby of photography also has come in handy.

Most of the overseas trips attracted little attention from the mainstream media, making our coverage all the more significant and exclusive. In most cases, the promoters of these events offered carte blanche invitations. What a deal!

Let's be honest. Users of the Directories buy them for the statistical information. But as an athletic director once told me: "These special features give the books documentary value. I keep all of my back issues."

In retrospect, it's no mystery why these travel adventures have wide appeal. Two of America's best-read and most prolific writers—James Michener and Sidney Sheldon—have carved out brilliant careers visiting the world's most exciting addresses. They just add believable characters and compelling plots, and bingo, best-sellers are created. In our case, college athletes comprise the cast and sports events the plots.

Tokyo is first.

14

BLAZING NEW TRAILS

There's Henry Ford with the automobile, the Wright brothers and their airplane and Alan Shepard, America's first man in space. All were pioneers in the world of travel.

Maybe it's a stretch to put them in that select company but the names of Chuck Mills and Utah State University should be lionized some day for blazing new trails in American football. In 1971, they made a 15,000-mile trip to Japan, becoming the first U.S. college grid team to perform overseas in a foreign country. A game that was dubbed the "Silk Bowl".

And it's an adventure I almost missed.

When rolling out of bed that crisp December morning, planning to rendezvous with the Utah State party in San Francisco, I found Amarillo nestled under an unlikely heavy fog. Now a fog in the flat, wide-open terrain of the Texas Panhandle is about as common as a tidal wave.

I paid little attention to its implications until arriving at the airport an hour before my 9:30 morning departure time. Upon finding everything completely socked in, I had reason to start worrying. No planes were landing and nothing was leaving the ground.

"What," I gasped, "if I can't get to Dallas?" My ticket had me going to Big D, then taking a direct flight to San Francisco, where the chartered Japan Air Lines DC-8 would jet us to Tokyo early next morning.

Weather cancellations cause major problems for all in air travel, but in my case it was potential disaster. If I don't get to San Francisco by the end of the day, it's sayonara even before the adventure begins. But somebody up there was looking out for me. After boarding our Braniff plane and waiting 30 minutes at the gate (with our fingers crossed), we started moving. With due concern and a rapid heart-beat, I watched out a window that revealed nothing but billowy white stuff. We started moving faster and faster. We were taxiing

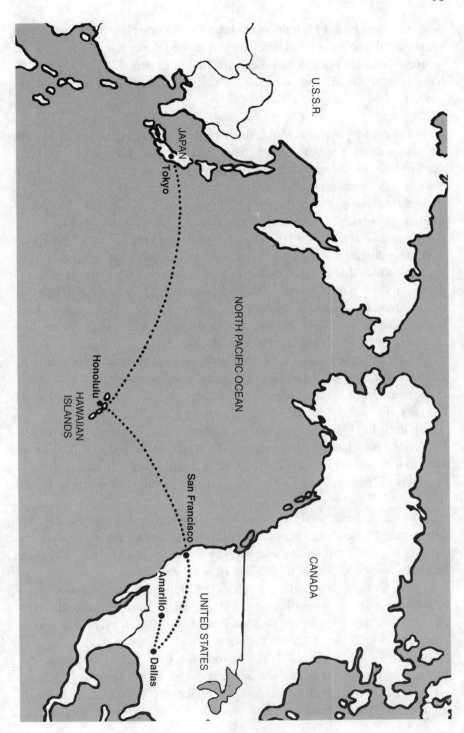

down the runway and I felt the plane lift off.   Seconds later there was bright sunshine. We found a small hole and had slipped through it.

How fortunate I had been I didn't find out until later. The unfamiliar fog hung around Amarillo all day and ours was the only flight to get off the ground.

Close call.

It was my first overseas flight, and except for a refueling stop in Honolulu, we saw nothing but water for 14 hours. There was little doubt we were heading for the Orient when petite Japan Air Lines stewardesses, clad in colorful silk kimonos, served our first meal with chopsticks.

Want to know the definition of "frustration"? Watching 250-pound football players trying to fill up on chicken and rice with chopsticks.

"I might be able to lose 50 pounds on this trip if I have to eat all my meals with these things." voiced a beefy lineman. He learned, along with the rest of us, that fish would be served in some form or fashion with every meal for 13 days. On the trip over, it was smoked salmon cocktail for lunch, fish cake for a mid-afternoon snack and crabmeat cocktail for dinner. In later years, I have learned that their affinity for fish is thought to be responsible for the low incidence of heart disease among orientals.

On our in-flight menu, I saw sake listed for the first time. Not a drinker, I didn't order any, but some adult Utah State fans confirmed that the alcoholic drink made from rice had a powerful wallop. It's the ethnic equivalent of Russia's vodka and America's bourbon whiskey.

Up until 1971, Hawaii had ranked as the ultimate in glamour excursions for American college football teams. So when we landed in Tokyo on an airstrip that juts out into the Pacific Ocean, I felt a flush. It was exciting to be a part of history, one of only two members of the U.S. media to record it.

Although international travel had been commonplace in other sports, this trip opened the floodgates for football excursions. Because of sheer numbers, football is a sport difficult to take overseas. Besides that, before 1971 there had been no one to play in this "Made In America" sport.

Today, however, it's a different story. U.S. college teams think nothing of boarding a plane at spring break and flying off to Europe, Australia, New Zealand or China. Even one invaded Russia in 1992, an event that will be discussed in great detail later in the book.

The games were one-sided, as everyone had expected. Utah State, who had just carved out an 8-3 season and had the likes of Texas and Oklahoma on their 1972 schedule, beat a contingent of Tokyo college all-stars, 50-6, in a game that was dubbed the "Silk Bowl". A few days later, they won in similar fashion from a squad at Osaka, 45-6, a game I didn't see. I chose to fly back ahead of the team so I would be home for Christmas.

However, the scores of the games were only incidental. It was the person-to-person contact among athletes from different parts of the world that was really significant. The Japanese appeared elated to host the Americans, take them into their homes and show them their country. When they returned home, the Aggies found that their unforgettable trip had attracted world-wide attention. Congratulations were received from such far-off places as Australia, South Africa, Germany, France, England and the Middle East.

The games provided a study in contrasts. The Americans outweighed their adversaries from the Orient about 40 pounds per man and had nearly a foot height advantage. The heaviest player on the Japanese rosters was listed at 183 pounds. The disparity in experience was even greater.

"About 50 colleges were playing American football in Japan in those days," remembers Aggie coach Chuck Mills, who more than anyone else was responsible for the historical trip. "From occupational troops after the end of World War II, the Japanese first became exposed to U.S. football. They liked the game, and progress is being made."

In 1971, technique was hurting. The single-wing was still big in the Japanese's offensive arsenal, and the wish-bone was something they still related to chicken creole. "They were better on offense than I expected," said Mills in his best diplomatic voice. "They threw the ball well on the short patterns, and they are good pass receivers."

Mills added that few people knew the handicap their opponents were playing under in those days. He was referring to these facts:

1. Japanese players had to buy their own shoes, shirts, pants, pads, everything. Football is still a minor sport and there is not enough ticket sale revenue to finance the program.
2. None of the teams had a paid coach or trainer on the staff. Only one had a coach connected to the school and the others were volunteers who helped after leaving regular jobs. Many times they never made workouts.

Knowing full well they would be outmanned badly, the Japanese coaches were eager to schedule the international games anyway. Designed to bring national attention to football, and thus increase it's quality in all areas, the games did just that.

The Tokyo match-up was played in Olympic Stadium, an area that doubles as a golf driving range. Despite country-wide television coverage, the game drew 30,000, most of whom had not the slightest idea of what was happening. Tickets were priced at 1,000 yen or about $3.25 U.S. currency. This equated to four times the average price of a regular Japanese football attraction, which will attract about 3,000. By comparison, a high school baseball playoff game may draw as many as 60,000.

The exposure wasn't limited to the games. The giants of Utah State commanded attention everywhere they went. When they first boarded their JAL charter in San Francisco, the Aggies drew astonished looks from the tiny Japanese stewardesses. Along the Ginza of Tokyo, shoppers and businessmen gawked at the touring Americans. It was the same when they visited the Imperial Gardens or slipped into a jewelry store to buy the latest Seiko watch.

Called the world's largest city with more than 15 million, Tokyo is actually two metropolises in one. Old Tokyo, with it's narrow streets and sidewalk markets selling everything from fish to watermelons, is quaint and the gathering place for tourists. I spent most of a whole day browsing the area and taking pictures. One of my favorite shots was that of an elderly Japanese woman carrying a huge box strapped to her back. It appeared to be much too heavy for a person of her stature.

Then there's modern Tokyo, complete with skyscrapers and office buildings that remind you of Chicago or New York. Along the Ginza, sidewalks are crowded with shoppers, uniformed students and Western-attired businessmen darting around like busy bees. I saw many people wearing white face masks. I found out they were worn to help filter out the smog and other impurities of a big bustling city. American movies are big along the Ginza, usually shown with Japanese subtitles.

For our week-long stay in Tokyo, we occupied the Akasaka Tokyu Hotel, a modern structure located in the diplomatic area of the city and near the Imperial Palace and Gardens. Culture came into play when 6-4 football players tried to fit into beds designed for much shorter orientals.

"It was fun at first," related one of the players, "but the novelty wore off after a couple of days."

I roomed with Bill Harrington, a Salt Lake City sportscaster who was video-taping the game for delayed broadcast. Both of average size, we still had trouble getting comfortable. The rooms were smaller also and furniture set a little closer to the floor.

The dozen newspaper and TV stations of Tokyo conducted numerous interviews and covered routine workouts because a relatively-new commodity was being introduced to their people. They were curious about the players, asking such questions as: "How many of you are married?. . . What is your

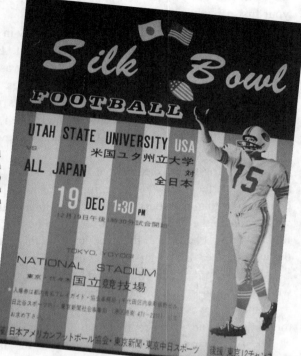

Posters of the Silk Bowl appeared all over Tokyo, printed in both English and Japanese. (Below) We flew Japan Air Lines with kimono-clad attendants from San Francisco to Tokyo.

major in college? . . . Do you plan to play professional football? . . . Is this your first trip to Japan?"

Being the first American college team to play in the land of the rising sun, Utah State was accorded the red carpet treatment. Even the U.S. ambassador to Japan, Armin Meyer, got into the act. He was present for the game in Tokyo, participated in the pre-game ceremonies and made the following observation: "In the stream of good-will sports visits to Japan, the great American game of football has unfortunately been slighted up to now. I am pleased that this oversight is being rectified by the visit of the fine Utah State team."

Famous for their conservative politeness and gift-giving, the Japanese played the perfect hosts. Sight-seeing tours and welcoming parties were more conspicuous than workouts and squad meetings on the Utah State itinerary. It was fortunate the Utags were not forced to be at top strength. The 14-hour flight over the Pacific had the Americans reeling the first couple days before the whirling-dervish social calendar took over.

At the receptions and other social gatherings, the pretty Japanese hostesses wore traditional kimonos, mainly ceremonial in nature.

"Japan has westernized in so many ways," observed Coach Mills, "and I think it's a shame. They're giving up a lot of their traditions."

The Americans found you can't outgive the Japanese. At the official welcoming party before the first game, a lavish buffet was served the players of both teams, coaches and booster club members with the Utah party. Expensive hand-painted bowls were presented to both athletic director Frank Williams and coach Mills of the visitors.

Satisfied that wasn't enough, Mikio Shinotake, head coach of the Tokyo team, slipped off his cuff links and gave them to his counterpart of the Utah State squad. Caught unaware and embarrassed, Mills reached down and took off his Super Bowl tie clasp (he's a former Kansas City Chief assistant.) When he gave it to Shinotake, the Japanese coach was already reaching for his tie chain and placed it in Mills' other hand. At this point, the American threw up his hands in despair and exclaimed: "These people are just too much . . . there's no way to match their generosity."

A similar incident occurred among the players after the Tokyo game. When it was over, the Japanese gridders dashed to the sidelines and came up with happy coats (kimono-style lounging jackets) for their American friends. In an impromptu act, the Aggies started peeling off their game jerseys and gave them away. But that wouldn't do. The Japanese came right back with their game shirts, specially-made for the All-Star game and much more expensive than the Aggie equipment. Pointing up the acute difference in size, some of the Utah State gridders had to take off their pads to get the Japanese jerseys over their shoulders.

Being in the land of the rising sun a week before Christmas afforded our group an interesting insight. Because Buddhism is dominant there, Christmas is not recognized by the majority of people. However, we found department stores gaily decorated with signs that said "Christmas '71" in both English and Japanese, and similar greetings. A lot of American dollars were being spent by servicemen in those days.

Playing the perfect hosts, families in Osaka took the American players and coaches into their homes on Christmas Eve, helping them celebrate the Christian event.

Although several Japanese officials spoke fair English, the language barrier caused some problems in the first U.S.-Japan Good Will football series. No one in the 125-member American group spoke Japanese. "One good thing about it," quipped Aggie quarterback Tony Adams, "we won't have to worry about them catching our audibles at the line of scrimmage."

How the games were scheduled is another story in itself. Utah State's fine 8-3 record qualified it for post-season play, but the groundwork had been laid long before the season started. It all began when coach Mills of the Aggies conducted clinics for U.S. military personnel in Japan in the summer of 1970. A few Japanese college and semi-pro coaches showed up for the classes, much to the delight of Mills and the servicemen.

Vigorous work by two former Aggies—Chris Pella and Bill Vasas (with U.S. Naval recreation departments in the Far East)—got the ball rolling. Mills and coach Ken Takeda, the Osaka coach who had spent two years at Michigan State getting his doctor's degree in psychology, then swung into action on their respective sides of the Pacific.

After the idea for the games had been tossed into the hopper, Japan Air Lines, a government-owned operation, insisted on flying the Utah State coach to Japan the summer before the game. He accepted, and after a week with Takeda and other Nippon officials, the plan was formulated. The next move was to get NCAA approval for Utah State. The first reply was anything but encouraging.

"We are not sure we have the machinery to approve such games," came the message from Kansas City. However, after a few weeks of reconsideration and some vigorous encouragement from the State Department in Washington, the NCAA okayed the international games in September, only three months before the scheduled trip.

That left one chore undone . . .financing the trip. Japan could offer no guarantee, but did agree to pick up all costs of the team after it landed in the country. They also agreed to split all profits after expenses, if any. The problem of getting the team to the Orient and back was still there.

Aggie officials huddled for several days and came up with a plan that could be called irregular, to say the least. But it worked. First, they asked every member of the coaching staff and all players to contribute $250 each toward air fare.

"Their first reaction was they couldn't come up with that kind of money," related coach Mills. "I told them, go borrow it from a relative or a bank . . . this is a chance of a lifetime."

As it turned out, only four players failed to make the trip because of finances. The backfield was hardest hit where three starters chose to remain in the snowy clime of Utah. All-American end Bob Wicks declined so he could participate in All-Star games in the States.

After 40 players and coaches brought in checks, athletic director Williams decided to charter a 140-passenger jet and sell additional space to boosters and alums. All but 20 seats on the DC-8 were peddled. More money was needed so coach Mills and his secretary sent out hundreds of letters to exes and top industries in the country, asking for donations. The request brought in about $5,000, including money from two professional football teams, several well-known businesses and area newspapers.

The trip abounded with a festive atmosphere from the very start. Aggie assistant coach Rich Groth used the event for a honeymoon. Originally planning to be married on the plane enroute, Groth and his bride relented to the whims of relatives and exchanged vows the day before departure.

And Bob Hope made a flitting appearance on the scene. The Utah State party was half-way between San Francisco and Honolulu when Hope and his Christmas show troupe pulled alongside in a military plane, heading for his annual trip to Vietnam.

"I wouldn't be surprised if you Aggies could beat the LA Rams," commented Hope over the plane's intercom. "After the Rams-Redskins game the other night (won by the Redskins), I'm what you might call financially clean!"

Reflecting back, it was an amazing experience and I'll always be grateful to Chuck Mills and Utah State for including me in the entourage. However, of all the major international cities I've visited, I found Tokyo the most uncomfortable. I'm sure the language and culture barriers are the big reasons. And I'm not a lover of fish.

Let me relate one experience. One day I took a cab from our hotel to the

The Ginza in the heart of New Tokyo bustles with people around the clock. I found few Japanese who could speak English. (Below) This picture illustrates the disparity in size of the Japanese and Utah State football players. The Japanese were outweighed 40 pounds per player.

Ginza to take pictures of Utah State players. We were given a card by officials that said "please show this card to the taxi driver; he will take you where you want to go."

When it was time to return to our hotel, I couldn't find the card that had "Akasaka Tokyu Hotel" printed in Japanese. Well, I went in one office after another, hoping to find someone who could speak English. No luck. They just threw up their hands when I opened my mouth. Finally, I had an idea.

"I'll try a department store," I thought, "one that has an English Christmas greeting on it's marquee." I guessed right. Because many customers were American servicemen, most sales girls were bilingual. One kindly scribbled the name of my hotel in Japanese and I was off to find the nearest cab. While I felt uncomfortable in Tokyo, a return trip to the Orient several years later with a church group was palatable. This time it was Hong Kong, much more western in atmosphere and bilingual.

While I had a difficult time warming up to Tokyo, the Utah State players didn't.

"Several of the boys who played in Japan have gone back to visit," recalls Coach Mills. "In '92 several players took their wives and children and looked up their Japanese counterparts. The American families visited in the homes, and had one whale of a reunion."

Twenty-five years after that pioneer excursion, Japanese football has come a long way. Instead of 50 colleges in 1971, more than 300 universities play the sport. In the early 70s, the college championship game attracted 10,000 fans. Today, it's more like 60,000.

Thanks to young Japanese coaches who come to the States to study technique and learn from the people who invented the game, their caliber of ball has made great strides. "They've recruited bigger kids from rugby and soccer," says Mills, who has made about 15 trips to the Far East. "They now execute as well as many American teams."

Now the athletic director at U.S. Coast Guard Academy, Mills has taken four more teams to Japan since 1971, and brought one over to play his squad at Southern Oregon. His contribution to athletics in the Orient has not gone unnoticed. In fact, he's a hero there. Each year, they give an award to the best Japanese collegiate player, their version of the Heisman Award.

It's called the Mills Cup!

15

RAH, RAH, MAGUIRE U.

Playful pranks have always been a part of athletics. Snoozing baseball players will eventually get the "hot foot" and short-sheeting a rookie's bed is commonplace.

Forget this small-time stuff. One of the most creative and funniest pranks happened in the fall of 1972, and the *National Directory of College Athletics* was the goat.

Keep in mind that during 23 years of publishing this annual book with multitudes of reference information, dozens of colleges are deleted and added annually. New schools are always popping up and old ones consolidate or go bankrupt. It's not uncommon to have a swing of 25 to 30 different listings yearly. But you can imagine my surprise, and dismay, when I picked up the February 19, 1973 edition of *Sports Illustrated* and read this sentence:

The latest hoax in college sports is on page 190 of the 1972-73 National Directory of College Athletics.

It carried the heading "Rah, Rah, Maguire U." and the nearly one-column long story was a part of the "Scoreboard" section, a weekly feature in *Sports Illustrated*. The story continued:

There, in company with Lynchburg State and the University of Maine, is Maguire U. of Forest Park, Illinois. Maguire has a president, Dr. Mel Connolly. Maguire U. has a nickname (the Jollymen), school colors (green and white) and an enrollment of 1,600. In reality, Maguire U. is a bar in Forest Park, and the school is named after it's owner, John Maguire. "President" Mel Connolly is a truck driver.

It all started back in 1963 when basketball interest reached a feverish pitch at Maguire's. And rightfully so. George Ireland's Loyola of Chicago team made it to the Final Four and a bunch of the boys decided to attend the tournament in Louisville. Bill Shay, then freshman coach at Loyola, hosted his pals from the bar and got them tickets.

They had such a great time (Loyola won the national championship, defeating Cincinnati, 60-58, in overtime), they began attending the NCAA Final Four every year. As a joke, they had T-shirts printed with "Maguire U." on them.

Then, in the spring of 1972 they got their chance for national recognition. By hook or crook, they got their hands on a Directory questionnaire. Maguire, the owner, and his friends gathered around a table and filled in the bogus information. Then they sent it in, along with a check for $8, price of the book.

Bill Shay became the "basketball coach", and another patron, Len Tyrrell, the "football coach". An Italian policeman who stopped in occasionally and was known only by his first name, Sal, was listed as Sal DeCopper, assistant football coach. Other customers were listed as coaches of additional sports, including track, baseball, tennis, golf, cross country and bowling. They even listed won-lost records in football and basketball for the previous year. It seemed authentic enough on the surface.

Once Maguire U. got into the Directory, all sorts of things started happening. Louisville Slugger, the bat company, wrote to "baseball coach" Ignatius Murphy trying to sell him bats. Then a real live basketball coach phoned one day to speak to Coach Shay. When told Coach Shay came in only on Friday nights, the caller asked: "What kind of a school are you running there anyway?"

If he read that 1973 issue of *Sports Illustrated*, he found out.

Long after this story got national attention in *Sports Illustrated*, there have been many sidebars to this prank.

"We are building a stadium for Maguire University, and planning to have it completed by the first football game."

With tongue in cheek, Jim Geurin, president of Southern Bleacher Company in Graham, TX, and a long-time advertiser, teased us in a letter after the prank was revealed.

He continued: "We want you to make the dedication speech. We are to be the hosts at the cocktail party following the first game. Please plan to have your entire group there as our guests."

Then, ten years after the *Sports Illustrated* story, I had a call from Vin

COLLEGE
01
CAA

ey

2400
Brewer
-9071
berger,

lassie
es Fox
sbury
rzenpa
roffitt

mas
tt
ger
x
homas
s Fox
erger
dge
L 3; T 1
W 19; L 9

LLEGE
t 05851

I, 1000

-3335
Bell,

ell
Bell
Owen
luntington
luntington

ntington

son
rell
ll
ington

EGE
St. Paul,

Baseball–Bob Sadek
Tennis–Jack Bachman
Golf–Ralph Lundeen
Swimming–Jack Bachman
Cross Country–Doug Bolstorff
Soccer–Ron Mettler
Ice Hockey–Bob Sadek
Trainer–Tom Coplin
1971 Football–W 1; L 7; T 1
1971-72 Basketball–W 17; L 9

MAC MURRAY COLLEGE
Jacksonville, Ill. 62650
Conference–Illinois-Indiana
Coll. Soccer, Midlands, NCAA
Enrollment–950
Colors–Scarlet, navy
Nickname–Highlanders
Fieldhouse–MacMurray, 1000
President–Dr. John J. Wittich

WALL
Ath. Phone–217-245-8707
Ath. Dir.–William L. Wall,
home 245-8608
Ass't Ath. Dir.–Peter George,
245-2473
Ath. Bus. Mgr.–William L. Wall
Sports Inf.–William L. Wall
PE Dir.–Dr. Marianne Torbert
Intra. Dir.–Doug Hunt
Basketball–William L. Wall
Ass't–Robert Gay
Track–Peter George, 245-2473
Baseball–Dr. Robert Gay,
243-3470
Tennis–William L. Wall
Golf–Peter George
Wrestling–Peter George
Cross Country–Peter George
Soccer–Dr. Robert Gay
1971-72 Basketball–W 4; L 22

MADISON COLLEGE
Harrisonburg, Va. 22801
Conference–Independent
Enrollment–4000
Colors–Purple, gold
Nickname–Dukes
Fieldhouse–Godwin Hall, 5000
President–Dr. Ron Carrier
Ath. Phone–703-433-6164

Wrestling–Dean Ehlers
Gymnastics–Hays Kruger
Swimming–Charles Arnold
Cross Country–Challace
McMillin
Soccer–Bob Vanderwarker
Trainer–Mike Null
1971-72 Basketball–W 16; L 7

MAGUIRE U.
7215 W. Madison St.,
Forest Park, Ill. 60130
Conference–Independent
Enrollment–1600
Colors–Green, white
Nickname–Jollymen
Stadium–Friar, 12,000
Fieldhouse–Lawless, 1800
President–Dr. Mel Connolly
Ath. Phone–312-366-2823
Ath. Dir.–Phil Farrell
Ass't Ath. Dir.–Billy Smith
Ath. Bus. Mgr.–Ed Gleason
Sports Inf.–John Maguire
PE Dir. (m)–Jim Cullerton
PE Dir. (w)–Gert Ireland
Intra. Dir.–John Rooney
Football–Len Tyrrell
Ass'ts–Sal De Copper, Red
Dwyer, Ed Hanrahan
Basketball–Bill Shay
Ass't–Ralph Hinger
Track–Wes Mason
Baseball–I. Murphy
Tennis–Bill Wallace
Golf–Bill Gleason
Cross Country–J. MacNamara
Bowling–Joe Vitiello
Trainer–Tom Monforti
1971 Football–W 6; L 4
1971-72 Basketball–W 15; L 10

MAINE MARITIME ACADEMY
Castine, Maine 04421
Conference–New England
Enrollment–500
Colors–Royal, gold
Nickname–Maritime
Stadium–Ritchie Field, 2100
Fieldhouse–Alexander, 1000
President–Edward A. Rodgers
Ath. Phone–207-326-4311
Ath. Dir.–Verge Forbes,
home 326-4913
Ass't Ath. Dir.–William Mottola
Ath. Bus. Mgr.–Verge Forbes
Sports Inf.–Chris Beardsly
PE Dir.–Verge Forbes

This bogus listing of "Maguire U." appeared in the 1972-73 edition of the National Directory of College Athletics and merited attention in *Sports Illustrated*.

Mannix, columnist for the Boca Raton, FL, News. "I just heard this classic story about Maguire U.," he started, "and I'd like to ask you some questions about it."

Jack Mehl, then Florida Atlantic University athletic director, told Mannix he was an Ohio State graduate assistant in 1975 when he attended the Final Four in San Diego. "There were four or five of us going out this one night," Mehl related. "One of the assistants at another school said he knew of a great hospitality room we should check out. Belonged to Maguire University.

"So we get to the hotel and, sure enough, there's this room with a big, felt banner with Maguire University on it. All these guys are wearing school blazers, drinking up and having a blast. It wasn't until some time later I realized it was a hoax. But I had a great time at the expense of old Maguire U."

After hearing this, Mannix did some super sleuthing. He found owner John Maguire had sold his bar and moved to Orlando. Maguire revealed to Mannix that Bob Lukstra, then a basketball assistant at U. of New Orleans, had secured the questionnaire that first landed the fictitious school in the Directory.

"He stopped in the bar one night with it, and you can imagine the fun we had with it."

Maguire U. may have lost its spot in the Directory, but the tradition lingers on. I was watching an ESPN feature prior to 1993's Final Four, and guess who was being featured?

Len Tyrrell, long-time patron of Maguire's and the same guy who was labeled as "football coach" in the Directory listing, was being interviewed. "Sure, we're still alive and well," he said. "We've got a bus filled, and Maguire's will be well represented in New Orleans."

Wonder if they've ever been on NCAA probation?

16

MISSION TO MOSCOW

Concerning World War II, Winston Churchill went on BBC Radio in October, 1939, and said: "I can't forecast to you the action of Russia. It is a riddle wrapped in a mystery inside an enigma."

Little has happened in modern years to change that characterization, and when the opportunity came to examine first-hand this country of mystique, secrecy and deception, I grabbed it.

It was August, 1973, and Russia, mired in a bitter cold war with most of the world, eased its guard for 18 days and hosted the World University Games. That's college sports' answer to the Olympics. Staged every two years in a different country, it is only a shade below the Olympics in quality and brings together many of the same competitors involved in the mother of all athletic conclaves.

Generally considered to be 50 years behind the rest of Europe in lifestyle, Russia took a bold, uncharacteristic step in opening its iron-clad doors to 3,513 athletes from 67 countries. An isolationist, the USSR had never hosted anything more than one-on-one international sports competition in the past. Its first appearance in the Olympics was 1952.

Yes, it was a sports extravaganza of historic interest. I still remember that Russia's diminutive Olga Korbut, the darling of the Games, dominated gymnastics, as she did a year earlier in the '72 Munich Olympics. And leaping David Thompson led the United States to a dramatic championship in men's basketball, gaining full revenge for the controversial loss to Russia in Munich a year earlier.

Officially, I was in Moscow for two weeks to prepare a story-photo feature for the *National Directory of College Athletics*. Robbins Flooring was sponsoring and picking up the tab. But, off the record, I was more interested in getting a peak at this unpredictable nation that must have been the

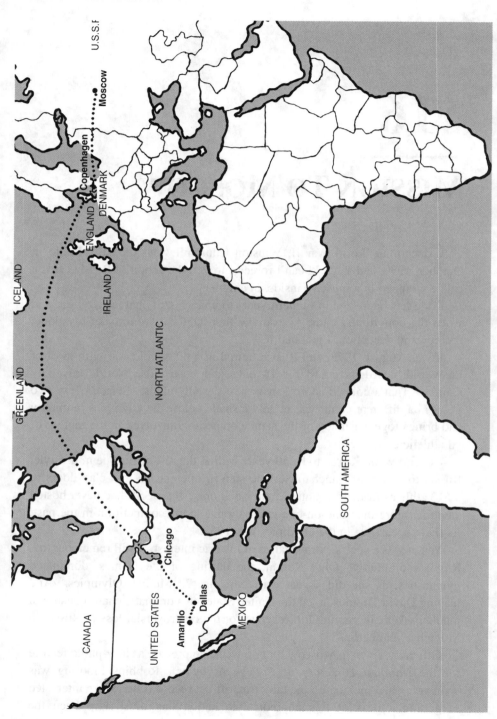

inspiration for Greta Garbo's famous quote, "I want to be alone." It's these observations I remember best.

If I had to select one word to describe the atmosphere of Moscow in 1973, it would be "intimidation". Yes, the KGB, Russia's much publicized secret police, was with us all our waking hours, a la James Bond. Everywhere you looked, there were police cars, police trucks and uniformed policemen. And keep in mind, the Soviets were putting their best foot forward, using these Games as a dress rehearsal for impressing Olympic officials. They eventually were awarded the 1980 Olympics, but USA boycotted because of the Afghanistan episode, tainting their success.

Like the trip to Japan with Utah State, I had to sweat out the departure. Although I had applied two months in advance for press credentials, they didn't arrive from Russia until the day before the American contingent of 300 athletes, coaches and officials converged on Chicago. Maybe the fact the envelope included no street address or box number delayed delivery. It was simply addressed to "Ray Franks, Amarillo, Texas, U.S.A." I was fortunate to get it at all, thanks to a caring post office employee who bothered to look up my street number. It was an omen of things to come.

The eight-hour Pan American charter flight from Chicago to Copenhagen, Denmark, was uneventful. After refueling, we were back in the air, arriving in Moscow three hours later. Then came the first hint of intimidation as we taxied to Moscow's archaic air terminal.

"We have been told by Soviet officials that photographing of the airport is forbidden for security reasons," announced an American official over the intercom. "And, yes, we have been warned not to bring any religious material into the country."

A maverick at heart, from my porthole window, I started snapping as fast as I could. Included was a picture of a Russian man coming toward us in something that looked like a golf cart. He was wearing one of those ever-present rabbit fur hats with the flaps, even in mid-August. I was carrying a small New Testament bible in my sport coat pocket, a gift of friend Jerry Young, and I wasn't about to give it up. I would make a lousy Russian.

It took three hours to get our luggage, probably because a little Russian man with a little golf cart had been entrusted with the bags of 300 people. But that was only the beginning. It got worse. When American athletes checked in a Moscow University, the world's largest single building school with 50,000 students and home base for competitors of the Games, they got a surprise.

"There's a problem," explained a Russian interpreter in fluent English. "Proper credentials for many of your people have not arrived."

George Killian, executive director of the National Junior College Athletic

Association and Chef de Mission for the Games, exchanged quizzical glances with other U.S. officials. Proper information had been mailed from the States in adequate time, and whether the packet had really been lost was a source of speculation. Probably not. New photos had to be taken and questionnaires completed again for 101 athletes, causing a 72-hour delay in getting the last American equipped with proper ID cards. Fortunately, the U.S. delegation arrived five days before the start of competition. The rooms were furnished adequately, comparable to dorm space on any American campus.

With other members of the media, I was assigned to Ukraine Hotel, an impressive Gothic-style stone structure that looks more like a county courthouse than a hotel. Checking in was a lesson in inefficiency. Or maybe it was merely intimidation. I was shuffled from one room to another and after five hours I got my key to room 633. An astonishing feat when you consider the Russkis have been leaders in space exploration and Sputnik circled the globe three times while I waited.

Although the hotel was only 16 years old and one of the country's finest, I could have done better with a room at a Route 66 tourist court 50 years ago. There was a tub-shower with no curtain and a single bed with a sagging quilt mattress.

In the corner was a desk with a radio that probably listened to me while I wasn't listening to it.

Once inside the room, it was time to play the popular Russian tourist game: "Search for the hidden microphone." I never found one but what do I know about electronics. The commies knew where I was though. I got a call one night and this sweet, heavily-accented female voice asked:

"Hello, mister. Would you like a party?"

I knew right off she wasn't talking about a Sunday School party. After the initial shock, I realized I was being propositioned by a Russian hooker. Other American men staying at the hotel received similar calls and we were told they most likely were linked to the KGB. Prostitution in Moscow is rampant, especially where foreigners lodge. It is said to be flourishing even more today with the advent of free enterprise.

In front of the elevators on each floor were stationed tough-looking, steely-eyed matrons who could hold their own at the wrestling arena on Saturday night. It was their duty to have every hotel guest sign in and sign out, noting the time with each entry. They also kept your door key. Another form of intimidation.

Before competition began, I wanted to do a photo shoot with U.S. coaches

When we landed in Moscow, we were warned not to take any pictures of the airport for security reasons. But the temptation was too great, and I snapped this picture of a Russian man wearing a rabbit fur hat coming to get our luggage in something no bigger than a golf cart.

One of my favorite pictures has Russian gymnastic superstar Olga Korbut wearing a USA warmup after the end of competition. At the direction of a coach, she held her arm over the "USA" patch until she got up to leave the press table.

The star of the American contingent was David Thompson, who led the basketball team to a championship.

and athletes at Red Square. You think we didn't attract attention when Coach Ed Badger and American athletes decked out in colorful sweats entered the scene. Then coach at Wilbur Wright Junior College in Chicago, Badger was the U.S. basketball tutor and later went on to the Chicago Bulls.

Dozens of curious Russians, mostly dressed in colorless clothes, started gathering around as I set up pictures for publication in the Directory. For the most part, they appeared to be sober, unhappy people, reflecting years and years of oppression. Occasionally, youngsters would ask for chewing gum, a delicacy behind the Iron Curtain. If you pointed your camera at adults, they'd turn away. I had motioned to one elderly woman wearing a black coat and black babushka that I wanted to take her picture. Each time, she ducked away. However, when I returned home and was looking through my prints, there she was. In a photo of the Americans in front of onion-domed St. Basil's Cathedral, she walked by just as the picture was snapped. A pleasant surprise.

By the same token, I unknowingly wound up in a Tass News Agency photo taken while we were executing our photo opportunities. I saw it on the press room bulletin board with a heading that read: "Americans at Red Square". It made a nice souvenir of the adventure and wound up in my briefcase before departing for home.

Red Square is breath-taking. It's one of those much-publicized places in the world that does not disappoint. I found it both exciting and eerie. It's the same brick courtyard where the young German boy outfoxed Russia's vaunted air corridor and landed his small airplane only a few years ago. It's also the same place where the once mighty USSR paraded its tanks and missiles on May Day, a scene that showed up on every TV set around the world.

Funny thing, when I returned home in '73, I told friends what I had witnessed in Russia had dispelled my fears. Long before President Ronald Reagan's tough stance broke the economic back of the USSR resulting in the fall of communism, I remarked, "I'm no longer afraid of Russia as a world power after seeing the general inefficiency of the country."

It turned out to be an astute observation.

Four-hundred-year old St. Basil's Cathedral, with its nine multi-colored onion domes, is Russia's answer to Disneyland and the darling of Red Square. One of the world's most photographed landmarks, it's a sight to behold at night with carefully-placed lights illuminating it against a dark sky. Built by Ivan the Terrible, who tortured and disposed of his enemies as easily as we swat flies, the structure was designed to be a Russian Orthodox church. With the advent of communism and atheism in 1917, it was converted into a museum.

In three trips there over 23 years, I still haven't seen anyone enter or exit the magnificent marvel. It's been said that after the edifice was completed in the 16th century, Ivan had the eyes of the architect gouged out, so the masterpiece would never be duplicated.

While St. Basil's attracts the photographers on the south side of Red Square, Lenin's Tomb on the west side was the biggest show in town in '73. In two trips there that year, eight-deep lines measured a half-mile long, discouraging me from taking a peek. They say the lines were still there, even in the midst of Russia's deep-freeze, bone-chilling winters. At one time, Stalin and Lenin were both stowed away in that granite mausoleum, but leaders in this fickle country often fade as fast as a West Texas sunset. Stalin's star has disappeared completely and today, there's no waiting for fast-fading Lenin. It's said he too will be removed as the truth about his ruthless regime surfaces.

Located just west of the tomb, behind a 30-foot stone wall, is the Kremlin, the heart of the communist party in '73. This completely barricaded 64-acre area encompasses museums, churches, government offices and the Grand Palace, where the party brain-trust met before Gorbachev's demise in 1991.

On the east side of Red Square is a landmark of less serious stature. It's GUM (pronounced "goom") department store, a government-owned grandiose building four blocks long that makes Bloomingdale's look like a corner convenience stop. With it's arched glass atrium and gothic columns, this 100-year-old, two-story store rates a 10 in architecture but a zero in efficiency. Mainly clothing, fur hats and the like are sold there, and I watched long enough to see how you shopped in the former Soviet Union 22 years ago.

To buy any item at GUM, you stood in three lines, which, I'm convinced is a national pastime over there. In the first one, you select your merchandise. Then in line two, you pull out your rubles and pay for it. A third line is necessary to pick up your merchandise with the sales slip you receive in line two. Can you imagine what Wal-Mart would do in the land of caviar and vodka?

Actually, without a knowledge of the language, I doubt that I could have succeeded in buying anything at GUM. Most of our group purchased samovars, balalaikas and hand-crafted items at hotel shops reserved for tourists. Russians were not allowed in these shops, and probably couldn't have afforded the items anyway.

Although the cold war was at a feverish pitch in the early 70s, the Russian people showed a genuine affinity for America, as demonstrated in the opening ceremonies. Even Bill Clinton was welcomed with open arms as a protesting college student a few years later.

"Without question, America's 217 athletes received the biggest ovation of any visiting delegation from 90,000 fans in Lenin Stadium," observed Bill Young, University of Wyoming Sports Information Director and Press Officer for U.S. media. An old SID myself, I found we had a lot in common and buddied around with Bill during those unforgettable two weeks. In Moscow, a monstrous city of eight million, it's not advisable to travel alone.

Probably the best illustration of the Soviets' affection for the USA came in a much-publicized early round basketball brawl between Cuba and the Yanks. It was an incident that attracted front page attention in the international press. At this time, Castro and Cuba ranked right along with the USSR as our mortal cold war enemies.

I had a front row seat with pad and camera in hand.

The situation was this. Cuba, blessed with a quick and talented men's team, was bristling from the start as it sought to upset the favored Americans. Cuban players often shook clenched fists in the faces of U.S. cagers following a basket or a good play. And all during the early going, when Cuba was making a close game of it, the predominantly-Russian crowd cheered the underdogs lustily.

The U.S. club maintained its poise, however, as it did all during the Games, and pulled away to a 98-72 lead with 1:30 left on the clock. At that point, Tom Burleson, the 7-4 North Carolina State giant, and a Cuban went to the floor for a loose ball under the American basket. The scrambling Cuban started kicking Burleson and that was the opening the badly beaten losers had been waiting for.

The Cuban bench erupted onto the floor, armed with chairs and glass water bottles. Some solid blows were struck by both sides, but the U.S. players generally chose to back off, whenever possible, for fear of getting disqualified from the competition. This they had been warned of by their coaches prior to the game.

It was bedlam for nearly 10 minutes. One Cuban grabbed the game pistol from the scorer's table and started shooting blanks. Another blind-sided team manager Duane "Moose" Woltzen with a chair, and he was knocked to the floor in a daze. Still another went after an American player with a glass bottle. Two Russian officials grabbed the Cuban, and as they were wrestling, the bottle fell to the playing floor and shattered.

During an early round, Cuba started a fight with USA in basketball competition that attracted international attention. (Bottom right) Moose Woltzen, the American team manager, was kayoed by a Cuban player swinging a folding chair. (Bottom left) Sportscaster Merle Harmon was interviewing American basketball coach Ed Badget after the US victory over Russia in the championship. In the middle of the interview, the lights were turned out by disgruntled Russian officials

When order was restored, the Russians started a deafening chant from the stands. An interpreter revealed they were shouting, "Cuba, Go Out." When the Cuban players came back on the floor to play out the final 90 seconds, they were bombarded with apples, paper wads and piercing whistles (symbol of booing in Europe) from Russian spectators. The Americans were greeted with thunderous applause on their return to the court.

"This action proved to everyone," reasoned coach Badger, "where the fault really lay."

During the fight, I got close enough with my camera to catch some of the action, until uniformed police pushed me away. The only photographer on the floor, I was contacted by the Associated Press for a print of Woltzen lying prostrate on the floor with officials huddled around. At that time, Woltzen was basketball coach at Lakeland College and almost 20 years later, I went with his travel agency to the Bahamas to cover the Goombay Shootout.

While Russian fans demonstrated a genuine affection for American athletes, they exhibited an equally ugly streak toward Israel and its representatives. It started during opening ceremonies when the small Israeli delegation was greeted with uproarious cat-calls and whistles. Even Russian television turned its cameras away from the tunnel when Israel entered the stadium.

Half the world's Jewish population resided in Czarist Russia at the turn of the century, and little has changed since those days of severe discrimination. The clincher came when Israel was scheduled to play a first round men's basketball game. Hundreds of Russian Jews showed up with valid tickets.

"The arena is full and you can't enter," the fans were told by a Games official. They were livid and asked me to come over and take a picture of them waving their tickets in the air. I did, although I was half expecting a policeman to snatch my camera any minute. We later learned why the small fieldhouse was full. The sneaky Russkis had filled the place with uniformed soldiers for two reasons. In addition to keeping Jewish fans out, they chided and derided Israel's basketballers relentlessly.

When Will Grimsley, the Associated Press's top sports chronicler for years, reported this in a story with a Moscow dateline, he was warned by the Soviets.

"Repeat this action and we'll pull your press credentials," they threatened. Another case of intimidation.

Led by the remarkable David Thompson, the U.S. basketball team won eight straight games, capped by a 75-67 win over Russia before 12,000 bitterly disappointed fans. Two funny sidebars happened during this event, one of only a few bright moments for America.

Most of the 220 U.S. athletes sat in a block at one end of the basketball arena. When their team began taking charge midway in the first half, they launched into some organized cheers. Things like "two bits, four bits, six bits, a dollar, all for America, stand up and holler!"

The somber, expressionless Russian fans were shocked. They'd never seen an outpouring of organized excitement like this. In a little while, five Russian soldiers moved down toward the end of the stadium, and stood guard in front of the cheering American delegation. They stayed there for the remainder of the game.

"I have no idea what they thought they were guarding," said one athlete. "Maybe they thought we were on the verge of mobbing the court. Strange people, these Russians."

Host officials didn't take the disappointing loss without retaliation. Immediately after the final buzzer, sportscaster Merle Harmon, who called the game for delayed telecast on Eddie Einhorn's TVS Network back in the States, was interviewing winning coach Ed Badger at courtside.

Pow! Suddenly the lights went out over the court, putting Harmon in near darkness. U.S. television officials cornered Russian authorities and pleaded their case. But to no avail. The interview was never completed. Another mark for intimidation.

Shortly before returning home, Harmon, former Milwaukee Brewers and Texas Rangers baseball announcer and later developer of the popular Merle Harmon's Fan Fair retail chain, was doing some work at a Moscow TV station. Standing in the driveway, he started panning the city for his personal documentation of the historic trip.

"Sorry," came a voice from behind, "that is forbidden." The Russian television official told Harmon he had just filmed KGB headquarters, took his camera and exposed the tape. From the first day we arrived, Merle had been putting together an extensive documentary. Then in an instant, it was destroyed.

After arriving home, I made duplicate prints of pictures involving Merle and events he covered. When he wanted to pay me for the mementos, I countered: "No way. But I've always wanted a Hank Aaron-autographed baseball." At that time, Merle was doing Milwaukee baseball with "Mr. Baseball's" Bob Uecker and the all-time home run champion was with that organization. The ball is one of my sports memorabilia treasures.

Unlike the Japan trip, this event was well documented by American media. In addition to Harmon, other TV personalities included Bud Palmer and Donna Devarona, former Olympic swim star and gold medal winner. Besides Grimsley of the AP, his counterpart, UPI's Bill Madden, was there from New York, No doubt, the setting had something to do with it.

I have made reference to the KGB several times and the most often question I've been asked is: "Do you think you were tailed?"

"Yes," is the answer, unequivocally. When Bill Young and I would be outside the hotel, walking the streets or riding the subway, we would see familiar faces. And unlike intrigue movies, where they are hiding behind flower pots and being more discreet, little attempt was made to hide their actions. On one occasion, a middle-aged man wearing a black suit and hat and sporting a mustache, approached us and made some small talk.

Speaking impeccable English, he asked me: "What part of the South are you from?" He was quite knowledgeable about the United States and got his paycheck from the KGB. He said as much.

Lest you think only foreigners are watched in Russia, think again. At an intersection near our hotel, I saw a plain-clothes policeman jump out of the crowd and grab a Russian teenager who had strayed maybe a foot outside the pedestrian crosswalk stripe. Once while riding a taxi, I saw the driver hailed to the curb, pulled out of his seat and roughed up for moving across a lane without a signal.

Gymnastics was treated as the showcase event of the Games, and elf-like Olga Korbut didn't disappoint the host country. Just 4-10 and 85 pounds, she was flawless and won everything in sight. No doubt about it, Korbut is responsible for propelling gymnastics to the forefront of international competition, especially the Olympics.

Married and now living in the U.S. at last report, the sandy-haired dynamo was the subject of my favorite photo of the entire trip. It's customary for athletes to swap warm-ups after competition and she switched with Terry Spencer of the U.S. At the final press conference, Olga and her dark blue jacket with red "USA" lettering were the center of every photographer. When a Russian coach went over and whispered in her ear, she quickly raised her left arm to cover the lettering. Playing the propaganda game to the hilt, these Russians are sneaky.

So are some of us Americans. At the conclusion of the press conference, Olga stood up to leave the table. When her left arm slipped down to her side, I snapped a full view of the pixie pig-tailed gymnast, getting equal billing for the "USA". Take that, you Russkis!

During the basketball championship game, about 200 U.S. athletes seated in the end section started organized cheers for their fellow Americans. The action so startled sedate Russians that five policemen went down to the area and stood guard the remainder of the game.

I took this picture of irate Russian Jews who weren't allowed to enter a gymnasium in which Israel was competing, even though they had tickets. They're waving their tickets for this photo protesting action of Russian officials. (Right) On a Sunday cruise down the Moscow River, I taught the son of the ship's captain how to blow bubble gum.

At all the competition, announcements were made in both Russian and English, generally accepted as the international language. Proving that something is often lost in translation, a woman interpreter was heard to say at a basketball game:

"That is Johnson's fifth personal foul, and she is ordered off the field." On another occasion, a double foul was described as a "mutual individual foul".

As I have hinted earlier, American athletes fared poorly, except for men's basketball and the swimmers, who contributed 30 of the USA's 53 medals. Track was the biggest disappointment, taking only two gold medals and a total of nine awards in a sport normally dominated by the red, white and blue. Russia stole it's own show with 134 medals.

One American athlete didn't win a competitive medal but deserved a purple heart. On his second day in Moscow and still trying to recover from jet lag, gymnast John Crosby complained of an excruciating pain in his side. A U.S. medic determined it probably was appendicitis and rushed him to a Moscow hospital.

There inside a high-ceiling, poorly-lit and scarcely-furnished operating room, Crosby had his appendix removed by a Russian woman surgeon who made the equivalent of $20 a month. Talk about bravery under fire. Despite the setting, Crosby made a quick recovery and was on hand to watch the gymnastics competition a week later.

As Yakov Smirnoff, the Russian comic now living in America, puts it: "In Russia, health care is free . . . and you get what you pay for."

Near the end of the trip, on a Sunday, members of the media were treated to a cruise down the Moscow River. After an incessant diet of sports activity, this was a pleasant change. The atmosphere was relaxed as we waved at Russians on holiday on passing boats. We detected a few smiles, a scarce commodity among the comrades. We were treated to a tasty lunch of finger sandwiches, pastries and the country's favorite soft drink, a bottled creation that tasted a lot like cream soda. And I taught the ship captain's 10-year-old son how to blow bubbles with bubble gum, an unknown quantity behind the Iron Curtain.

Out in the countryside, we saw one-family dwellings for the first time in almost two weeks. They were wooden shacks, small in size and in disrepair. Everyone in Moscow lives in apartments, crowded apartments, very crowded apartments. Often, four families share one kitchen and one bathroom, our college student interpreters revealed.

In a rare moment of confession, one of our translators told us there was much internal unrest in her country. "We hate this way of life and are watched constantly," a young girl confided. "Apartment living makes it easy for informers to keep track of others and organized meetings are next to impossible."

Night life in Moscow is almost non-existent. Few can afford leisure activities, but when they can, it's usually the circus or ballet. We had time for neither on this trip. Actually, Sunday is the only day hard-working Muscovites can call their own. A typical activity is making a trip across town on Moscow's famed squeaky-clean subway, or a stroll through the park with an ice cream bar or cone in hand.

Two things about this land of mystery impressed me. One was it's quality ice cream, something similar to our Eskimo Pies. I tried the ice cream, purchased from sidewalk vendors, and it was good. The other its Metro. At least one generation behind the West in most areas, the Russians do excel in underground railroads. And as Bill Young and I rode a sleek, glistening car to Lenin Stadium one day, we wondered why?

Why would a country bordering the poverty level for centuries spend so much on lavish subways nestled in elegant stations boasting marble floors and walls, huge bronze statues and beautiful brass chandeliers? It's spotless, no trash as you would most certainly find in New York. A showplace for visitors and natives alike, the system was started in 1935 and services nearly all the vast metropolis. It's another paradox that boggles the mind.

The Metro is Russia's main mode of travel because few can afford cars. On our bus trips around town, we would be riding wide boulevards marked for six lanes of traffic and see only five or six cars, small cars of poor quality. It was scary. Most of the Russian-made Volgas we saw belonged to government officials.

"How was the food?" is another most-asked question about Russia. Like night clubs, restaurants were lacking and McDonald's was still only a farm at this point in time. Away from the sports scene, most of our time centered around stoic, very formal Hotel Ukraine.

I like basic food and did well with potatoes and bread, items they prepare well. I felt safe with chicken Kiev, a dish I had eaten in America, and borscht, a typical Russian soup with beets and cabbage. Accustomed to the best beef in the world living in West Texas, I found Soviet steak as tough as a ditch-digger in Siberia. As in most European cities, ice is scarce and not normally served with cold drinks. Most grumbled about the food, but I found it acceptable. I'm not too difficult to please in this department.

While we weren't eating or sleeping at ol' Ukraine, we sat around the hotel and listened to a Russian jazz band that delivered "Body and Soul" and "Woodchopper's Ball" with surprising authority. In Russia, all American music is craved, from rock and roll to country-western. Even sitting in our hotel lobby, we would look up and wonder: "You think that chandelier is bugged?" And it probably was.

For more than two weeks, I looked around, studied and tried to figure out this odd country, the one Churchill labelled an "enigma". It was a strange departure from the U.S.; no noisy traffic, no colorful clothing and no flickering neon lights.

"What in the world do eight million people do in their spare time with only a handful of entertainment and recreational attractions around?" I asked Bill Young. Especially, when you remember the average salary barely covers necessities. Before the break-up of the Soviet Union in the early 90's, this sheltered country comprised one-third of the world's surface.

It was virtually impossible to talk to the people, especially those on the street. We later learned they were discouraged from talking to strangers, another security measure no doubt. Oppressed and brain-washed by czars for centuries, and then by communism for another 75 years, the damage had been done.

"The American Charge d'Affaires and Mrs. Dubs request the pleasure of the company of Ray Franks at a reception on Thursday at 6:30 o'clock." This invitation bearing the gold-engraved seal of the U.S. Embassy announced the highlight of our social activity in Russia.

Wearing our best threads, we arrived at the much-photographed high metal gate in Moscow's diplomatic area, where two grim Russian soldiers were guarding the premises. After showing proper credentials, we ascended a long staircase to a huge ballroom filled with American coaches, Games officials and the media. Security was the first item to be addressed.

"Don't say anything you don't want the Russians to hear," was the opening statement we heard from Embassy officials. "I don't know anything that would be of value to them anyway," remarked Marge Fieber, long-time NCAA business manager who was serving as secretary of the U.S. delegation.

It was a laid-back, pleasant evening hosted by Adolph Dubs, who was bridging the gap while the Embassy was between ambassadors. I was saddened to see on the news a few years later that Dubs was killed when the U.S. Embassy was stormed by rebels in the nearby country of Baluchistan.

The American athletes fared poorly in the Games, except for men's basketball and swimming. However, they too were treated to an evening at the Embassy the night before returning home. The media was included again, and all of us gulped down those good ol' American staples, hot dogs and cream puffs. You think the athletes didn't appreciate that menu after two weeks of European dining and no fast food fixes?

But the real cheers came 24 hours later when we landed at O'Hare Airport. We returned via the same route, with a stop-over in Copenhagen. At touchdown on American soil, the entire plane erupted into uproarious spontaneous applause. Normally blasé college students had learned an important lesson 18 days behind the Iron Curtain—freedom should never be taken for granted.

We found communism despicable. But we also discovered one reason why Russians are a grim and sad lot.

Even today, there's not a single golf course in the entire country.

17

DAY WITH ORAL ROBERTS

With Oral Roberts, there's no middle ground. You either love the guy and trust him unequivocally or you are prone to ridicule him and question his motives.

One thing is certain, he and his life have never been dull.

The son of a poor Oklahoma Pentecostal Holiness preacher, he ran away from home as a young teenager, barely survived tuberculosis when it was a deadly untreatable disease, launched a world-wide "faith healing" crusade and founded a multi-million dollar university bearing his name.

His latest endeavor, an ambitious modernistic City of Faith medical and research center, never quite made it. The patients didn't come in the numbers expected and needed to make it economically feasible. Now only partially utilized by a number of organizations, this futuristic 1.9 million square-foot facility is mute evidence of a philosophy that was designed to unite medicine and prayer in the healing of mankind.

But it was a quotation on a newspaper sports page in the early 70s that aroused my curiosity for a feature in the National Directory of College Athletics. "I want our basketball team to make a strong and powerful witness wherever it plays," was the statement of this controversial evangelist turned university president.

My oldest son Randy, who was employed at the Ranch at the time, accompanied me to Tulsa. It was a six-hour drive and after turning south on Lewis Avenue, we passed the famous Southern Hills Country Club, site of many major golf events.

Then, we saw it. Looming on the horizon was a complex of futuristic buildings that looked more like a Martian city than a college. No ivy-covered red brick buildings here. It was spectacular, eye-popping and most impressive.

When Evangelist Oral Roberts launched an NCAA Division I basketball program in the 70s, he granted an interview to our publication. That's son Randy on the left.

"Wow, I had heard it was different," said Randy, "but I wasn't ready forsomething like this."

No, we hadn't taken a wrong turn, and yes, we were approaching Oral Roberts University, a brand new religious-oriented school of 2,000 with an ambitious athletic program. After finding athletic director and basketball coach Ken Trickey at his desk in Mabee Center, I saw the figure of another person sitting across from him. The man with thick dark hair, long sideburns and a ruddy complexion looked familiar.

"Come on in, boys," motioned Trickey, "and you're in luck. I'd like you to meet Oral Roberts."

We were indeed fortunate to find the human dynamo relaxing for a few minutes. After all, he was carrying the load of two full-time jobs, radio and TV evangelist and president of Oral Roberts University. On this occasion, he was merely an avid basketball fan, trying to get a line on ORU's opponent in the final home game of the season. He knew our mission and thanked us for coming in to do a special story.

It was mid-afternoon, a good four hours before tip-off time.

"Would you like to look around our wonderful new facility?" asked Roberts. "It's all paid for," he said gesturing to plaques at various locations, indicating names of donors. An effective evangelist, he has always been a dynamic fund-raiser.

"In addition to being a beautiful basketball arena that seats 11,000," related Roberts, "it's extremely flexible."

He explained that it could easily be converted into a theater seating 3,000, and was the scene of all regular "Oral Roberts Presents" TV shows, featuring his son Richard and the World Action Singers. It's equipped with a hydraulic orchestra pit and elegant curtains that crop from the ceiling. It's first-class in every way.

While standing in the middle of the playing floor, emblazoned on two sides with the slogan, "Expect A Miracle", he outlined his philosophy for a big-time basketball program.

"I feel a strong basketball team, exemplifying the Christian spirit at all times, can make a powerful witness wherever it appears," remarked the man who for 20 years criss-crossed the world with massive tent revivals practicing faith healing.

"Many people are not as faithful in church attendance on Sunday mornings as they once were. But 40 million men read the sports pages on Sunday morning. In this ministry, we try to reach people where they are."

He had a phone call and our discussion was over for the time being. However, before the game that night and all during the contest at the press table, he consented to a lengthy interview, giving us all the time we wanted. At basketball games, the personable Roberts often sits in the press area, visiting with the media and staying close to the action. Basketball affords the busy religious leader a release from the pressures of his work.

"I can relax and get ready for the next day while watching a basketball game," he reasons.

Rarely will he sit still in one place for an entire game. He may start in his reserved seat, then wander down to the press area or any remote part of Mabee Center, shaking hands or talking to friends. Son Richard, a TV personality in his own right, is just as rabid about basketball, and is a frequent visitor to the press area.

The minister recalled his school's first trip to the National Invitation Tournament at Madison Square Garden. "I don't believe I got to see more than a few minutes of that game," he said. "The people up there were just beautiful . . . and so friendly."

Since that episode, Roberts made a practice of sitting on the ORU bench at road games. "By being down on the court with us, we could shield him somewhat from the crowd," said Tricky, who no longer coaches at ORU after two stints. "President Roberts is constantly being mobbed wherever he goes."

The notoriety has its benefits too. A household name for years by way of weekly radio and TV shows, President Roberts lends a helping hand in recruiting. He's been known to call prospective athletes on the phone or drop by in the school's private jet to see a boy and his parents. Even Bobby Knight doesn't have that kind of clout.

He takes a lot of good-natured kidding about his deep concern for sports and basketball in particular. But he takes it in stride, and laughs about it when relating stories. In an appearance on the Johnny Carson Show, he was asked by the host about the school's basketball team.

"Right at this minute, they're getting ready to tip off against Marshall University out in Huntington, WV," informed the personable evangelist, placing his hands together under his chin in a gesture of prayer.

"That Marshall team doesn't have a chance," laughed Carson. When Roberts returned to his hotel that night, there was a telephone message from Coach Trickey indicating ORU had won an upset, 81-76.

The 72-73 season was the first for the University to have a full-time trainer, and Roberts, who advocated "healing of the whole man" in crusades of the past, gets ribbed about that. "With President Roberts around, we haven't needed a trainer," explained an athletic official with tongue in cheek.

During the interview, he explained his deep interest in basketball. "At 6-1½, I played center on my high school team," he started. "I loved every minute of it after making the starting team, but my playing days were cut short by a freak situation.

"It was during the championship game of the Oklahoma Seven Tournament, and I was driving down the court for a lay-up. All of a sudden, everything began to blur before my eyes. I stumbled and collapsed on the gym floor."

Living in Atoka, Oklahoma, after running away from home at an early age, he lost consciousness briefly and began hemorrhaging with every breath. The 16-year-old was diagnosed as having tuberculosis and since penicillin had not been discovered, his chances of survival were thin. After being bedfast for 63 days, he went from 160 pounds to 120, and doctors threw up their hands. They could do nothing more.

His brother, Elmer, no more religious than Oral in those days, heard about a tent revival in Ada, where a preacher was praying for the sick. "God is going to heal you," said Elmer, "Now get up and let's go."

The young boy was literally carried to the tent and when it was time for the divine healing portion of the service, Oral was placed on the stage in a rocking chair. "The preacher put his hands on my head and said a short prayer: 'Thou foul disease. I command you in the name of Jesus Christ to come out of this boy's lungs. Loose him and let him go.'"

The next thing he knew Oral was racing back and forth on the platform, shouting at the top of his voice, "I am healed, I am healed." A stutterer and stammerer, even though he had been named "Oral", Roberts took the microphone and spoke to that crowd without hesitation. He never again had a speech problem.

That experience convinced Granville Oral Roberts that God had spared him for a reason. He added: "From poverty, to a runaway, to deathbed, and healing—it all combined to make me a preacher." Within two months of his total healing, he delivered his first sermon.

Giving God total credit, Roberts said he has seen thousands made well through divine healing. But there have been some rough times too. Like the year he was run out of Australia by hoodlums and hecklers who threatened to burn his tent. And the time he was in Amarillo, Texas, when a tornado-like wind blew down his tent and 7,000 people escaped without a serious injury. Once in Tulsa at an early tent revival, he was shot at and nearly hit by a man "who was tired of his crusade lingering on."

The ORU basketball story has been a roller-coaster ride. At the outset, Roberts and Coach Trickey set a 10-year-old goal of national recognition. Incidentally, Trickey moved to ORU from Middle Tennessee State after having visited the campus for a game and "being most impressed". Middle Tennessee had trounced the Titans and Roberts too had been impressed with Trickey, calling him for the job when an opening occurred.

They were right on target. In the first eight years, the Titans compiled a record of 160 wins against only 51 defeats; earned two NIT bids; and in 1971-72 set a new all-time NCAA scoring record of 105.1 points per game. They had the attention of the sports world.

In those early years as an independent, scheduling was tough. However, after achieving Division I status, they moved in and out of the top 20 teams with regularity and once got as high as 11th. Continued success followed the Titans into the 80s, but like many small schools around the country, the money crunch caught up with them.

Currently, ORU plays a low-key schedule, but still spices its season with some of the biggies. It's not the same quality, but those ORU scores still appear on the daily sports pages. In his late 70s, Oral has relinquished many of his responsibilities to son Richard, including the presidency of the college bearing his name.

"What about Oral Roberts, the man?" I've been asked. A charismatic TV personality for years after those 20 years of tent revivals, he's misunderstood by many.

"I know better than anyone that Oral Roberts can not heal people," he says. "Men like myself are only instruments of God."

Like other people of controversy, Oral Roberts is a complex person and difficult to comprehend. I won't attempt to judge him after spending most of one day in his presence. After all, only one judgement will be important in the end.

18

TIME-OUT FOR HEART SURGERY

My travel aspirations, my career, in fact my whole life came to a standstill in January, 1977, when I underwent open-heart surgery.

Red-neck humorist Lewis Grizzard wrote an entire book around his first open-heart surgery, titling it *"They Tore Out My Heart and Stomped That Sucker Flat."* The least I can do is devote a short chapter to the same experience.

On a routine physical examination, I reported to my doctor I was experiencing general sluggishness and a "tightness" in my left arm. A heart catherization showed 90% blockage in the left anterior descending artery. That was the only one of significance filled with plaque, but it's also the one doctors call the "widow maker". It distributes more blood to the body than any other.

My doctors said I was a borderline candidate for by-pass surgery, a procedure that had been performed for about five years in Amarillo hospitals. A good lawyer friend, Elton Cox, was the first I knew who experienced the operation in the early 70s.

He seemed to be doing well and after praying over the matter and talking to my wife, I opted for surgery. If I had known then what I know today, I probably would have made the other decision. So much more is being offered now less radical than surgery and I was only 47 at the time. I turned 48 three days later.

"A perfect surgery", assured Dr. R.D. Sutherland when I first recognized him in CCU. With my Southern Baptist faith and Christian friends praying for me, I honestly faced it with a minimum of fright. Daughter Debbie saw me just after leaving recovery and almost fainted. She later described me as "looking like a dead man."

As with most heart surgeries, I was pushed out of bed for my first walk only hours after completion. Dozens of tubes and wires were still attached. The first meal was a shocker too. It consisted of string green beans, mashed potatoes, a bowl of jello, a roll and BARBECUED BEEF. I ate it, and survived, but it didn't appear appropriate for someone just out of the operating room. After eating questionable dishes like shark fin soup and squid in the Orient, I'm convinced I have a cast-iron stomach.

The operation, performed quite often today on people in pressure professions, was the subject of a story in the 1977-78 *National Directory of College Athletics*. Heck, how many jobs can you think of with more pressure-cooker implications than those in college athletics?

It really developed, however, after a strange turn of events at the 1977 NACDA (National Association of College Director of Athletics) Convention in Las Vegas.

Robert Macken, Athletic Director at Dominican College in Blauvelt, New York, had just seen his name drawn as the winner of a free trip for two to Majorca, Spain (compliments of NACDA). It's an annual drawing in the area of exhibitors designed to stimulate traffic among commercial exhibits.

As Macken, his wife and daughter passed the booth of the *National Directory of College Athletics*, a happy Mrs. Macken remarked to my wife: "I guess this is Robert's reward for just having had open-heart surgery." Floy couldn't believe her ears. She related that her husband also had experienced the same operation in '77, and set out to arrange a meeting between Macken and myself.

In a brief conversation that followed, we compared operating procedures and general information about open-heart surgery. We agreed testimonials about our experiences might benefit others in the stress-saturated business of athletics. The following comments were related by Macken on his return from the convention:

"I am happy you decided to write about our heart surgeries in your fine Directory. If we can help just one person, it will be well worth it.

"In reviewing my situation, I feel that the most important thing to do is go to your doctor if you have the slightest pain or discomfort. Accept the possibility of a heart problem, and do not delay treatment that can save your life. No one really wants to undergo open heart surgery, but as we both know, it's the only way to correct blocked arteries.

"I have been active all my life as an athlete and coach, and felt I would always enjoy good health. It was difficult for me to accept the fact that

Iwould get winded just walking across the room, and I knew I needed medical assistance.

"Taking the stress cardiogram was most important, and it indicated my trouble was in the coronary arteries. My heart was not getting the proper flow of blood when I was active on the treadmill. I had taken previous EKG's while lying prone and there was no indication that anything was wrong with my heart. Stress tests are musts.

"After tests proved my need for surgery, I decided to accept the challenge. I prepared myself physically, emotionally and spiritually for the operation. I had to lose 40 pounds. I had great faith in God and put my trust in Him. I am Catholic and was happy when my college had a Mass said at the exact time of surgery. The prayers and wishes I received from friends and coaches also gave me a great confidence that God would take care of me. It was certainly a great feeling knowing that people from all denominations and colleges we compete against were praying for me.

"Now that the operation is over, and I am on the road to recovery, I am sure I made the right choice. If I hadn't undergone surgery, who knows?"

The operation took care of Bob Macken's needs for 15 years, but he died in 1992 after a long and illustrious career in college athletics.

19

ROAD TO RIO

It was April, 1977. Riding along a main thoroughfare of Rio de Janeiro, Brazil, then Arkansas basketball coach Eddie Sutton gazed out the window and mused:

"This has got to be the most spectacularly beautiful city in all the world."

To fellow passengers on the team bus he added: "It reminds me of several cities all rolled into one. The architecture and beaches make me think of Miami. The hilly terrain looks like San Francisco."

Romantic Rio is all that and then some, as we found out on a two-week "Partners of the Americas" goodwill tour of Brazil. Actually, my wife, Floy, and I had been invited by Gary Neeleman of the international organization to do this story a year earlier.

Marquette, the NCAA champion in 1977, was the college selected to represent the USA on the same trip the previous year. When I approached Coach Al McGuire at the National Sporting Goods Show in Chicago about accompanying his team to South America, he threw up his hands.

"No, absolutely not," he said, "we don't want anyone covering our trip to Brazil."

I took the hint, backed away and scratched my head.

"Why?' I asked myself. To this day, I still have no clue.

However, it was a blessing in disguise.

The reception from Sutton and his Arkansas Razorbacks couldn't have been warmer. Since that episode, the personable coach has been at Kentucky and Oklahoma State, where he presently controls the destinies of his old alma mater.

But let's back up and provide another piece to this equation. Without sponsorship, out trip would not have been possible. At this time in history, Braniff International owned the air routes to Central and South America, and

it's sports director, Bob Sign, was looking for new promotions. When I approached him with the idea of an advertising travel tradeout, he grabbed the ball and ran. We quickly seized the opportunity although I was only three months past heart surgery.

Because Arkansas' expenses were picked up by the organization "promoting an interchange of information and technology in basketball", they flew Varig Airlines, the Brazilian company, from Miami. We went Braniff all the way. The route was Dallas, Miami, Panama City, Lima and Rio, almost totally in darkness. The return was the same, leaving from Sao Paulo instead of Rio. We hooked up with Arkansas in Rio, the first phase of basketball action.

Going through customs in Brazil, we quickly learned to be on the defensive. When our luggage was checked, we were told all aerosol products like deodorant and hair spray would have to be checked in another area. Officials took them away and we never saw them again. An international rip-off we might have expected in Mexico, but not Brazil.

"Hey, where's our deodorant?" I asked before leaving the area. Nothing but blank stares.

Before spending almost two weeks in the country, Brazil meant three things to me . . . soccer, coffee and piranha (the flesh-eating fish that is found in the Amazon River). At the beach, we saw youngsters kicking soccer balls instead of beach balls. In late afternoon when the sun would hide behind the office buildings, pick-up games of soccer were common-place on the beaches.

Next door to the basketball arena in Rio was Maracana Stadium, the world's largest soccer edifice with a seating capacity of 200,000. Evangelist Billy Graham and Pele (Brazil's legendary soccer hero) have filled the giant stadium on several occasions. And this before the 1994 success of winning the World Cup.

To no one's surprise, we found coffee to be the national drink of Brazil, and it is huckstered by brightly-dressed vendors at sports events. At the basketball games in Rio, the peddlers' coats blared "Cafe Pele." We learned that the all-time soccer great lends his name to the sale of coffee in Brazil similar to Joe DiMaggio's endorsement of a coffee-maker in the States.

The closest we got to a piranha was the stuffed variety, which we found in a Japanese souvenir shop. The ones we brought home resemble large blue-gill (about 8-9 inches long) with one very significant exception. The piranha is reinforced with razor-sharp teeth that leave little doubt why they are carnivorous. What great line-backers they'd make!

But of course, we found this huge country that occupies about half of

South America to be much more than that. Traveling in the company of a college basketball squad had its advantages. And the Arkansas contingent, which had just completed a 26-2 season and won the Southwest Conference, were perfect goodwill ambassadors.

"This is unquestionably one of the finest groups of young men to visit our country," praised Jose Claudio dos Reis, Vice-President of the Brazilian Basketball Confederation and "Mr. Basketball" of all South America. "The United States can be proud of its representative . . . not a single time did the players lose their composure."

On the court, the Arkansas squad waded into tough international competition and did remarkably well. They won five and lost three against national teams of Argentina and Brazil in three tournaments and two exhibitions. They captured the plum of the tourneys—the Governor's Cup at Sao Paulo—a feat even more remarkable when you consider the defending NCAA champs, Marquette, failed in their attempt to do the same thing a year previous.

Out of their basketball regalia, the Razorbacks, most of whom had never wandered far from the hills and hollows of Arkansas, were even more impressive. Cavorting on beautiful Copacabana Beach in Rio, the Hogs attracted huge throngs of young people, seeking autographs and just wanting to talk. They found Rio particularly alluring and fascinating because of its many beaches, majestic mountains and casual atmosphere. Many of the home-grown Razorbacks had never seen a beach before, and Rio was just as exotic and fun-loving as movies and travel folders had pictured.

In the same haunts Bob Hope, Bing Crosby and Dorothy Lamour had glamorized on the screen, the North Americans were trying to teach natives their famous "hog call." At the same time, they were learning the meaning of "carioca" and "cruzeiro", the latter Brazil's monetary unit that changed in value almost daily.

In Sao Paulo, an industrial metropolis of 12 million and still growing, the Hogs continued to get "A's" in diplomacy. On a free afternoon when it would have been more fashionable to shop, five of the players volunteered to travel across town and conduct a clinic for junior high and high school basketballers. Several of the youngsters attended the game that night, leading cheers for the Hogs.

Visiting the interior cities of Goiana and Brasilia, last stops on the tour, their popularity never diminished. Besieged by autograph-seekers and souvenir hunters, they obliged all reasonable requests. Floy and I skipped the last two stops, opting to get back to the States to take care of business.

Copacabana Beach in Rio de Janeiro seems to stretch forever. This picture was taken from our hotel room. (Below) The Franks took advantage of the famous beach on the last day of the season and only three months after I had survived open-heart surgery. That's Sugar Loaf mountain in the background.

Brazil's news media couldn't have been more cooperative and the country of 110 million people was well aware of the U.S. team's presence. Coach Sutton and his players were constantly being interviewed by sportswriters, and the games were carried live on national radio and TV. It was estimated 25 million watched the finals between Arkansas and Brazil in Sao Paulo.

What effect does an international swing like this have on the players? "It's a marvelous educational experience," voiced Sutton, named "Coach of the Year" by the U.S. Basketball Writers and NBC Grandstand in '77. The mild-mannered tutor continued: "This is a great bunch of kids, and a trip like this helps develop togetherness. I believe our actual play here was secondary to the real importance of coming to Brazil."

The Razorbacks were not sharp in the early going. The 6,000 mile, 24-hour trek from Fayetteville to Rio, by way of Dallas and Miami, took its toll. Also, the international play came nearly two months after the close of the '76-77 season, and Coach Sutton felt 10 days preparation time was inadequate. This was no schlock American basketball team. It had been the darling of the past college season, losing only two games, and had key personnel returning for 1978.

In the first tourney, the Cup of Rio, they lost to both Argentina, 77-75, and Brazil, 84-77. Both games, which could have gone either way, were played in 24,000 seat Maracana Zinha Arena. For the final game against Brazil, an enthusiastic crowd of 9,000 turned out.

After a two-day break, the teams moved on to Sao Paulo for the granddaddy of Brazilian tournament play, the annual Governor's Cup. The Hogs had been in the "coffee capital" of the world for a week now, and displayed the same caliber of play that elevated them as high as seventh in national polls during the season. Led by All-Conference performers Marvin Delph, Sid Moncrief and Ron Brewer, Arkansas lambasted Argentina's best, 90-73. They came back the next night and surprised Brazil's National squad (the team that represented them in World Cup competition), 73-69. A stingy defense was the key to that win.

"It just took us a while to get adjusted to international rules," asserted Delph, a 6-4 jumping jack from Conway, Arkansas. An active worker in Fellowship of Christian Athletes, Delph added: "This is a lot rougher than college. We learned a lot from the games in Rio."

The big 10,000 seat arena in Sao Paulo had been booked for the Ice Follies, and the games were moved to a private athletic club with a gym capacity of 4,000. It overflowed for the big U.S. - Brazil encounter, despite being televised in Sao Paulo and the remainder of the country.

The last tournament took the touring teams to the interior of Brazil. Goiana is a city of 600,000 and close to Brasilia, the modern capital where the U.S. entourage had an opportunity to sight-see the day before the first game. In 1956, Brasilia was proclaimed the country's new capital in an effort to spur inner development of the vast nation. At Goiana, Arkansas reached its offensive peak of the trip with a 106-92 romp of Argentina. The following night, however, Brazil got sweet revenge with an 89-66 win over a tired and home-sick U.S. team.

"It was our worse game of the South American swing," surmised sports information director Butch Henry. Jetting back to Rio the following day, the Razorbacks defeated the Flamengo Club in an exhibition and then hopped a plane that night for the welcomed return home.

Was Coach Sutton surprised by the caliber of play from Argentina and Brazil? "They were good basketball teams," he observed. "They can beat a lot of college teams in our country."

Sutton praised their great shooting ability. "They are not afraid to take the long shot . . . and their accuracy is uncanny." The Arkansas coach played under Hank Iba at Oklahoma State, where patient basketball was the game and percentage shooting prevailed. His teams play virtually the same style, and found it unnatural to cover far out and stop the long bombs.

One of the objects of the U.S. team's visit to South America was to help stimulate interest in basketball throughout a nation where soccer reigns supreme. Jose Claudio, the Brazilian cage impresario, was asked how it ranked as a spectator sport.

"Is it No. 2 in popularity?" he was queried.

"No," answered Jose with a wry grin. "I would say basketball ranks about sixth. Soccer is first, soccer is second, soccer is third, fourth and fifth . . . and then comes basketball."

Soccer may be king in Brazil, but fans do vent their emotions at basketball games. Sutton and the Arkansas bench were pelted with paper wads and debris all during the championship tilt with Brazil at Sao Paulo. Intermittent crescendos of "Bra . . . zil! Bra . . . zil!" rattled the rafters.

A year before, Coach Al McGuire of Marquette experienced the same situation. "It was unbelievable . . . 25,000 people booing and throwing garbage at us. It was just like playing Notre Dame."

During a two-week visit to a foreign country where language and customs are different, a number of humorous stories are bound to surface.

The Arkansas players found Brazilian food tasty and many dishes familiar. Beef steak, grilled chicken, spaghetti, roast pork and fresh fruit were on restaurant menus. Occasionally, though, the chef would slip in a surprise like fried bananas or palm hearts, and some of the players would cast a wary eye.

After a week away from home cooking, Ron Brewer eased over to Coach Sutton and confided: "Coach, you know what sounds good? A peanut butter and jelly sandwich."

That afternoon, Sutton found a supermarket in Sao Paulo and bought the biggest jar of peanut butter and strawberry jelly he could find. He took it to the pre-game meal that night, and needless to relate, Brewer and his surprised mates inhaled it in record time.

Brazil mainly is still free of the influence of U.S. fast-food chains. A couple of ambitious scouts did report finding a "Burger King" and "Jack-In-The-Box."

Official language of Brazil is Portuguese, and that proved an insurmountable barrier at times. One of the first nights in the country, sports publicist Butch Henry volunteered to take some of the players to a Rio sidewalk cafe and help them order with his scant knowledge of the language. After assisting the players, Henry informed the waiter he wanted a "batida," Portuguese for a mixed drink. Apparently losing something in his pronunciation, Henry was served an order of "french-fried" potatoes.

Rio's beautiful pristine beaches and the clear blue-green surf of the Atlantic fascinated the U.S. contingent of 15. One morning when the North Americans and several hundred Brazilians were enjoying world-famous Copacabana, a rain-shower moved in. The natives quickly scurried to their cars and went home. The Razorbacks, relishing every minute of the jet-set atmosphere, stayed on and had the beach to themselves.

Floy and I spent an entire day at Copacabana Beach, in my estimation the most gorgeous in the world. It winds for about four miles along the waterfront through handsome residential sections, bordered by a beautiful sidewalk of white marble inlaid with brilliantly colored mosaic work. We were there the last day of beach season since winter was arriving south of the Equator.

A Brazilian custom the Razorbacks had trouble adjusting to was extremely late starting times. Their tournament games never got underway before 11 or 11:15 p.m. The dinner meal is eaten quite late in Brazil, and Arkansas normally played the second game of a double-header. The team usually finished off post-game sandwiches and soft drinks about 2 a.m., and Coach Sutton reasoned that this adjustment in eating and sleeping habits probably had some effect on their performance at the outset.

Players from all teams stayed in the same hotels and usually ate at

A gracious Eddie Sutton, Arkansas basketball coach, and wife Patsy allowed the Franks to accompany the Razorbacks on a spring tour of Brazil.

At the beach, Brazilian youngsters took time out from their soccer games to visit with the Arkansas players.

Instead of customary soft drinks, peddlers sold hot coffee at sports events. The famous Pele loaned his name to the product.

adjoining tables at meal-time. It afforded all of them excellent opportunities to trade equipment and souvenirs, and joke with each other. Marvin Delph, high-scoring senior, had fun teaching a big Argentine center the meaning of "cool, daddy." English slang wasn't easy for someone who barely understood a few words of the language, but one morning the Argentine stepped off the hotel elevator and greeted a group of Hogs with a recognizable rendition of "cull, doddy!"

Officiating was unpredictable all during the tour, and an incident during the game with Argentina at Sao Paulo had the North Americans shaking their heads in disbelief. Junior guard Trey Trumbo was shooting a free throw just before half-time. The ball went directly through the hoop, hit the bottom of the tight net, and popped back out. The Brazilian referee signalled "no good," and Trey was forced to convert a second time, which he did.

Television coverage of the games was thorough and one colorful announcer was so bold he made Howard Cosell look like a shrinking violet. Working the sidelines during timeouts, he would take his microphone and jump into team huddles while coaches were barking instructions to their players. On occasions when the referees and coaches would get into controversies, he would be right in the middle interviewing both parties. It was a first for Sutton.

The sight-seeing excursions kept the Razorbacks hustling in their spare time. In Rio, they were escorted to world-famed Corcovado Rock where a 132-foot statue of Jesus Christ looms over the city and can be seen from any point in this sea-side resort spa. Tourists must climb 280 steps to reach the base of the five-million-dollar structure after a long winding ride up the city's tallest mountain. Another afternoon was spent riding the trams out to Sugarloaf Mountain, affording the visiting cagers a breathtaking view of Guanabara Bay, Copacabana Beach and other spectacular sights of Rio. Several of the players, along with my wife, thought the ride across bottomless canyons was more "breathtaking" than they desired. They waited behind and found comfortable benches.

In Sao Paulo, we visited the country's largest and best-stocked zoo and found the downtown malls meccas for souvenir shopping. Called the New York City of South America, Sao Paulo boasts hundreds of skyscrapers and is the industrial capital of South America. It is a stark contrast to the laid-back sea and ski metropolis of Rio de Janeiro, where having a good time seems to be the native's No. 1 objective.

One incident in this massive metropolis gave us pause for thought. We were picking out some fruit from a wagon peddler when we heard this shrill siren scream in our ears. Not knowing what to do, especially when Brazilians started scurrying off the street and finding shelter in nearby stores, we followed a couple into a souvenir shop. The owner promptly pulled down an overhead metal door and locked it. "Gangs sometimes attack downtown shoppers and stores," we were told, "and that's the reason for the siren."

The unforgettable trip down under was a fitting climax for an Arkansas squad that was named the "surprise team" of the '77 season, and an appropriate prelude to 1978. With the terrific trio of Delf, Moncrief and Brewer returning, the Razorbacks won the Southwest Conference once again and made their first trip to the Final Four, joining Kentucky, Duke and Notre Dame for the big dance.

It was an equally memorable experience for a couple of tag-alongs who were mesmerized by the majestic beauty of Rio and the massive size and modernization of Sao Paulo. On a day set aside for sight-seeing in Rio, we received a special treat. We called a Southern Baptist missionary couple and asked them to join us for breakfast in the penthouse restaurant atop the France Hotel overlooking Copacabana Beach.

Church friends Bryant and Floy Flores had given us their names and we hit it off immediately. What started out as a breakfast meeting turned into an all-day visit, one in which Ron and Marilyn Boswell gave us a personal tour of their chic adopted city. The highlight was a tour of H. Stern Jewelers, home base for a famous world-wide operation. We observed gem cutting and wound up buying a pear-shaped aquamarine ring, a stone found almost exclusively in Brazil. A perfect memento.

In general, we found Brazilians to be warm, friendly and pro-American. This despite the fact that in the late 70s there was tension between the countries in nuclear matters, coffee prices and human rights policies. Jimmy Carter could not have won a popularity contest in Brazil, and he wasn't doing much better in the States.

As Gary Neeleman, America's representative for "Partners of the Americas", observed: "This good-will tour couldn't have come at a better time."

20

FUNNY THING HAPPENED ON WAY TO HULA BOWL

Don't get me wrong, Hawaii in the dead of winter is a wonderful place to be. But research on the Hula Bowl All-Star game proved almost incidental when we were there in January of 1978.

After all, few all-star games pump up much excitement and are rarely more than a television showcase for individual performances. Dull is more like it. And most college players normally have better things to do in Hawaii than play football.

Then consider it was the Franks' 25th wedding anniversary, and we did something a bit bizarre. We took along our grown children—Debbie, Randy and David, and son-in-law Tim Sharp. None had ever been to paradise.

Our first distraction came in LAX, Los Angeles International Airport, while waiting for our Braniff flight across the Pacific. I believe it was Debbie who struck up a conversation with Bob Burt, an assistant football coach at University of Hawaii. While waiting for a hop back home, he volunteered: "Oh sure, I use the *National Directory of College Athletics* almost every day in my work. It's a great book." Then he added: "I've just appeared on Family Feud, and our family won quite a bit of money. It really wasn't that tough to get on, and it was great fun."

As we became more interested in what he had to say, and since every member of our family had always enjoyed the show emceed by Richard Dawson, he asked the question: "Hey, why don't you guys audition for the show? You'd have a great chance to make it."

Fast forward eleven years. Son David and wife Sandy, working in Dallas, decided in early 1989 to take a vacation to Southern California. A video editor and director, he was looking for possible relocation and invited Floy, daughter Debbie and me to join them. He had made an appointment to audition our clan for Family Feud, fulfilling an ambition that had been planted in that airport waiting area more than a decade ago.

In a second-story office building on Wilshire Boulevard, we were greeted by a bubbly receptionist who immediately gave us name tags and took a polaroid picture of the Franks troupe. Then along came lengthy questionnaires and a few verbal questions. Six or seven other families were doing the same thing.

The next step was to go head-to-head in simulated competition with another family in the first round of auditions. A young male assistant lined us up against a wall facing a family from California.

"Give me names of European capital cities?" was the first question. The captain of our opponents shot up his hand first and answered, "France." Of course, that wasn't on the list of correct answers because it's a country, not a capital city. Being the captain of our squad, I answered, "London".

It was first on the list of popular answers and our team named "Rome", "Paris" and all the other European cities on the answer sheet without getting a single strike. So far, so good.

After playing a second match with the same family, which we also won, our group was ushered into another small room with a dozen or so chairs. When we asked the young girl leading the way how we were doing, she replied: "Passing the first audition is the hardest part. Not many make it this far."

Now we were in the presence of Howard Felsher, a gray-haired, 60ish type with an unmistakable Eastern accent and the producer of "New Family Feud." The "new" tag was added to the title after being off the air a couple of years, and a different emcee, Ray Combs, was installed.

"Is your wife your best friend?" the long-time producer of Mark Goodson Productions asked me. When I answered in the affirmative, he wanted to know why. After learning I was a publisher, he asked if I knew the meaning of the word, "colophon". I didn't. He explained it was a symbol used by publishers at the end of manuscripts, mostly in the 15th and 16th centuries. Heck, I should have known that.

Then he queried Floy about her name. "Is that a nickname for something like Florence?" He asked Debbie about her homemaking activities and David and Sandy about their jobs in Dallas. After making small talk with members of another family, he lined us up for a second mock television match.

"Name the qualities of a good school teacher," was the first question thrown out for grabs. The opposition jumped in first and named something at the bottom of the list. Felsher turned to me, and I answered, "knowledgeable". It was near the top of replies in a poll of 100 people and our family gained control again. We won the round without letting the opposition get back in the game.

"Name false things that women wear," was the category for the next match. Floy gained control with the answer "eyelashes". And with "wigs", "boobs", and "fingernails", the Franks remained undefeated. The competition was over and we heaved a huge sigh of relief.

We giggled like little school children all the way down the hallway and on the elevator after being told we would hear from them by letter if we were accepted for the television show. Assistants to Felsher told us we had done well as we left the audition area. "How can we miss?" grinned David as we all felt contented and confident with our performance. For good measure, we presented producer Felsher a framed wall-hanging of the Family Feud logo which Sandy had cross-stitched.

The next day, on a tour of CBS Television City in Hollywood, we got to see the set of Family Feud first hand. "This week a celebrity match between the Super Bowl teams is being taped," said our guide. "The San Francisco 49ers and Cincinnati Bengals". The names of Bengal quarterback Boomer Essiason and other lesser known players were printed on place cards. As we canvassed the stage area and empty studio, we smiled and thought: "It won't be long until we're right here as contestants."

A week after returning home, the letter came. It was from Howard Felsher himself on a Mark Goodson Productions letterhead. It read:

Dear Family:

Congratulations! I hope it pleases you as much as it pleases us to tell you that you are eligible to appear on the "New Family Feud". Your family is now in our file of accepted contestants. Of course, we cannot guarantee appearances.

If we contact you for an appearance, it will be approximately one week prior to the tape date. The wait for our call could involve several months.

If you change your address or phone numbers, please let us know by calling 213/965-9999.

You have invested a lot of time and effort with us. We recognize it and appreciate it.

Thank you,
Sincerely,

HOWARD FELSHER, Producer
New Family Feud

On our 25th anniversary, the Franks took everyone to Hawaii. From left are Randy, son-in-law Tim Sharp, Debbie, Floy and David.

Weeks passed and two phone calls to California produced comments like "your family is still in our files." I'm guessing the Franks family application was either decimated by moths or gathered more moss than you'd find at Forest Lawn Cemetery. What really happened is of little importance now since the show is off the air. Besides that, former host Ray Combs recently committed suicide.

The reality that "congratulations" really meant "maybe" was tough to digest but the most difficult chore was explaining to relatives and friends. As recent as a year ago, I've been asked: "Hey, when were you guys on Family Feud? I must have missed it."

Another interesting sidebar to our Hawaiian holiday, again completely unrelated to the Hula Bowl, started on a browsing trip through Ala Moana shopping center. As we turned into the Center Art Gallery of Honolulu, an unusual oil painting caught our attention.

In fact, Floy and I did a double take. Right in the middle of a wall of beautiful, serene still life paintings was an oil treatment of a panic-stricken Woody Woodpecker, the colorful cartoon character, paddling for all he was worth in the waters of Waikiki Beach. In hot pursuit was a big-toothed shark ready to make a kill. It was precious.

We learned from a sales clerk that Walter Lantz, the famous creator of Woody Woodpecker more than 50 years ago, had turned his talent toward "Happy Art", still life oils incorporating his stable of cartoon characters. Producing cartoons had become a thing of the past because of the high cost of production, and he studied under the great Robert Wood before jumping into his new venture.

The oil of Woody and the shark was out of our financial reach but we purchased a 9x12 pen and ink original of the famous woodpecker doing the hula, one of several such pieces also available at this exclusive showing. An innocent letter complimenting Mr. Lantz on his ingenious works of art triggered a pen-pal relationship that lasted several weeks and produced a personalized drawing I still treasure.

"I would like an oil painting of yours and have an idea for one," I wrote.

"Here in West Texas the windmill is a standard fixture against the horizon and is painted many different ways in artwork. The wind does blow frequently and with a lot of velocity. My thought for a truly original Western painting would be a wooden windmill in the throes of a gusty windstorm with Woody hanging on for dear life. A tumbleweed or two could be swirling across the terrain or a cactus bending in the breeze. I think this could be the basis for a clever piece of Happy Art."

That letter was sent January 14, 1980. A week later, I received this reply

When we interviewed for "Family Feud", this photo was taken by officials for the files. Behind me are Floy, David, daughter-in-law Sandy and Debbie. (Below) This original drawing with a West Texas flavor was done by Walter Lantz, creator of Woody Woodpecker.

To ~ Ray Franks ~
Walter Lantz
FEB. 1, 1980

from the Academy Award-winning giant who has been described as a "totally humble man".

> *Dear Mr. Franks:*
>
> *Thank you for your letter of January 14.*
>
> *It is very rewarding when I hear from people who have bought one of my paintings or drawings, and, also, hearing how much pleasure they get from them.*
>
> *I like your idea of Woody on a Texas windmill. If you will send me a picture of one, I'll see what I can do with it. Don't worry about the price. I know I can come up with something you can afford.*
>
> *The Gallery sets the price on my paintings, but we'll handle this as a personal matter.*
>
> *I donate practically all of the money I receive from paintings to charity.*
>
> > *Sincerely,*
> >
> > *Walter Lantz*

After gathering up a couple pictures of vintage windmills and sending them off to his Hollywood studio, I received the following letter three weeks later. Along with it was a 9x12 drawing.

> *Dear Mr. Franks:*
>
> *Enclosed is an original drawing that I have made for you of Woody Woodpecker on a Texas windmill.*
>
> *I couldn't make a painting, because I have an exclusive arrangement with the Center Gallery of Honolulu to sell my paintings. They would sell a painting like this one for $9,000.*
>
> *I am giving you this drawing. If you would like to make a donation to the Braille Institute Auxiliary, and take a tax deduction, I would appreciate it.*
>
> > *Sincerely,*
> >
> > *Walter Lantz*
>
> *WL:db*
>
> *P.S. The drawing has been treated, so it won't rub off.*

The drawing is precious, exhibiting the talent and humor that made Lantz one of this country's greatest animators until his death in early '94 at age 93.

Appearing in this chapter, the personalized work has an exasperated Woody hanging from a whirling windmill in a West Texas windstorm. It's all in pencil except Woody with his red shock of head feathers, yellow beak and blue body, a look many of us can associate with in hundreds of cartoons featuring the famous bird.

Not only did he take my idea and produce an original drawing with a Texas twist, but he did it out of the goodness of his heart. It was a freebie. That's a quality rarely found in people of that stature. And that's not all. For eight years after this episode, we were added to the Walter and Gracie Lantz's Christmas card list. Until his eyesight started failing, each December we received a colorful "Happy Art" card incorporating his cartoon characters in a winter scene.

In subsequent correspondence and conversations with his secretary, Dorothy, we learned that wife Gracie was the voice of Woody Woodpecker in most of the cartoon productions. Mel Blanc was the first Woody. But when he became exclusive property of Warner Brothers, Gracie applied for the job. Unknowingly to her husband. Her tape of the raucous "heh-heh-heh-HEHHHH-heh" was chosen by an impartial panel of judges.

As a die-hard Woody fan, I also learned that his character was inspired when the Lantzes were honeymooning at a California lake cottage in 1941. The incessant rapping of a woodpecker outside their front door prompted Gracie to suggest creating an animated character based on the bird.

"Woody started out as a supporting player", Lantz once said, "but he became a star in the second picture. And he's been a nest egg ever since."

Back to the Hula Bowl and Hawaii. It proved to be one of the Franks' best ever family vacations. Our children, normally late morning risers, were on Waikiki Beach at the crack of dawn. We literally had to beg them to make one island sight-seeing excursion, including a visit to Pearl Harbor and its memorials.

I soaked up far too much of the Hawaiian sun. The top of my feet got sunburned and I had to fly home wearing the minimum in footwear.

21

CHICKEN DELIGHT

My nomination for the No. 1 sports figure in America today isn't Troy Aikman, Barry Bonds or Shaquille O'Neal. In fact, he's not even an athlete. It's a chicken, The Famous Chicken.

The genius inside the bright red, yellow and blue costume is Ted Giannoulas, an ex-San Diego State student who has taken an innate talent and clever idea and parlayed them into a big-bucks, seven-digit entrepreneurship. And that ain't chicken feed.

At major and minor league baseball parks, college football and basketball games and about anyplace else people gather, he packs 'em in with routines that captivate, entertain and double you up with laughter. This chicken doesn't lay eggs. In fact, at last count he had performed live to more than 55 million people in 50 states and nine countries, including presidents and luminaries in all walks of life.

In my books, he's an American icon, a national treasure.

Our paths first crossed in 1978, four years after he introduced a regional character called the KGB Chicken in San Diego, California. Ted has used the *National Directory of College Athletics* for a reference tool most of those 20 years he's developed into a huge national celebrity. In two editions, he bought full page, four-color ads, one of which appears in this chapter. It's a classic, typical of the wit that emanates from this brash but lovable character. The headline reads: "He Has an M.A. in Drawing Crowds. And That's No B.S."

The Chicken's story started rather innocently when a San Diego radio station, with the unlikely call letters of KGB, hired a college student with gymnastic talent to do some part-time public relations work in 1974. Most thought it would be just another zany promotional gimmick, one that might be amusing for a short time and then fade into oblivion. That's usually the pattern of radio station ideas.

His first costume was awful, which prompted Ted to say he was once "an ugly duckling". The eyes had a goofy glaze, the comb was droopy and the colors were weak. But the idea worked, bad costume and all. This new character on the block appeared at civic happenings, restaurant openings, hospitals, children's parties and most anywhere people could use a good laugh. After dropping in on a San Diego Padre baseball game one night and dazzling 40,000 fans, his success was sealed.

He was still pretty much a regional fixture when I first saw his act at the inaugural Holiday Bowl football game in December, 1978. The Directory had been invited to chronicle this new sports event, which was a dandy. The Naval Academy came from behind to clip Brigham Young, 23-16, in an exciting game that thoroughly thrilled 52,000 fans and assured the new bowl a permanent niche in post-season football circles. Besides that, San Diego is a great place to be in the winter, what with its marvelous weather and varied tourist attractions.

But not all the entertainment came from the teams. The bowl had an impressive list of celebrities on hand. There was President Gerald Ford, looking out for Navy's interest; the president of the Mormon Church, doting over BYU; Donnie and Marie Osmond, who sang the National Anthem; and the KGB Chicken. All except The Chicken had been invited.

"The San Diego Chicken wanted to be here tonight," another sideline photographer told me, "but he was asked not to show up. Something about being a distraction to the game."

However, midway in the first quarter, I saw this strange-looking creature resembling an overgrown chicken, feathers and all, come skipping down an aisle, flailing his brightly-colored wings. Like a conquering hero, he leaped over the rail onto ground level amid resounding cheers from the crowd.

But uniformed guards went after him. Two, three and four took chase and finally got him cornered. At this point, The Chicken plopped down on the ground in a prone position, flat on his back, as if to say "if I'm leaving, you'll have to carry me out." When the officers reached down to pick him up, the hysterical crowd started chanting: "We want The Chicken, we want The Chicken".

The officers looked at each other, thought about the situation, and realized they were by far the most unpopular people in a packed stadium. They sheepishly backed away and received an ovation of their own. The Chicken leaped to his feet and started beating his chest with his arms, uh wings. Winner and still champion – The KGB Chicken.

With photo passes, son David and I worked the sidelines and made acquaintance with Ted. I snapped a picture of David and his feathered friend, arms around each other, and the poster still graces our game room wall. Another good pose had him petting the Navy goat, which was utilized in the Directory story. "A very nice guy and great fun," remembers David. It was a memorable evening for both of us and the start of a long relationship with one of the best mimes to ever don feathers.

Shortly after the Holiday Bowl, The Chicken's notoriety began mushrooming. Another Ted, Ted Turner of Atlanta, Georgia, contacted him. At a time when his baseball team was doing little entertaining and finishing last in pennant races, he invited Giannoulas to fly the San Diego coop and move to Georgia. Although a reported offer of $100,000 a year was tempting, the answer was "thanks, but no thanks".

Realizing his potential as a national sports figure, Mr. G attempted to break with the regional radio station in San Diego. By now, it was clear to many that a special life was being breathed into this many-feathered character, and the attraction was much more than a zany costume.

"No way," responded KGB officials. "The Chicken is our idea and he belongs to us." A lengthy court battle ensued before Ted eventually got his freedom. He had to alter the uniform a little and get a new name. First the "KGB Chicken" and "San Diego Chicken," he took the label, "The Chicken." He later became "The Famous Chicken", and now answers to any or all of the above.

After winning his case, Giannoulas concocted an ingenious idea to launch his new career. On June 29, 1979, before 47,000 cheering fans at San Diego's Jack Murphy Stadium, he staged a "Grand Hatching". The start of the San Diego-Houston baseball game was delayed 30 minutes and media from all over the country came in to cover the event. It was televised live on local stations.

With all the pomp and circumstance of a royal coronation, a huge egg was hauled into the stadium by an armored truck, escorted by a California highway patrol motorcycle brigade. After baseball players lifted the over-sized egg off the truck, it rolled around on the ground a few minutes, cracked and out emerged a sleepy-eyed, wing-flailing Chicken. The fans leaped to their feet and gave him a long, boisterous ovation equal to that afforded any sports hero in American annals. The Chicken would not be denied his roost and he was now a "free bird".

Part of this enchanting character's mystique is keeping the identity of Giannoulas low key. I've seen this master entertainer perform a dozen times, talked to him on the phone on several occasions and have had considerable

He has an M.A. in drawing crowds. And that's no B.S.

You never know to what degree the Master of Antics will go. The Famous Chicken. America's feathered phenom has performed before more than 50 million fans since he "hatched" in San Diego in 1974. When it comes to entertaining crowds, The Famous Chicken rules the roost. A storied fowl who's ready to help you boost attendance for any sport. So call or write today. With *this* bird in hand, you could fill your stands.

The Famous Chicken®

This four-color ad that appeared in the National Directory of College Athletics reflects the hilarious humor of The Famous Chicken.

correspondence over the past 17 years. Yet, I had never met him in person until the summer of 1994.

It was prior to an Amarillo Dillas baseball game and the Class AA organization was bringing in The Chicken for his second appearance of the season. On the way to the hot dog line, I bumped into a long-time friend, radio announcer Jerry Webb, and mentioned I'd never met the evening's key attraction.

"I saw him around here not long ago," remarked Jerry.

When I returned to the picnic table near the visiting team's dressing room with my hands full of Polish dogs and cola, there stood a trim, handsome man of about 40 brandishing a full head of black hair and an impressive mustache.

"Hi Ray, I'm Ted Giannoulas," he said, sticking out his right hand.

"So this is the genius behind that lovable character I've admired for many years," I replied, while introducing him to wife Floy and good friend Bill Chandler.

As we started chatting about the Directories and the baseball strike, Chandler stepped back a few feet to take a snapshot of Ted, Floy and myself. Out of the corner of his eye, Giannoulas saw what was happening and turned toward Chandler.

"I'd appreciate it if you wouldn't take my picture out of costume," he asked politely. "I'm not in this for personal glory; I want The Chicken to be the focus of everyone's attention."

We got our pictures at the end of the game, with Ted in character. As with every personal appearance, Ted sticks around to complete every autograph and photo request, regardless of how long the lines are. The consummate entrepreneur, his retail products now include tee shirts, color photos, pens and a 37-minute video labeled "The Chicken's Greatest Bits." It's a classic, a collection of antics from live performances. Our five-year-old granddaughter, Alexandria, prefers it over Disney videos.

In the 15 minutes we visited, I found Ted to be an extremely gentle and humble person, almost shy in demeanor. It isn't unusual for performers in the entertainment industry to be opposites of the personalities they portray.

And when he goes into action at a baseball game, usually after the second inning, it's pure magic. After a stirring musical intro from the public address system, this strange-looking character decked out in blazing colorful feathers, web feet and an over-sized beak leaps onto the field and dashes straight for the home plate umpire.

When the ump sticks out his hand, The Chicken pulls his back and lifts his leg to zap the man in blue's backside. An old trick with a new wrinkle, and the crowd goes bananas.

The ump is the target in other hijinks. In one episode, he pulls out a shoeshine rag and proceeds to polish the umpire's shoes. When finished, he holds out his hand for a tip. After the umpire shakes his head negatively, The Chicken starts jumping up and down and finally kicks dirt on the freshly-shined shoes. That brings the boot from the ump, who winds up carrying him off to the dugout. It's a brilliant piece of pantomiming.

Two favorite posters The Chicken pulls out of his bag of tricks are an optometrist's eye chart, which he flashes in front of the ump, and one that reads: "Will Ump For Food." Another popular stunt is to demean the opposing team. After moving cautiously toward their dugout, he turns and hexes them with hand motions. Then, when he takes the first base coaching position, he pulls out large posters of scantily-clad girls to distract the opposing pitcher. That one brings down the house.

Always a crowd-pleaser, he uses four local youngsters in one scene. Dressed in identical chicken costumes, the baby chicks follow Ted around the diamond single file, emulating his every move. That includes kicking dirt on the umpires and making gestures at the opposing players.

"Much that I do is spontaneous and improvisational," he told Sam Waller of the Amarillo Daily News. "But I have more than 200 routines that I draw from. I could do an entire homestand without repeating a single trick."

In interviews I've done concerning my book on college nicknames, titled *"What's In a Nickname?"*, I have often given credit to The Chicken for expanding the role of mascots in athletics. I told Chris Cox of the Boston Sunday Herald: "In the wide world of sports B.C. (Before Chicken), mascots usually were relegated to the sidelines with the cheerleaders. Now, however, mascots are considered a bona fide promotion, a public relations and entertainment vehicle."

Giannoulas normally travels with an associate who also doubles as a bodyguard. People are constantly tugging at him, jostling him or just wanting to get close. However, an incident reported in a book he wrote back in 1978 landed him in big trouble, even with an able-bodied assistant.

I have followed the career of this brilliant showman with more than casual interest, and this is one of the funniest stories I've ever heard. In the early days of his existence, The Chicken appeared at a lot of rock concerts in the San Diego area, including the likes of Elvis Presley and Paul McCartney. On this night, Aerosmith was in town.

The Chicken and his good friend and bodyguard, Ralph Haberman, arrived at the Sports Arena at intermission after what had already been a long, gruelling day. A Continental Airlines promotion had taken him to Denver and back earlier, followed by a gig at San Diego Stadium, where the Padres beat the Giants, 2-0.

Down by the floor seats, Ted was doing a little dancing, pantomime and general clucking about when he caught the attention of one of the band members. He liked the act so much that he invited Chicken to join Aerosmith on stage for a number.

Relishing the prospect of performing before 10,000 rock fans on the same platform with Aerosmith, he readily accepted, but added credentials would be needed. The band member agreed and hurried off to secure official okay. In the meantime, the show had begun and Ted turned to watch the action on stage as the lights dimmed and the spotlight hit the group.

In his own words, The Chicken continues the saga:

I was standing off to the side of a corridor when I looked back to see that Ralph was having a problem with one of the bouncers hired for security at the concert. Ralph was explaining that we were waiting for credentials which would be coming in a minute.

I was content that Ralph could take care of the matter easily and continued to fix my attention on stage, as I would be up there in just a few moments.

Then, all of a sudden, I felt a jerk; it was one of the arena bouncers, whom we'll call "Bigfoot." He grabbed me and dragged me to the floor as I wondered what in the world was going on. My anxiety was temporarily relieved, though, for Bigfoot soon had to contend with Ralph, who rushed to my rescue as soon as he saw what had happened.

They started grappling, exchanging wrestling holds, with Ralph trying to tell Bigfoot to cool it. He wouldn't, but Ralph quickly got the upper hand. However, that didn't help, for Bigfoot responded by calling in his confederates. Outnumbered three to one, Ralph offered no resistance. All this was going on while Aerosmith was rocking away on stage, with most of the crowd oblivious to our little scuffle.

As soon as his cronies came to his aid, Bigfoot took advantage of the situation. He hit Ralph while he was being held by the others. Then Ralph was shoved into a back room just off the corridor. Even though no one was paying attention to me by this time, I followed, frightened for Ralph's safety. Once inside, I saw my friend in a compromising

Three generations of chicken-watchers are included in these pictures. Besides granddad at the bottom are son David (top) and five-year-old granddaughter Alexandria at far right. The Famous Chicken's costume in 1978 (with David) is a far cry from today's version.

position: His legs were buckled, his hands raised.   Ralph was cornered. Bigfoot, the head of security for the arena that evening, was slowly applying a black leather glove to his right fist. He was glaring at Ralph.

"Turn around with your hands up against the wall," he ordered ominously. With that, he pounded Ralph with his gloved hand. With Bigfoot's two colleagues there for support, I felt helpless, but I had to do something.

"What is this?" I yelled after Bigfoot hit Ralph. With that, Bigfoot turned on me and screamed: "I want you up against the wall, too!"

He then hurled me toward the cement wall, which I hit head first. It was a kayo in the first round.

After regaining consciousness, The Chicken and Ralph were taken to the police station on a citizen's arrest lodged by Sports Arena security. Officers couldn't believe their eyes as the feathered one and his friend walked through the door. At first, they thought the new sensation in town was there to entertain the troops. Smiles were everywhere.

Then a silence came over the place when the escorting officers explained the duo had been placed under arrest. The atmosphere quickly changed from party to professionalism. The Chicken's account continues:

It was eerie. I was led into the holding tank where now it was the inmates' turn. They broke out into applause and whistles and I felt like Johnny Cash doing an encore at Folsom Prison. There were about 20 fellow inmates waiting to be processed, and the questions started flying immediately.

"What are you in for, brother?" asked one.

"Impersonating a chicken," I deadpanned.

"Did you take a urine test?" another inquired.

"No, I didn't study for it," I replied. Even with the joking, I still had a hollow feeling.

"Why did the chicken cross the street?" another inmate shouted.

"To get away from stupid questions," I countered.

Another prisoner asked: "Waft nurph yeek doog rah?"

That guy was drunk.

After calling his boss at the radio station, The Chicken was processed and released. As he joked, "That's better than being processed and served for Sunday's dinner." He was being fingerprinted with one hand and signing autographs with the other. It was really crazy.

Expecting nothing more than a small blurb in next day's paper, if that, Ted gazed in awe at what he saw. There was a front-page photo in the Evening Tribune with the following headline: "KGB Chicken Roosts in County Coop After Fuss."

22

DALLAS COWBOYS AND
A CHEESY SANDWICH

"Public relations" is one of those terms that can be as real as a hot Texas sun in August or as nebulous as the air we breathe. Any way you cut it, it's an ingredient that I feel is vital to a successful operation. So much so, that we have used the letters "PR" as a double entendre on our business logo for years. Not only does it suggest "Publishing Ranch" but also "public relations".

This may seem like a trivial illustration but I still remember a good example of bad public relations, even though it happened 15 years ago. It was Sunday night and after church our family sought out a snack with friends Rod and Jeanelle Saylor and their children, Jeremy and Julie.

We found an ice cream parlor that also served sandwiches. Since a scrumptious, high-calorie ice cream concoction of some variety was the big attraction, Floy and I decided to split a grilled cheese sandwich prior to dessert. We asked for an extra saucer.

When reaching the cash register ready to pay out, I noticed an unaccounted for "50 cents" on our ticket.

"What's the meaning of this charge?" I asked.

The cashier looked at the ticket quizzically and analyzed the order.

"Oh yes," he answered. "That's for the extra saucer you used with your sandwich". I couldn't believe my ears. After mumbling something like "I didn't want to buy the saucer, just use it" and embarrassing members of my family and our friends, I paid the bill.

"I'll never spend another dime here," was my parting shot. And I didn't. In fact, the last time I looked, the store was out of business.

On the other side of the coin, I would like to use an illustration of impeccable public relations displayed by the Dallas Cowboys. Not the current organization, but the vintage Cowboy group that included Tex Schramm, Gil Brandt and Tom Landry a few years back. I doubt that either of the new honchos—Jerry Jones or Barry Switzer—knows the meaning of "public relations".

I chose to cover the annual American Football Coaches Association Golf Tournament and Convention in the summer of 1980. My wife and son David were also invited to the social functions that made it the most popular event with college coaches and their families.

The 54-hole Florida scramble golf tournament was played at beautiful Los Colinas Country Club in the shadow of Texas Stadium in Irving, and about 10 sponsors put together a schedule that was keeping guests hopping like Texas jackrabbits. On the first night, the Hyatt Regency Hotel hosted a dinner and dance at renovated Union Station, a classic job of bringing back the beauty of yesteryear for today's enjoyment. The menu was huge shrimp from the Gulf of Mexico, frog legs and barbecued ribs. The music was country western, of course.

On the final night when golf awards were made, Dr. Pepper, with corporate headquarters in Dallas and a long-time friend of college athletics, hosted a "Be A Pepper Night" at the Hyatt Regency ballroom. CEO Foots Clements remembered the days he was an end candidate at Alabama when the starters were Bear Bryant and Don Hutson. It was a class affair in every way.

But the Dallas Cowboys, one of the event sponsors, outdid 'em all on Monday night. With the indefatigable Gil Brandt calling the shots, they delivered a short course on public relations that would warm the cockles of a rattlesnake.

From the time we first entered the Stadium Club at the far end of Texas Stadium for an old-fashioned barbecue, we got the VIP treatment. Hostesses preparing the "drink of your choice" served them in personalized plastic cups. Names of everyone in attendance—coaches, wives, sponsors and the media— were printed on the containers, along with the date and picture of Texas Stadium, home of the Cowboys. A typical cup read "Tom and Alicia Landry Are Here—June 2, 1980," and it was the challenge of guests to find their own imprinted souvenir before the evening ended. It was a delightful way to meet a lot of people you didn't know.

Then, as we wandered around trying to find our monogrammed cup, we noticed clever and thoughtful hand-lettered signs on the walls. One of them read:

"From the Dallas Cowboys, That Team in the Blue,
We'd Never Make It Without People Like You."

The meal was wonderful—barbecued ribs, beef, sausage and chicken with a distinctive Texas mesquite favor. But the clincher, the choicest bit of ingenuity displayed all evening, was a photography gimmick. While guests visited or danced to the strains of a live Western band, Cowboy photographer Bob Friedman was coaxing couples over to one corner of the club. He stationed them near the glass window overlooking Texas Stadium and snapped pictures as their names appeared on the huge message board at the other end of the playing field.

In most of the photos, the message center flashed a simple statement: "Cowboys Welcome . . . Ray And Floy Franks, N.D.C.A." On others, clever limericks were prepared, again reflecting the creativity and sense of humor of someone in the organization. One of the better ones involved then Indiana football coach Lee Corso:

"I Hear Lee Corso, Because of Fright,
Hired a Body Guard, Some Guy Named Bobby Knight"

Another dandy featured UCLA football coach Terry Donahue:

"When Bruins Are Going Strong,
Terry's King of the Hill;
But When Things Aren't So Great,
He Changes His Name to Phil"

When the 1980-81 Directories came off the press in early August, Terry called our office wanting to get a copy of that picture. "What a great idea," he effused, "and I was surprised to see it in the Directory."

We had used the photo of Terry and his wife, Andrea, in the AFCA feature, and informed him that he soon would be receiving an 8 x 10 glossy from the Cowboys. Everyone who posed that night was mailed similar photos, the ultimate souvenir of an extraordinary evening.

While doing research on this chapter, I came across some interesting names who were in attendance at the Cowboy bash.

"This is the only time you can sit around and enjoy life," said Jimmy Johnson, then head coach at Oklahoma State. "You're not playing each other head to head, or recruiting. It's just a heck of a lot of fun."

Wonder if JJ had the remotest thought that night of winding up in the same

The Franks get the VIP treatment from the Dallas Cowboys at a barbecue in Texas Stadium.

Cowboy cheerleaders added charm to the golf tournament as they traveled around the course serving refreshments. Here they are shown with football coaches Sark Arslanian of Colorado State and Lee Corso of Indiana.

stadium a decade later, leading the Dallas Cowboys to two Super Bowl championships? And then getting fired a year later for no apparent reason?

Then consider the trail of the young coach who won the golf tournament. John Mackovic, coach at Wake Forest in 1980, may never rival Arnold Palmer as the No. 1 Deacon golfer, but June in Dallas belonged to him as he won by one stroke over Jackie Sherrill, then of Pittsburgh, and Dave Maurer of Wittenberg.

Mackovic, who roomed with the late Brian Piccolo when they played at Wake Forest, must have been impressed with the "PR" that night. His career has had a distinctive Texas flavor ever since. He was with the Cowboys as an assistant for a few years, and then returned to the Lone Star State as trail boss of the Texas Longhorns after a stint at Illinois.

The Dallas Cowboy magic didn't stop after their big bash on Monday night. All during the golf tournament, they had their famous Cowboy cheerleaders in attendance. The appearance of the much-publicized and exuberant Texas beauties picked up the spirits of everyone. They served as official hostesses, flitting around the course in golf carts iced-down with Dr. Pepper and beer.

Tex Schramm, Gil Brandt and Tom Landry are no longer around Valley Ranch, but the Cowboys still enjoy success with sports fans today. Nice guys and super athletes, Troy Aikman and Emmitt Smith have a lot to do with that image, and the magic is still working in spite of an over-bearing, egomaniac owner.

Oh yes, the AFCA Convention is still as huge as ever in Big D each summer, but the picture-taking gimmick by the Cowboys was discontinued a couple years ago.

23

MENAGERIE AT THE RANCH

Mention "Fighting Irish", "Crimson Tide" and "Nittany Lions", and most sports fans can readily tell you these are famous nicknames for the athletic teams of Notre Dame, Alabama and Penn State.

But follow this up with the names of "Polar Bears", "Saxons" and "Judges", and even the most avid sports buff will be scratching his head in dismay. It would be rare indeed to find anyone who can match these athletic mascots with Bowdoin College, Alfred University and Brandeis University.

An intense national interest in nickname trivia and a personal insatiable appetite for the subject launched a research project in early 1981 that was laborious, to say the least. The first letter produced about 25% response from colleges. Then second, third and fourth inquiries followed. Ranch associates Shaine LeGrand and Randy Franks manned the telephone lines for the stragglers.

Eighteen months after research started, all loose ends were pulled together and a 208-page paperback book, *"What's In a Nickname?"*, was off the press. The first book of its kind to include nickname and mascot information on more than 2,000 senior and junior colleges in the U.S. and Canada, it also boasted more than 1,200 pictures and logos. Only one school—Illinois State—refused to allow its mascot to be included, "unless we paid them". In all probability, its presence would have saved countless inquiries to the school's sports information office.

Designed to be an off-season project of the coaching directories, it mushroomed into one of the most satisfying challenges in my 50 years in sports. Everybody loved it. College sports information directors used the book for instant clip art. Newspapers gleaned it for limitless column material. Libraries stocked it for their reference centers. And of course, radio talk shows found it bountiful fodder for their many hours of air time.

I've been interviewed on at least 200 sports talk shows, three times on WHO, the 50,000-watt station in Des Moines, Iowa. On KLIF, a strong Dallas sports station, Norm Hitzges started an interview that was designed to last 15 minutes. We were still on the air an hour later, overwhelmed with endless questions about nickname trivia.

But the biggest surprise of all came in the fall of '82 when I picked up the October 4 issue of *Sports Illustrated*. There on page eight, bigger than life, was a half-page review under its department title, "Booktalk". Authored by H. Brooks Clark, a staff writer, the subtitle read: "Here's a compendium of the whys and whences of college nicknames." This opened the floodgates for the biggest audience of all, the nickname trivia nut.

We had not sent out review copies. Apparently, *Sports Illustrated,* who buys dozens of Directories yearly, received one of our advance flyers and wrote the favorable review after spending $12.95 for an early copy.

We were flattered, and deluged. After being unsuccessful in finding an Eastern publisher to handle the book, we self-published and sold Nickname by direct mail only. At first, we thought interest would be limited to the same people who bought the Directories. With *Sports Illustrated's* massive circulation, you can imagine what happened. The review noted that the unique publication "was compiled by Ray Franks and his staff at their Publishing Ranch in Amarillo, Texas." That's all, no address, no phone number.

The phone lines started lighting up, but few got through. The correct listing of our business in the phone book is "Ray Franks Publishing Ranch", and just plain "Publishing Ranch" had operators scratching their heads. So what did potential buyers of the book do next? They called *Sports Illustrated*. And they were deluged.

But the staffers at the world's most-read sports magazine were good sports. They passed on address information and trivia buff business ran hot and heavy for several weeks. The original printing of 5,000 sold out and a second run still attracts customers almost daily, twelve years later.

Since that first compilation, a few colleges have changed nicknames, mainly due to outside pressure. The Ed Asners and Jane Fondas of the world have not limited their whining to Vietnam, nuclear weapons and abortion. And for some unknown reason, colleges have been listening to these misfits who have nothing better to do than wander around the country carrying protest signs.

The subject of "Indian" nicknames has been given a lot of attention by the

The Tufts Jumbos took their name from a famous elephant of the 1880s.

Donald Duck quacks for the University of Oregon.

media and why, I don't know. In recent times, Stanford has changed its label from "Indians" to "Cardinal" and Siena has switched from "Indians" to "Saints". I call colleges "wimps" who buckle under to this political pressure that has little or no input from the real native Americans.

Let me explain. Out in Grand Forks at University of North Dakota, more native American students graduate yearly than at any other college in this country. And about their athletic nickname, "Fighting Sioux", they're proud of it.

"We, of the University of North Dakota, can do no better than to instill in our young men and women the values attributed to the Fighting Sioux of the Great Plains," said former athletic director Dr. Carl Miller.

Professor Art Raymond, UND Director of Indian studies, added: "Those values of fortitude (some call it guts), of individual freedom, of generosity and sharing and respect for the old ones built a way of life which set them apart. These same values in our day can and do contribute to our way of life."

Besides that, my wife is one-fourth Choctaw and she calls the controversy "silly". So, lighten up out there, Ed and Jane, and devote your time and attention to the important things in life. Instilling Christian morals in our young people would be a great place to start.

"How can anyone take logos seriously?" wrote Herman Masin in *Scholastic Coach* magazine. "They're just fun things; they make no statement whatsoever about Indians. Think about it. Would schools pick a nickname that didn't mean something special to them, that they didn't admire? To almost all of us growing up on the legends of Custer and Geronimo, Indian remains a symbol of the American experience, signifying fierceness, strength, pride and indomitability."

Well said, Herman! I have contended in interviews that mascots and nicknames give athletic teams and student bodies something to rally around. Nothing more, nothing less.

The airheads who have levied attacks at schools using Indian names also are trying to influence other colleges for equally outlandish reasons. At Auburn, some want to eliminate the "Senator" mascot because "he's white, male and could be a plantation owner." He could also be a major league baseball player who performed in Washington, D.C.

A lot of print was given to some protesters who insisted U. of Massachusetts at Amherst eliminate its "Minuteman" label. "It's too macho, white and violent," said the dissidents. "If you're a woman or a person of color, he really can't represent you."

After much controversy, Chancellor David Scott and other school officials stood firm and ignored the protest. Hooray for the Minutemen; that name will always have a soft spot in my heart. As it turned out, only a few disgruntled people lodged the protest, and the students (the ones that really count) wanted to retain the name that reflects rich historical heritage. It's too bad other colleges haven't displayed the same kind of good common sense.

But the corker of all was the guy who complained that "nicknames should not be derived from anything alive." He said he preferred something "inanimate." Like, maybe, the Fighting Mineral Salts.

While response to the Nickname book was overwhelming, some letters were downright hilarious. Take the one from Gary Lee Clothier, radio station WEEU in Reading, PA:

"I have spent the better part of a year sending letters to book stores, publishing companies and finally the Library of Congress to get the name of your book, "What's In a Nickname?". Someone walked off with my often-used first copy and I couldn't remember the name to reorder. I recommended the book many times on the air and had several people call me later to say they bought and thoroughly enjoyed it. My pleas to get my stolen copy back failed to produce results."

From K.G. (his name is withheld for obvious reasons) in Lakewood, CO, came this letter: "Recently, I toured my nearby library and to my excitement, found a book entitled *"What's in a Nickname?"*. I was eager to check it out and bring it home but I found it to be a reference only book. I could have stoled (sic) it, but no I thought, someone else would no doubt like to find this interesting book. Here's a check for my own copy."

Jack Hepfer, a lawyer in Seattle who might have caught one too many gavels to the head, wrote: "I was tickled to discover your entertaining and informative Nickname book at Seattle Public Library today. The recent NCAA playoffs got me going on team names. There are some real gems. How about the Red Foxes of Marist? The U. of Washington Bookstore advises that, yes, the book is still in print, but for some reason it always takes 'four-to-six weeks' to get anything. In this age of instant communication, I don't understand that, and I echo the Thurber cartoon child: I say it's spinach and the hell with it.' I will take my chances and go directly to the source, relying on Texas speed and cunning to beat the above time-frame. Go you Red Hot Franks!"

Three years later, I got another letter from the same zany Mr. Hepfer: "One of my associates has a burning desire for Nickname. Can't blame him, can we? I appreciate that there is no doubt a heavy surtax for autographed copies but . . . he is a worthy young man so perhaps you can list this as part of your pro bono publico work. Thanks, Ray, some day the autographed copies are going to be worth big bucks."

I still think ol' Jack is looney tunes.

Then from Norma Linton in Champaign, IL, I received this commentary: "I am writing a dissertation in anthropology on sport team mascots and have found your book to be an invaluable source work. Since I cite it frequently in my text, I would like to know the following about it. Are all your descriptive passages verbatim quotations from various sports information people who wrote to you? In those instances where you gathered information by telephone or in conversation, did you tape record the speaker, or paraphrase?"

Huh?

For Ed Tinucci in Shamong, NJ, the book is a way of life. Here's an excerpt from his letter: "I have a thirst for college mascot names and other related information, and your book is placed on the table next to my easy chair for constant review. It has been the source of a lot of enjoyment for my friends and me, and has settled many an argument about sports trivia."

While talking to his wife about an additional order, she confirmed, "Yes, my husband does have your book on a table right next to his chair. It has become a part of our home and our lifestyle".

Many sports fans are fanatics about nicknames and mascots but one of the most visible in the field of show business is Bob Barker of "The Price Is Right" television program. Bob, who often makes reference to nicknames when a contestant is wearing a college sweat shirt, has a Nickname book. His secretary, Kathy "Fingers" Greco, wrote a note relating, "Bob knows he will enjoy it very much and use it constantly."

Only recently, I heard the silver-haired game show veteran say to his sidekick announcer, Rod Roddy: "Hey, I like that purple coat you're wearing. I'll bet it's because you attended TCU."

Roddy smiled and nodded his head. "How many people in this country would know that the colors at TCU are purple and white?" asked Barker. "And that their nickname is the Horned Frogs." He was correct on both counts.

Another television show has been guilty of calling on information from the book. Several weeks after Jeopardy had ordered a copy from its California office, I was watching the show. Lo and Behold, one of the categories that was listed by host Alex Trebeck was "college nicknames".

Then, not long ago came this cute note from Kathie Tryson of St. Louis. "This book is a gift for my son Alex's 12th birthday, and it would be great if you could autograph it for him," she wrote. "Alex discovered your book in the reference section of our local library and was distressed to learn he could not check it out. He's a big Penn State fan and always wondered how the Nittany Lions got their name. Your book was the first place where he could find that information."

Only recently, Disneyland ordered a copy. Maybe the executives are looking for some new friends to go along with Mickey and Pluto. While Walt Disney was still alive, his studio created artwork for the U. of Oregon Duck and four lesser-known colleges.

My candidate for one of the most obsessed nickname freaks is Frank Mauz, a teacher in Hawaii. Calling Nickname "the best book I've ever read," Frank stumbled onto the publication shortly after it was available and writes about every couple years. It's a page-long letter with complimentary comments like, "Since my original letter, I've had time to read your book much more carefully and each time it is more fascinating and enjoyable."

Then he comes up with new schools and nickname changes that he has researched, in case an updated version is published. And guess what? He teaches at a school (Honolulu Community College) that has a nickname (Cougars), but no sports teams. In his last epistle, Frank added: "At this time, I am attempting to organize a campus contest to change our nickname from Cougars to something more exciting. In spite of the fact we cannot afford sports teams, there is excitement about the nickname contest."

Now that's commitment.

And there's a postscript to Frank Mauz's association with nicknames. In the summer, he teaches at St. Andrew's Priory, a school with many sports teams, but no nickname.

To what extent the Nickname book is used has no bounds. I had a call one day from Kal Silverberg, who works for Burlington Northern Railroad in Fort Worth. "You'll never guess why I'm ordering this book?" he teased me. "We have names for all our railroad cars and we use your book to pick them."

Then, this one from Kelly Finnegan in Kearns, Utah: "Every year when March Madness begins I think about having all of the college nicknames available to quiz friends and know the stories behind the Salukis and Hoyas. I didn't think such a thing existed, and was thinking of putting one together, myself. Then I found a copy of your book, *What's In a Nickname?*, at the library. It even has more information than I had hoped for."

Not long ago, I received a letter with an unusual request. Aaron Boxerman, a student at U. of California @ Riverside, said he was going to be the school mascot (a bear in a Scottish outfit) the following year. He inquired: "Since you wrote an extensive book on the subject, I was wondering if you know of any sources where I could get ideas for mascot routines."

That was easy. Just call The Famous Chicken!

Despite numerous interviews from many people, the favorite question invariably is: "What's the most popular nickname among colleges?"

Used 72 times among 2,000 colleges, it's the Eagle. I feel the large bird of prey soared to its lofty perch for a number of reasons. Several colleges chose it because the Bald Eagle is the national bird. Some went a step further and combined it with school colors of red, white and blue. Many made reference to the prominence of the Eagle in the Bible. Scripture from Isaiah 40:31 appears at the bottom of the Asbury College (Kentucky) athletic letterhead: "They that wait upon the Lord shall renew their strength, and mount up with wings as eagles."

Nor far behind and the pick of 68 senior and junior colleges is the Tiger, largely due to the influence of that sleek and graceful animal at Princeton U. Rounding out the top ten in the world of mascot mania are Cougars, Bulldogs, Warriors, Lions, Panthers, Indians, Wildcats and Bears.

Actually, if all names associated with the American Indian were grouped together, that category would be the unquestionable winner. In addition to Indian, such labels as Redmen, Warriors, Savages, Braves and Chiefs show up

172

frequently as athletic mascots.

"What's your personal favorite?" is another often-asked question.

Because a lot of ingenuity has been used—exploring history, special events, geography and other factors—there are dozens of names that could be given the blue ribbon. But when I have to choose just one, I always select the "Jumbos" of Tufts University. The story surrounding this choice at the Medford, Massachusetts, school is a dandy, and spans more than a hundred years.

The Tufts Jumbos derive their nickname from Jumbo the elephant, who was a gift of Phineas T. Barnum, the famed circus owner and former trustee of the Massachusetts college. In 1885, Barnum presented Jumbo's hide, weighing 1,538 pounds, to the college to be stuffed and displayed in Barnum Museum, another donation of the circus owner. The largest elephant of his day, Jumbo was a part of Barnum's circus before being killed in a collision with a freight train in St. Thomas, Ontario, Canada.

Legend persists that Jumbo herded a baby elephant, Tom Thumb, and his trainer off the tracks before colliding with the freight. The elephant measured 12 feet high and 14 feet long when mounted in Barnum Museum. He was on display there from 1885 to 1975 when a fire destroyed the elephant hide and the museum itself. However, a resourceful administrator in athletics, Phyllis Byrne, scraped the elephant's ashes into a peanut butter jar (what else) and returned it to her department, where it is kept in a safe. It has become a tradition that Tufts athletes who rub the jar before entering competition are usually successful.

24

A ROYAL AFFAIR

The Canadian Rockies in July sounded tempting. That relentless Texas summer sun can take its toll.

But it was only a passing thought being batted around until the BIG announcement was made. After the blockbuster news that Prince Charles and Lady Diana would be on hand for the opening ceremonies of the World University Games in Canada, all systems were go. The timing was perfect and inclusion of a feature on this embellished sports event seemed like a natural for the upcoming 1983-84 *National Directory of College Athletics*.

Like the Southwest Airlines "Friends Fly Free" commercial, members of the Franks family became exceptionally chummy. The decision was made; everyone could be utilized at this event, college athletics' answer to the Olympic Games. Oldest son Randy grabbed a note pad, David (home from college) loaded a camera, and wife Floy packed our bags and took care of plane tickets and press credentials.

From the time we landed at Edmonton, in the province of Alberta, all the talk was about the royal couple and their forthcoming visit to this thriving city of 750,000. The University Games now had become secondary. Even today, after divorce, the famous principals still command mounds of attention.

Located above Montana in Western Canada and called the "Gateway to the North", Edmonton is dissected by the North Saskatchewan River. It was this vast river, which we crossed daily on our shuttle bus, that initially brought traders in the 1790s to Fort Edmonton, the Hudson's Bay Company post that was the start of the present-day metropolis. Before leaving Alberta's capital city, we were to use it as a springboard for a thrilling tour of the nearby Canadian Rockies, truly one of God's greatest creations. Indeed, what had initially intended to be the sports event of the decade for

Edmonton was fast becoming the social event of the season also. Remember, this was less than two years after the fairy-tale marriage of the Prince and Princess of Wales, and no one could suspect it would be reduced to charred ruins a decade later.

Opening ceremony day arrived and while the city found itself gripped by an uncharacteristic euphoria, an overcast sky and threat of rain kept Games officials nervous and looking upward. The die was cast for an extraordinary day, one that would be eternally etched in my memory.

"I'm taking my rain hat and jacket," advised my wife, who still wasn't convinced the weatherman was going to cooperate. When we arrived at Commonwealth Stadium, a handsome new structure that seats 62,000, clouds were moving away and the prospect of clear weather was increasing. All the time the electricity was building among those who were arriving early for this "once-in-a-lifetime" opportunity.

The fact we got there before the gates opened at 12:30 reflects our enthusiasm. Precisely at 2 o'clock, with a full house in place, hundreds of teenagers dressed in white and carrying white pom-pons ran into the stadium and ringed the inside of the track. Minutes later a hundred-piece bagpipe band, decked out in colorful Scottish-plaid kilts, roared into the arena and we knew the star attractions wouldn't be far behind.

At 2:10, right on the heels of the pulsating band, Charles and Diana made their much-awaited appearance in the back seat of a white Cadillac convertible. Waving and smiling profusely, they circled the track before exiting the car and entering the royal box. The crowd roared its approval and you sensed something special was taking place.

Our seats were not more than 50 feet away; close enough to see that charming Charles was wearing a dark blue suit with red and blue stripped dazzling tie and Diana was stunning in a blue dress with pink polka dots, a pink jacket and blue hat with a blue plume. My wife volunteered this vital information.

"A photographer's dream," observed David, who was using a telephoto lens to capture Diana's every move.

Even though Charles is destined to become the King of England, this was Diana's day. It was her 22nd birthday, and not only was the ravishing brunette the focus of royalty watchers in the stands, she was the favorite of the athletes. As they passed by the reviewing stand, most of them aimed cameras at the smiling Princess. One Belgium even broke ranks to move in for a "close-up".

Coincidentally, it was also Canada's Independence Day, the equivalent of America's Fourth of July. No wonder Canadians were bubbling over. A rain-

Prince Charles and Lady Diana made the 1983 World University Games a royal affair in Edmonton, Alberta. They circled the track in a white Cadillac before joining the packed stadium. (Below left) The great Romanian gymnast Nadia Comaneci drew star attention also.

out would have been incomprehensible.

Following the parade of athletes, cut short by "no-shows" from 30 nations, Prince Charles stepped to the microphone. Like a pretty girl's mini-skirt, his opening speech was long enough to cover the subject and short enough to be interesting.

I tape-recorded the six-minute address, delivered with an eloquent British accent befitting royalty. I found it to be short, crisp and poignant. Here it is, in its entirety:

Ladies and Gentlemen and Competitors:

Today is a very special day for three reasons:

It's the birthday of my dear wife. Not only that, but she had the good sense and the excellent taste to be born on Canada's National Day, which we celebrate today, the 116th anniversary of the Confederation. Today also sees the start of the World University Games and both of us are delighted to have this opportunity of being with you all to set the proceedings in motion.

It is our last event in Canada before we return to Britain and we shall leave here with our hearts overflowing with the warmth and friendliness and hospitality of the Canadian people. All this has been showered on us during the past 17 days.

Having visited the Athletes Village briefly yesterday, we very quickly experienced the atmosphere of excitement, shared enthusiasm, and friendship which is engendered by such a gathering of students from so many countries. How they manage to combine their sports with their university studies remains a mystery, but I sincerely hope that many of them will not only bring glory to their families and countries, but will also succeed in their chosen careers.

These Games exemplify that great platonic principal of the interaction between a healthy mind and a healthy body. With that in mind, my wife and I wish good fortune to all the competitors in these contests, and may they continue to preserve those qualities of good sportsmanship which are the essence of such amateur games.

I now declare open the 12th World University Summer Games of Edmonton!

Following the torch ceremony, dancers, flag-wavers and huge inflated rubber creatures entertained before a flurry of balloons and a flyover by a Royal Canadian Air Force stunt team capped off festivities. It was a program fit for a king . . . and a prince and princess.

This was the last event of a busy 17-day schedule in Canada, and after departing the stadium, the royal couple boarded a plane for a non-stop return flight to London.

"The Edmonton segment was so relaxed, so happy, and so smooth," observed Steven Wood, a London Daily Express photographer and veteran of a dozen royal tours. "It was the savior of the Canadian trip."

The day previous, Charles and Diana had demonstrated a personal touch by making a surprise visit to the Athletes Village. They made stops at the Canadian and U.S. quarters, shaking hands and greeting athletes. A couple athletes were granted permission to give Charles a peck on the cheek for photo shoots.

Following such an auspicious opening, the Universiade would find it difficult to maintain that same level of interest the next 10 days. When 30 of the 79 countries scheduled to compete didn't appear, problems started. The chain of events disrupted pairings in early round competition and left many fans with nothing more than a sack of popcorn and a Coke in empty arenas.

Another disappointment was the lackluster performance of the large USA contingent, which finished a poor second to Russia in the quest for medals. With its men's and women's basketball teams back home polishing up for European competition, Russia completely dominated the gold medal race, capturing 59. In all, the USSR took home 115 medals, including 29 silver and 27 bronze.

In comparison, the Americans managed only 12 gold, 22 silver and 20 bronze for a total of 54 medals. Canada, upsetting the USA for the coveted gold in men's basketball, kept 38 medals in home trophy cases including nine gold.

Russia's dominance of what was termed "a preview of the '84 Olympics in Los Angeles" was tarnished by the accident which befell diver Sergei Chalibashwili two days before closing ceremonies. While attempting a difficult, high-risk dive in 10-meter platform competition, the 21-year-old student cracked his skull on the platform on the descent. To the dismay of other athletes and fans, he plunged into the water feet first bleeding profusely. He died in an Edmonton hospital less than a week later, two days after his teammates returned home.

Ironically, the Russian was attempting a dive that was successfully completed by Greg Louganis, America's bright light in water sports. He took gold in the three-meter springboard and 10-meter platform in an otherwise disappointing showing by the U.S.

Spending five days at the competition, the Franks family enjoyed gymnastics, volleyball and basketball in large doses. With full photographer's privileges, David had access to a number of telephoto lenses, free film and a well-supplied darkroom. The press was taken care of in grand style.

"We should have won it all," said a dejected Norm Stewart, the U.S. head coach from University of Missouri. "Especially since Russia didn't enter." Charles Barkley was the biggest star on mostly a no-name roster. But it was a sweet victory for the home country when Canada nipped the U.S., 85-77, in the semi-finals before a packed house of 10,000. Coached by American Jack Donohue, the magic continued in the finals. They defeated Yugoslavia, 83-68.

Even the peppery Bobby Knight of Indiana University came to the Games. He was there to scout U.S. athletes for the '84 Olympic Games, where he was taking over the head post. Even though the men faltered, American women brought home a gold in basketball. They easily handled Romania, 83-61, in the championship round.

Speaking of Romania, one of the darlings of the Games was a gymnast who captured the hearts of all fans in the 1976 Montreal Olympics. Her name was Nadia Comaneci of Romania. Still in competitive shape, she had advertised that she might compete in Edmonton, but backed out at the last minute. Instead, she helped coach her country's talented team, and spent much of her time signing autographs. A world champ at 14, she's now 33 and living out her dream of residing in the United States, married to former American gymnast Bart Conner. Showing she still has a big heart, Nadia donated $120,000 to the Romanian gymnastic team for the 1996 Olympics in Atlanta.

"She still looks like a little school girl," observed my wife, who like the rest of the Franks family, was more impressed with Nadia than the competitors in that event. Just 21 in Edmonton, she had stunned the sports world seven years earlier by scoring seven perfect 10s in the '76 Olympic Games, replacing Olga Korbut as the darling of gymnastics.

Tales of hardship and misadventure are a big part of any international sports spectacle. The 1983 Universiade had its share.

Take Rwanda's volleyball team, for example. The 14 members of this small country's squad had never flown before, and had never been to another country. Their practice sessions had been limited to dirt courts, outdoors of course, before arriving in Edmonton.

Libya's contingent of 50 athletes experienced less than normal eating procedures during the Games. They were in the middle of Ramadan, a holy month of fasting in the Moslem year, and could not eat or drink from sunrise to sundown. Normally, that wouldn't be a big problem, but Edmonton in the summer time is something else. During the Games, sunrise would occur about 4 a.m. and sunset around 10 p.m.

"We don't usually schedule athletic competitions during this holy time," said volleyball coach Omar Tafour after the first loss, incurred after the team had gone 23 hours without sleep or anything to eat or drink.

One American water polo player found out Universiade officials really took accreditation seriously. He was refused entrance to the Athletes Village late one night because he had forgotten his card at the Kinsmen pool lockerroom. After hitchhiking back up to the pool in a rainstorm, he was picked up after midnight on his way back by a Games volunteer who was taking translators to the housing facility. The athlete remarked to the van driver, "Without this little card, you're nobody."

When the Hong Kong volleyball team was being formulated, it learned the government was paying only 15 percent of expenses. The players were faced with the monumental task of raising $300,000 Hong Kong dollars (or $40,000 U.S. dollars) to attend the Games.

"We scheduled exhibition matches with Chinese television stars," admitted men's coach Keung Leung. "We also held a jog-a-thon, auctioned off personal articles of TV stars, and then pitched in $4,000 each to reach our goal. Plus, our people were still taking exams two days before departure, leaving no time for practice."

But buckle your seatbelts, you haven't heard anything yet. The most incredible tale of all involved the Peruvian men's basketball team and its trip to Edmonton.

The players' troubles began when they qualified for the Games and were told by their government they had to pay their own way. "We tried to raise a respectable amount of money by holding bingos and basketball exhibitions." related player Gonzalo Galdos, "but that didn't get much."

The team purchased their own uniforms and hitched a ride to Washington, D.C. on a Peruvian Air Force jet. "When we got to Washington, we thought our troubles were over," laughed Galdos. "But we were mistaken, they were only beginning."

In Washington, they lost their head coach when he received word his mother had died in Peru. But the players continued on.

They boarded a bus to Buffalo, NY, and another to Toronto, where they walked the streets all night because they couldn't afford a hotel.

At sunrise, they hopped another bus for Edmonton and arrived to find their room and board at the Games Village had not been paid. Members of

Edmonton's small Peruvian community went to work and helped take care of that need. When hearing the story of the team's plight, an American television announcer pulled $500 out of his pocket and made a donation. Similar contributions helped get the squad back to Washington, where it was scheduled to board the same Peruvian Air Force plane bound for Lima.

After playing their games, members of the Peru team were seen scurrying to the sidelines, getting their cameras, and taking pictures of their opponents. Despite a number of crushing defeats, including the 134-25 loss to the U.S., the team was anything but depressed.

"We are very, very happy to be in Canada," said Galdos, the team's leading scorer and spokesman. "We came here to compete and to learn."

Traveling to Canada and not inhaling the natural, world famous beauty of the Rockies would almost smack of blasphemy. Especially when you are only a stone's throw away. With pressing deadlines at home and final proofs coming due, I had to design a plan that would later be referred to as "the longest day" in Franks family annals.

We had 24 hours in which to do a week's worth of sight-seeing. "Since days are long and nights short up here in July", I reasoned, "let's do something that's complete lunacy."

When I suggested picking up a rent car at 4 a.m. and drive until dark, which is about 10 p.m., at this time of the year, I thought I'd be voted down.

"Sounds good to me," voiced David.

"Sure", added Randy. "David and I can do the driving and you and Mom can relax in the back seat."

And that's what we did. Plus take pictures.

After leaving a 3 a.m. wake-up call, we were headed west out of Edmonton an hour later on Highway 16. Our objective was to negotiate a huge triangular-shaped sweep through the vast and rugged countryside called Western Alberta, stop at the major attraction and be back in Edmonton by nightfall. Quite an assignment.

After driving along the flatlands of central Alberta for 200 miles, we pulled into Hinton for breakfast. The foothills of the famous Canadian Rockies loomed on the horizon.

Then we entered Jasper National Park, a wonderland of picturesque mountain resorts, towering peaks, crystal clear lakes and rolling alpine meadows. After passing through the small town of Jasper, we saw the famous Athabasca Falls and the cavernous gorge at Sunwapta.

"This has to be God's creation," observed Floy. "The beauty is simply breathtaking. It looks like one big travel poster."

That's son Randy taking in one of the greatest scenic spots of the world, Lake Louise. The Franks family arrived for the opening ceremonies well ahead of most of the crowd in the picture below.

At Jasper, we hit Highway 93, also called the Icefields Parkway, and acknowledged by many to be the most spectacular scenic drive in the world. Now riding south on the eastern side of the Continental Divide, we stopped at the most-famous of all glaciers, the Columbia Icefields. Only a short hike from the highway, we walked over to this vast sea of glacial ice that feeds the Pacific, Atlantic and Arctic Oceans. Probably 40 or 50 other tourists in RV's, cars and buses were there at the same time.

The splendor of this drive is such that we constantly took pictures through the car windows, not exactly the best way to capture raw beauty. However, we would never have made it back to Edmonton had we stopped each time a photo opportunity presented itself. I was taking pictures out of one side of the car and David the other.

After leaving Columbia Icefields, we entered Banff, the first and most famous of Canada's national parks. Truly one of North America's most exhilarating and spectacular resort areas, it represents an incomparable combination of snow-capped towering peaks, multi-hued lakes, massive glaciers and keen mountain air. The mountains in the Canadian Rockies impressed me as being the tallest I've ever seen, much more majestic than the Alps in Europe.

A roadside sign confirmed we were right on target. It read: "Lake Louise, 76 km; Banff, 132 km."

"Look," gestured Randy, pointing to a big black bear standing in a meadow not more than a hundred feet from the highway. We snapped pictures from the moving car as it turned and stared at us with unconcern. We had been told that black and grizzly bears were plentiful in this part of the country.

At last, we drove under a rustic board sign that confirmed we had arrived at "Chateau Lake Louise". In all the world, maybe there are half a dozen landmarks that defy description. This is one of them.

Labeled the "Gem of the Rockies", Louise is a gorgeous, emerald-colored lake nestled at the feet of tall pines and steep mountains. Looking out the huge plate-glass windows of the Chateau, you see that the mountains form a perfect frame for beautiful Victoria Glacier, a picture that resembles frosting on a giant cake. Breathtaking!

At one time, only the wealthy could afford to stay at the hotel and make periodic visits to this paradise. The likes of Theodore Roosevelt, King George VI, Cole Porter and Jack Benny have been guests. When we walked through the elegant hotel lobby and adjoining rooms, we detected a distinctive European flavor; an attractive woman was playing the harp and formally-dressed men and women were sipping tea.

"A perfect spot for a honeymoon," observed my wife, always the romantic one. David was married four years later and Louise was on his short list for honeymoon sites. However, he and wife Sandy opted for another lake, Tahoe, an equally charming choice and a little closer to home.

The sprawling green-roofed hotel rests on a giant ridge that also serves as a dam for the huge body of water. A lush lawn separates the hotel from the lake and there must have been 40 or 50 tourists toting cameras and browsing the premises. Talk about a photographer's dream.

Reluctantly, we piled into our rent car and left Lake Louise, all of us vowing to return sometime when we could spend more than a couple hours feasting on this superlative resort that attracts trailers and tour buses like honey lures flies.

Still traveling south on Highway 93, we motored 36 miles down to the town of Banff, another famous year-round resort area of 4,000. A bright and bustling community that caters to both winter skiers and summer vacationers, it is the home of the famous Banff Springs Hotel, a story-book castle in a lovely mountain setting. Natural hot springs, which first drew tourists to this area years ago, still are popular attractions.

We took a side trip into the breathtaking mountain and lake area surrounding Banff, and it cost 50 cents at the gate. "What a rip-off," grinned David, who added "this has got to be one of the most dramatically-beautiful places this side of heaven."

After overdosing on unbelievable landscapes for most of the day and running through four rolls of slide film, the family left Banff National Park and headed directly east to the city of Calgary.

We ate our evening meal in this metropolitan city of 750,000, known the world over for its famous stampede each summer, and caught our second wind. Started as a Northwest Mounted Police post in 1875, Calgary attracted homesteaders and ranchers at the turn of the century and then really blossomed with an oil boom that still prospers the city.

The last leg was a 220-mile stretch directly north to our home base in Edmonton. When we pulled into the rent car lot, the sun had nearly slipped behind the horizon. Our watches indicated it was 9:55 and the odometer told us we had traveled exactly 810 miles. Whew!

Our final day in Western Canada had been one of those memorable moments you don't soon forget, and it was a tough decision. Was it more exciting than the first day when Prince Charles and Lady Diana charmed us at the Games? I don't think anyone bothered to call for a vote. We were too tired.

25

~~~~~~~~~~

KISS

If there is one underlying strain of philosophy that has permeated our business at the Publishing Ranch all these years, it would be "keep it simple".

There's an old joke about the coach who was sitting at the head table waiting to make a banquet speech. His wife passed him a note that read in big bold face letters, "KISS".

"What a sweet thought," he mused. Then he looked a little closer, and below those initials, she had scribbled, "Keep It Simple, Stupid!"

Keeping it simple at the Ranch has meant holding overhead to a minimum. Up until 1991, when we sold the Directory portion of the business, we made it just fine without printing equipment, typesetters, postage meter machines, fax equipment, an 800-number and yes, computers. My idea of modern technology is graduating from manual to electric typewriters.

Because our Directories were produced only once a year, we parcelled out the typesetting and printing portions of the operation to specialists. It would have been financially foolish to tie up hundreds of thousands of dollars on equipment for seasonal printing.

Despite frequent, almost yearly, suggestions from the post office people to lease Pitney Bowes postage meter equipment, we elected to do it "the old-fashioned way" for two reasons. Reader surveys show that people respond more favorably to mail bearing a stamp as opposed to metered correspondence. Even though some mailings numbered several thousand, we hand-applied first class stamps to each envelope. We also affixed first class stamps to enclosed questionnaires to encourage high response. The questionnaire information comprised the heart of our Directories and the extra cost was well worth it.

Just as regular as clockwork, we received about 50% response on mailings that included questionnaires. The second mailing to colleges that didn't respond the first time would produce 50% return again. A third mailing would do likewise. For deadbeats who failed to open their mail, we would use the phone for last-minute changes.

Because we were a seasonal publisher, we had the luxury of extra time, and I believe it paid off to go the first class route. Some companies use bulk mail to save money. We never did and I believe its sheer stupidity. At home or at the office, I never open mail not bearing first class postage. It goes into the trash can without a second look.

The second reason for not leasing a postage machine amounted to a savings in personnel expenses. Instead of hiring someone to affix metered labels to packaged Directories in our office, we took them to the post office. They allowed us to use their loading dock in the rear. Then they provided an employee to affix the metered labels to the packages, which we had separated by zones and weight. It worked quite nicely for both parties.

August was harvest time at the Publishing Ranch. It was an exciting time, reminiscent of the days on the farm when we gathered and sold watermelons and cantaloupes. First, my trusty secretary and assistant, Shaine LeGrand, prepared advance order lists and typed gum labels. She did this while the printers were winding up their operation.

Oldest son Randy, who worked at the Ranch for 15 years, was in charge of mailing. Wife Floy and dear friends Judy and Heather Gibson would keep the month of August open and handle the packaging chores. Even after the Gibson family moved away from Amarillo, Judy and Heather would return in August and stay in our home. As soon as daily shipments of Directories would arrive from the printer, they would get the jiffy bags, staplers and brown strapping tape flying. Randy, who also assisted in the individual packaging, would haul books to the post office twice daily.

That routine was repeated each working day until the many thousands of advance orders were filled. At the time the Directories were sold, circulation for both the men's and women's editions had reached 25,000. And about 90% of those were dispatched during August. While small orders were mailed via the postal service, larger amounts that were boxed went by United Parcel Service. Finances dictated that procedure.

About modern technology. I must confess if we had kept the Directories another year or two, we probably would have purchased a fax machine to stay current with advertisers. Oh, we huddled quite often around the office and discussed the possibility of adding computers, wats lines and new equipment. Each time, we would come up with the same conclusion: "If it ain't broke, don't fix it."

"Card files and manila folders have worked just fine all these years," reasoned Shaine. "Let's not change a thing until it's necessary."

Two years before the Directories were sold, we did put our school listing information on computerized equipment at TypePros, a professional typesetting company in downtown Amarillo. We furnished the changes and they did the updating. Prior to that, we had used another old-fashioned method for more than 20 years. The info had been compiled in hot type, and the world's most accurate linotype operator, Charlie Higgins, made the corrections each year. He then pulled slick camera-ready proofs for publication.

Trafton Printers produced our college directories for 15 years, and its president, Rick Trafton, would shake his head when talking about our operation. "I don't know how they get away with it," he would say, "but I can't knock it; it's working for them." Before Trafton, it was Craftsman Printers in Lubbock, and it's owner, Ron Peters, probably gave me more good advice about printing than anyone.

Without change, I'm well aware the United States would not be the industrial giant of the world. While I might be slow to doing things differently, I would never fight it. My problem is changing "just for the sake of change."

The computer craze, and all its ancillary businesses, boggles my mind. I know this megabucks industry is here to stay, but I saw a story in the *Los Angeles Times* recently that caught my attention.

It seems that Cliff Stoll, an astrophysicist and one-time champion of technology, now is having second thoughts. A best-selling author from the Silicon Valley in California, he is switching gears and sounding a warning about cyberspace.

"One of the problems of technology is that people think it's a substitute for real life," he says. "I don't have to deal with my neighbor when I can log onto the Internet for two hours a night. It's a weak substitute, an ersatz community. I'm beginning to think seriously that there are people who really would prefer to talk to a machine than a human. But this is not a society I want my six-year-old daughter to grow up in."

Don't worry about me, Cliff. When I hear the word, "web", I see a Rawlings baseball glove. "Net" conjures up a picture of a 30-foot jump shot making string music with a basketball goal.

I'm writing this book on a 20-year-old IBM Executive electric typewriter that seems like part of the family. It's like a favorite saddle on a favorite horse. It just feels good. And it's dependable—no unexpected shutdowns, no glitches.

The conservative approach to our operation was not necessarily a practice in frugality. While it might appear that way, just the opposite was true in many aspects. Think of the first class postage stamps. We spent thousands more in postage going first class on our mail-outs. The high quality of our Directories also reflected no short cuts or cheap materials in our operation. We constantly received letters and phone calls from customers, complimenting the staff on "a quality product."

When I think of simplicity in business, I'm always reminded of the Wal-Mart versus Sears story. After many years of success with a catalog and retail business, Sears constructed a huge tower in Chicago and employed hundreds of executives. With a plain two-story building in Bentonville, Arkansas, and a handful of employees, Wal-Mart elected to keep it simple while fighting for the same business. You already know who's winning that battle. Wal-Mart is the dominant retailer in the world today.

Another good lesson I've learned at the Ranch is "pay cash when you can". I keep on my desk a quote from F.W. Woolworth, the founder of the chain that bears his name. He claimed that straight-laced Dutch businessmen of Puritan stock taught him how to flourish in business.

"They ran their stores on the same policy for more than half a century," he related. "They did not progress except as a tree progresses in size. They grew wealthy slowly but surely. They never went into debt; they always paid for what they bought, and paid with cash."

That advice seems just as appropriate today, and I've tried to follow it. To protect what you have and make it grow, it may be good to think like the Dutch businessmen. I'm certain my early years on a Midwest farm managed by my German grandfather served me well and helped formulate my conservative approach to finances. The horrendous waste I witnessed those four years in the Air Force also taught me a lot about how not to run a business.

"Shun credit as if it were a poisonous snake," advises Don Taylor, a business consultant who writes a weekly column, "Minding Your Own Business". He adds: "Learn to live within your means, even if you have to cut up your credit cards. The easy payment plan may make you feel rich for a time, but in reality it will keep you broke."

To the new entrepreneur, I would advise "be careful of early success". A few years ago, a new magazine went into competition with the locally-produced *Quarter Horse Journal*, the official publication of the jumbo-sized American Quarter Horse Association. My artist friend, Glenn Zulauf, did work for them so I had a front row seat.

The new publication did well in the beginning and there was plenty of room for two good magazines in that fast-growing field. But flushed with early success, the publisher started chartering private planes and making huge unnecessary expenditures. Guess what? Expenses soon began exceeding income, and the venture went under. It was a good idea, well conceived, but his initial triumphs caused him to lose sight of the total picture.

Here's another good argument for keeping close control of your costs. In Sam Walton's book, "*Made In America*," he offered this revelation: "Recently, we analyzed the top American retailers' annual financial statements. Wal-Mart's operating expenses, compared to sales, are nearly a third less than No. 2 K-Mart and less than half of No. 3 Sears. That takes dedicated control."

Then there's another side of the publishing business at the Ranch that reflects our "simple approach." Because of our strong advertising base and general success, we periodically were being asked to take on additional publications. Things like house organs, quarterly magazines, etc.

We refused every offer. "Do the best job in whatever you do", is old advice I've tried to follow. Which, to me, means don't spread yourself too thin. It has never been my goal to build an empire; only to mold a successful business in a field I enjoy, make a comfortable amount of money and have time for family travel and other avocations. It's been as simple as that.

I like the quote by Steve Allen, reflecting on the fact he came along too early to make the big TV bucks: "Who cares? I can only drive one car at a time, wear one outfit of clothing at a time and eat three meals a day."

26

NUTS TO MACADAMIA NUTS

Lest you get the opinion ol' Franks hasn't made some business mistakes along the way, think again. I lost my tail in the stock market in 1993, a year when nearly everyone else was doing well in a bull market mode.

If I had followed advice I heard years ago, I wouldn't have been there in the first place. "Don't invest in something you know nothing about", is a line I've heard that made good sense. And in the stock market, only brokers have the cinches. They make commissions when buying for customers and commissions when they sell.

Here's how it happened. A few years back when the bottom was falling out of CDs (certificates of deposit), I took much of our retirement nest-egg out of the bank and invested in a relatively-safe New York Stock Exchange company, Southwestern Public Service. A conservative utility company that fluctuates little in the market, it yielded a nice 7.5 percent dividend quarterly at the time.

In early 1992 with the threat of interest rates escalating, my broker and I got nervous. Traditionally, when interest rates increase, utility stocks go south. From a business newsletter, I got a glowing report on a "safe conservative stock" that looked too good to be true. That should have been my first clue to be suspect.

Priced at 8½ dollars a share on the New York Exchange, Mauna Loa Macadamia Partners of Hawaii was paying an outrageous 14.5 percent dividend each quarter. This was at a time when you could get no more than 2 or 3 percent from CDs at the bank. What a deal. Besides that, the newsletter suggested: "Buy this stock, take a periodic trip to the islands and deduct it as a legitimate business expense."

Well, the evidence was overwhelming, especially when you realize my stock broker's parent company had labeled it "a strong buy". So, I sold all my utility stocks and purchased 5,000 shares of the world's largest grower of macadamia nuts. I started packing my bags for a vacation to paradise; palm trees, hula dancers and beaches were swimming in my head.

Then a series of bad things started happening. A month after buying the stock, the *Honolulu Star-Bulletin* ran a story accusing Australian macadamia nut farmers of flooding the market, causing a 20% decline in that product's spot market price. Mauna Loa's stock also dropped drastically from 8½ to 5½.

But that was just the start. A couple months later, a hurricane roared through Hawaii causing considerable damage to the macadamia crop. The stock price dropped even further. Then the worst news of all came from the home office. They decided to cut in half the fat 14.5 dividend yield, the best reason for buying the stock in the first place.

Despite the fact the stock had dipped to 4 on the New York Exchange, less than half of my purchase price, I stuck with it for another year. It didn't rebound like I had hoped and sold out in August, 1993, at a net loss of $23,309. When I last looked, the company was still floundering around the same price.

The glamour trip to Hawaii never materialized either. Who needs a business write-off when you take that kind of hit?

I should have been wary when first seeing Mauna Loa's symbol on the stock exchange. Its code letters are NUT.

We can't leave the subject of dumb decisions without relating the Snapple Beverage story. It doesn't represent a large loss in finances, just a missed opportunity.

In late 1992 when I was still looking for places to invest CD retirement money, I heard Rush Limbaugh do an advertising spot on Snapple drinks, a small Eastern company with a new approach to bottled beverages, including iced tea. Limbaugh's show was going through the roof, so I figured anything he was selling would be worth considering. Besides that, I bought some of their peach iced tea and it was wonderful.

Snapple went public as an over-the-counter stock at 20 dollars a share on December 15, 1992. Twelve days later when I decided to jump in with 500 shares, it had already zoomed to 38½, almost double in value. Guess what, it quit zooming. It appeared I had bought at the top. In fact, more investors started selling than buying the hot stock and soon it had lost back to 32. It laid there like a wet dishrag for three months, and I was getting nervous. When it rebounded a little, I instructed my broker to sell out at a small loss. I don't have the patience or savvy for the stock market.

That was Snapple's cue to go gangbusters. Not long after cutting all ties,

I saw the small beverage company run up to 60 on the NASDAQ board. It split and continued its miraculous surge without skipping a beat. It jumped back to 60 once again, and ecstatic board directors called for another split. All this in only a few months.

These "home runs" don't happen every day in the stock market, I'm told, but imagine my poor stomach as I continued to sneak a peek at Snapple in the morning newspaper reports. Had I stuck around until the second split, which is unlikely after the quick big run-ups, I would have been the proud owner of 2,000 shares of Snapple at $30 per. It doesn't take a genius to figure out that my original investment of $19,250 would have escalated to $60,000, or a hefty $40,000 profit, in less than a year. Ugh!

My original instinct was right on, but I didn't have the patience to stick with it.

Will Rogers had the best advice for making money in the stock market: "Buy some good stock, hold it 'til it goes up and then sell it. If it doesn't go up, don't buy it."

27

ARCTIC BOWL

It was New York's Kennedy Airport and the U.S. customs agent stopped the two Americans with four bags and a reindeer skin.

"Where you coming from?" he asked.

"Finland."

"Been on a vacation, I suppose?"

"No, we've been covering the first Arctic Bowl football game only a few miles from the Arctic Circle. A game between an American college and a Finnish team."

The agent raised his quizzical eyes up from the bags, paused and blurted out, "You've got to be kidding."

As bizarre as it sounds, such a game was played in June, 1985, and it afforded my wife and I a memorable 11-day adventure in Scandinavia, our first such visit to that part of the world. Finland, with a population of five million in an area the size of Montana, is bordered by Sweden on the west and Russia on the east.

It all started with a phone call the previous fall.

"Dr. Franks," came the voice at the other end, and I immediately knew it was Sam Ketchman calling. Sam, a longtime football coach and athletic director at Ferris State in Michigan, had always called me that for no apparent reason.

"I'm putting together an unusual bowl game involving American and Finnish football teams," he continued, "and I'd like you to go. We'll pick up the expenses."

Ketchman is an unusual man. I first met him when both of us were publishing high school coaching directories 40 years ago. After retiring from the world of college athletics, he moved to Sarasota, Florida and started international match-making.

"It keeps me busy," he related, "and it has exceeded my wildest dream."

Alma Coach Phil Brooks took his own cheerleaders to Finland, wife Rose and daughters
Patti, Julie and Tresie.

He does his booking through a company called Athletic Enterprises, which he
recently sold but hangs on to as an adviser.

Ketchman, who still plays tennis and rides his bicycle daily at 80+, got the
idea for an "Arctic Bowl" in the spring of '84 while accompanying U.S. teams
to southern Finland and West Germany. My son, Randy, made that trip with
William Jewell College when a conflict deemed it impossible for me to go.

"Sam called me when he was in Helsinki," recalled Jarmo Karpakka, a
young doctor living in Oulu, just 150 miles south of the Arctic Circle. He
went down to Helsinki and they worked out the details for the game in his
hometown of 95,000, the largest city in northern Finland. At that time, Dr.
Karpakka was president of the Oulu club team and also playing defensive
tackle.

A mail-out to the nation's small four-year and junior colleges produced
several inquiries but Alma College in Michigan seemed to fit the bill. Playing
predominantly regional talent, Alma is a Presbyterian private school of 1,200,
many of whom have Scandinavian ancestors.

The pieces were falling into place and we had our tickets and itinerary in
hand when we got a call from Sam only days before departure.

"Guess what," he said in a depressed tone. "I'm going to miss the trip." During a routine physical exam, his doctor had found some artery problems. Open heart surgery was scheduled.

"Sorry, I won't make it," he continued, "but first things first."

On the precise day of the Arctic Bowl game, Ketchman underwent four-bypass heart surgery in Sarasota and sailed through it without a hitch. His good health had been a factor.

Phil Brooks, Alma College's efficient and mild-mannered athletic director and football coach, assumed most of Ketchman's travel responsibilities, and the party of 53 players, coaches and fans left on schedule. Floy and I joined the group in New York, where we all departed for the six-hour, trans-Atlantic flight to London.

Facing a layover of several hours at Heathrow Airport, the Americans were treated to an exceptionally thoughtful move on the part of Finnair, Finland's national airline that was taking us on to Helsinki. Realizing most of the group had never been to London, and may never return, the thoughtful airline scheduled a bus and took us on a two-hour tour of England's capital city. We made picture-taking stops at Parliament, home of Big Ben, St. Paul's Cathedral, Westminster Abbey, Piccadilly Circus and Hyde Park.

The flight from London to Helsinki was easy enough and the hour hop on to Oulu afforded us our first view of the Finnish countryside. We saw miles and miles of trees and water, just about what I'd expected. Even though the calendar said June, we encountered 40-degree temperatures when landing in Oulu, second only in size to Murmansk, Russia, in the Arctic region. We soon realized our wind-breakers would be inadequate for the brisk weather we would be facing.

After 24 hours of rest and jet lag rehabilitation, we were taken to a leisure fair Sunday afternoon, an experience akin to a small county fair in America. Popcorn, cotton candy and other snacks were sold while campers and other recreation equipment were being promoted. Dancers graced a stage for free shows and even Santa Claus showed up. Yes, in the middle of June. The Finns were exceptionally friendly to our group and the football team reciprocated by staging a light workout at the fair. The young Finns, especially, gathered around for their first look at American football.

On Monday, we were honored in a special ceremony at City Hall, and then taken on a tour of Oulu that included visits to a leading dairy and the University of Oulu. Tuesday morning was free for shopping and resting prior to the 6 p.m. kickoff that evening. Game day had finally arrived.

The following represent opening paragraphs in my story that appeared in the 1985-86 National Directory of College Athletics:

> *World history has taught us that Finland is famous for long summer days and short nights. The closer you get to the Arctic Circle the more the sun shines. In fact, because of the phenomenon, this country steeped in reindeer and saunas has gained the label "land of the midnight sun."*
>
> *On an early June night in the port city of Oulu, Finland, just 150 miles south of the Arctic Circle, local residents detected a special luminous glow on the horizon, a sight brighter than the aurora borealis would normally produce.*
>
> *A closer look revealed a 21-gun fireworks display, an explosion triggered by visitors from Alma College and the USA, playing American-type football within a snowball's throw of Lapland country.*
>
> *It was called the Arctic Bowl, and the Yanks easily defeated Oulu's club team, aptly-named the "Northern Lights." The final score was 72-0, but that was incidental to the occasion.*
>
> *Alma had been invited to Finland to help stimulate interest in American-style football and after all, the one-sided score had been expected. The powerful Michigan team had averaged 39 points a game against American opponents in 1984, leading all NCAA Division III colleges in total offense. It was no fluke.*

"We knew there would be a lot of disparity in the strength of the two teams," commented Alma's Coach Brooks. "But we also knew the spirit of international competition would be more important than the final score. Don't forget, also, this is a game that was invented in America. They've been playing here only three years."

"It was a learning experience for us," remarked Karpakka, the young medical doctor who was serving without pay as Oulu's president, defensive tackle and chief bottle-washer. "The Americans helped us in clinics and would even stop and tell us what we were doing wrong while the game was in progress. We want to learn from the best."

From the start, everyone knew it would be one-sided. Technique was the big difference. So starved for something to yell about, Finn fans cheered lustily when their team made a first down. Brooks echoed the fact it was a learning experience for his players too. Not necessarily in terms of football, but in world travel and culture. "Many of our players had never flown in a plane much less gone overseas," he revealed.

While soccer is still king in all European countries, the Arctic Bowl did attract about a thousand fans for the six o'clock kickoff. Lights were never turned on because it doesn't get dark until 11:45 in midsummer in Finland. It was played in a soccer stadium that had to be re-marked, and the cost was 20 Finnmarks, about $3.15 in U.S. currency.

The Americans, including eight parents who sat in the stands, were treated to a different look in sideline activities. Instead of brassy marching bands, Finn officials offered recorded disco music and lively chatter by a fast-talking announcer between plays. He started on the initial kickoff and went non-stop through the final play.

The pre-game show was big time. Four parachutists dropped out of the sky with colorful silks and the game ball to trumpet the beginning of the Arctic Bowl. Even the town mayor was there to execute the mock opening kickoff, soccer style. Cute Finnish girls with pom-pons were recruited from a local dance school to serve as cheerleaders for the Northern Lights.

Probably the biggest physical difference in U.S. and Finnish football was displayed in the uniforms. While American jerseys reflect no more than a number, and sometimes a player's name, the Oulu performers looked like walking billboards. Names of commercial sponsors, logos and emblems decorate the top of the helmet down to the knee stockings. A prominent Oulu night club reserved advertising space on the rear end, a choice position when the team goes into a three-point stance.

"Advertising on the uniforms of the players, officials and cheerleaders produces about 40% of our income," revealed Karpakka. Since football is a club sport and not affiliated with a college, no well-heeled alumni are available to pick up the shortages.

Since the make-up of the Finnish teams is club in nature, a check of the team roster produces interesting data. In addition to Karpakka, a married doctor, the Oulu squad included an architect, a chef, a clothing designer, a mental nurse, city workers and some 20 students. Ages ranged from 18 to 29.

While Karpakka is quick to share credit with several others, there is no doubt he was the pioneer in the development of organized football in northern Finland. His first exposure to the American game came in 1975 as an exchange student in Minnesota.

"I didn't play the sport in the States," he confessed, "but I wish I had. At that time in my life, I was too busy chasing the cheerleaders." Jarmo, who could pass for an Ivy Leaguer and speaks near-perfect English, related how he got into the football business back in his home country.

"I was driving along the street one day and saw two guys tossing an

The Arctic Bowl was played about 130 miles from the Arctic Circle (notice misspelling of "Arctic") on the poster. The Finns utilized all areas of their uniforms for advertising revenue (far right). (Below) The team landed in Oulu after the long flight from Michigan.

American football to each other. I pulled over immediately and out of curiosity went over to talk to them. I found out they too were interested in getting a team started in Oulu and one thing led to another."

The six-foot, 200-pounder, whose earlier athletic activities had been devoted to distance running, has a keen sense of humor. He told the story about an opposing quarterback getting decked on a blitz by the Oulu team. While the dazed player lay on the ground awaiting attention, Jarmo walked over from his defensive tackle position, looked down and said to the puzzled opponent: "I'm a doctor, can I help?"

Another typical Oulu player was Markku "Nappi" Ilonen, an ex-hockey player who is in construction. "I prefer American football to soccer," he explained, "because there's more team play involved. Although most people think otherwise, it really isn't as dangerous as soccer. Just this past year, our local volleyball team had five broken legs compared to just two in American football."

About half the team works out all year long, so strong the dedication. On the other side of the coin, players have been known not to show up for a game, and report later, "I had to attend a wedding."

Since the exposure of American football to Finland in the early 80s, a number of American retired coaches and recently-graduated players make summer trips to Europe. Some new graduates both play for the Finns and serve as coaches. Many responded to ads in the *NCAA News* that read: "Spend an expense-free summer in Europe coaching football."

Former Grand Rapids Junior College coach Dick Smith did it. "These guys are very industrious and give it everything they have," he remembered. "We worked out seven days a week. They have the size and a great attitude. All they really need is improvement in technique."

The next morning after the Arctic Bowl was a day I'd been eagerly awaiting. We boarded a tour bus bright and early and headed due north to the Lapland capital of Rovaniemi. I'd read and heard a lot about this intriguing part of the world and now I was going to see it first hand. We saw little but thick green forest that lined the paved two-lane highway. After a three-hour ride, we arrived at the Arctic Circle, which is marked by a large pole and sign that proclaims the words, "Arctic Circle," in six languages. A nearby well-stocked gift shop yielded reindeer skins to the Americans, along with other Finnish souvenirs.

We spent several hours in Rovaniemi, a town of 30,000 that was completely destroyed by the Germans in World War II. The sun shines 24 hours a day in mid-summer. The Laplanders' influence was everywhere but not more evident than in a local museum.

Lapland is the northernmost part of Europe, we were told, and spreads over parts of Finland, Russia, Sweden and Norway. It is not an independent country, more a lifestyle, and most Lapps reside in Finland. Nomads at heart, they can ski almost as well as they walk, and pack reindeer are used to pull sleds over the deep Arctic snow. Reindeer is vital to their existence. Milk and meat provide sustenance and hide and furs are used for clothing and shelter. We viewed a typical hut and tent constructed by the tough Lapps to withstand the long cold winters. Until recently, it was the custom for a man to buy a wife by giving her father a certain number of reindeer.

Guides told us Lapland has only two seasons, "day" and "night". The night season is about nine months long and extremely cold and dark. The day season, or summer, lasts only three months. It's a time for storing food and performing those errands that require daylight.

After arriving back in Oulu that night, I took a picture from our hotel window at exactly 11:35 as the last glimmer of sunlight was dropping behind the horizon. While browsing through a Finnish travel magazine, I noticed that an "annual midnight golf tournament" was scheduled for June 15.

The social highlight of our Finland adventure, a sauna party capped the day of our trip to the Arctic Circle. Host families, Northern Lights players and townspeople applauded as the chartered bus drove up to a huge Nordic ski lodge six miles out of Oulu. In the setting of a beautiful wooded area and a cool stream trickling down the hillside, principals from both countries shared laughter, good company and good food. Floy got my share of the salmon soup. Not one of my favorite foods, fish is a staple on Finnish menus.

I asked young Karpakka, the remarkable doctor-football player, if the close proximity of Russia made the Finnish people nervous. Remember, this was before the fall of communism and not that long after Russia had taken Finnish land by force in the 1940s.

"We don't pay much attention to them," he said. "We're aware of the guard towers and physical barriers on Russia's side of the border, and there are occasional attempts by Russians to escape to Finland."

He was asked if Finns had ever tried to cross into Russia. "Only one," he recalled with a wry smile. "But he was quickly caught and returned to the insane asylum."

After five days in Oulu, the American contingent flew back to Helsinki, the capital city of 600,000 only a stone's throw across the Gulf of Finland from St. Petersburg, Russia. We shopped and did little the first day. However, on Friday, we were taken on a tour of the city, which with its big department stores, modern facilities and intense shoppers looks like any typical American metropolis. A strange contrast to the lifestyle of Russians only a few miles away.

We visited Helsinki's famous port, walked through the open markets and took pictures at Senate Square, the equivalent of our Capitol Building in Washington. The highlight was a short boat ride to Fortress Island in the mouth of the Baltic Sea, a famous historical landmark.

That night in a soccer stadium adjacent to Olympic Stadium, Alma's football team played its second game in four days. They defeated a team of Helsinki All-Stars, 53-0, but it was much more difficult than the win in Oulu. The American game had been around for six years in southern Finland, and a vocal and knowledgeable crowd of 2,000 attended.

At this time the czar of Helsinki football was blond-haired Jari Narhi, a 24-year-old engineer who also had been an exchange student in the U.S. The Finnish American Football Association plays 10 games during the months of June, July and August, closing down before the long cold winter swoops down out of the Arctic. In mid-season each year, Finland's National All-Star team participates in a European Playoff Championship that rotates among the competing countries. In '85, it was staged in Milan, Italy.

When interviewing Narhi, he made an interesting observation. "American football is getting big in Europe," he proclaimed, "and I don't think it's out of the question to consider Russia as a future expansion areas." Four years later, his prediction became a reality.

Alma College players received a bonus on this trip that Americans traveling overseas rarely enjoy. While Floy and I, coaches and parents stayed in hotels, the players resided in Finnish homes. Partly to save on expenses being picked up by the host country's football associations but mostly to afford the Yanks a rich cultural experience. Strong friendships were formed in a short time and saying goodbye wasn't easy.

Lars and Eija Nylund were typical hosts. He is a banker and she's a teacher in Oulu, and they took in Alma footballers John Quinn and Dennis Reinhart. Lars related they especially wanted the experience of keeping American athletes because of their two boys, Wille, 12 and Johan, 7.

"Our sons went on a soccer tour to the south of France last year and stayed in homes," informed Lars. "We heard about the American team coming to Oulu through a friend and wanted to do something likewise. It was a wonderful time our boys will always remember."

This picture was taken from our hotel room at 11:35 p.m., showing that the Arctic truly is the "land of the midnight sun".

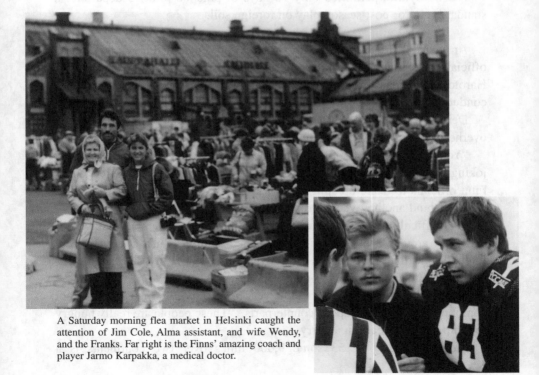

A Saturday morning flea market in Helsinki caught the attention of Jim Cole, Alma assistant, and wife Wendy, and the Franks. Far right is the Finns' amazing coach and player Jarmo Karpakka, a medical doctor.

Alma's European tour was not your usual trip to the corner drugstore. In the first place, players were asked to raise their own air fare, $1,300 (it would be double that now). Even though they have limited funds in a neophyte program, the Finnish hosts offered to cover internal costs. That included room and board, sightseeing tours and other incidentals.

After being selected by Athletic Enterprises to represent the U.S. in this most unusual bowl game, Alma officials then had to secure approval from the Michigan Intercollegiate Athletic Association and the NCAA. That was completed in January.

As a fund-raiser to help meet their financial obligations, the athletes conducted a "Lift-A-Thon." Sponsors pledged funds for each pound a player lifted. With support from Alma friends along with their home communities, the Scots came up with a big chunk of their money in that February event.

For Alma's seniors it was a surprising bonus to an outstanding 6-3 season, and a chance to hook 'em up one more time. Defensive back Rob Cwik was quoted: "This was so exciting for all of us. The football was fun, but the tours in Finland and stopovers in London and Sweden made it a great educational experience."

NCAA bylaws permitted only 10 days of practice prior to departure, a standard rule for post-season play on foreign soil.

An unusual sidelight to the tour was the presence of three U.S. football officials. Insurance agent Stan Kemp, attorney Jim Mullendore and teacher Harold Deines paid their own way to help officiate Alma's games and later conduct clinics for Finnish officials.

Deines was calling a girls basketball game at Alma College when he overheard Coach Brooks announce plans for the tour.

"You want to work the first Arctic Bowl in Finland?" Brooks asked, half-jokingly. That was the seed that evolved into another "first". All three joined Finn officials to make up split crews for the two games, then Stan and Jim stayed behind another week to direct clinics.

"It's difficult at best to referee a sport even when you've grown up with it and been around it all your life," explained Kemp. "In a country where football is still so young, we thought we could really be beneficial." American and Finnish coaches concurred.

Mullendore, who had worked a year in the USFL, had nothing but compliments for the European counterparts. "These people are really hungry for help and they learn in a hurry."

Moving a party of 53 some 9,000 miles over two continents is a monumental challenge, especially when the director is home recovering from open heart surgery. The only incident resembling a problem occurred in Helsinki on arrival from London. Coach Brooks was informed that only 23 seats were available on the last leg of the trip to Oulu. That left 30 people with valid tickets but no transportation to the northern port. Host families were waiting to pick up players, that was the last flight of the day and no train connection could be made.

The stranded Americans were hustled off to Helsinki's Inter-Continental Hotel (sans luggage), fed an evening meal and put on the first flight out the next morning, all compliments of Finnair. Problem solved. Floy and I were in the second group, but we saw it as a bonus. It allowed us another night in Helsinki, an exciting city that isn't normally included on your typical European tour package.

Before saying farewell to Finland on Saturday, the Franks found a side of this Scandinavian nation that's as American as apple pie. Just like Peoria and Chattanooga, Helsinki has a weekend flea market near the downtown area. Among the "treasures" we found on card tables and blankets scattered over several vacant lots was a second-hand colorful red, white and blue Laplander costume hat. It made the top rung of our entry halltree back in Texas.

Because of pressing deadlines back home, I returned to the States two days ahead of the Alma College family. It wasn't without its rewards though. We were given first class seats on Finnair all the way to New York, thanks to an advertising vice-president, Jerry Zaboroski. It was nice and plushy, our first and only experience in that strata. From the time we first buckled up, we were wined and dined like royalty.

Finland is a country after my heart. For years, they had to fight off first Sweden, and then Russian and German aggressors. Proud people, the Finns were the only country after World War I that insisted on paying back money borrowed from the U.S. The pro-American spirit prevailed during our time there.

And what about the principals in this saga. Ten years after the adventure, Coach Brooks has opted for a more laid-back lifestyle. He's coaching a high school team in Saint Joseph, Michigan, and involved in running a motivational program. His former assistant coach, Jim Cole, has replaced him at Alma. Two years after our trip to Finland, the Finn All-Stars came to the States and played Alma College and Grand Rapids Junior College.

Football, American-style, continues to mushroom in Finland and other European countries as more and more U.S. colleges take their show overseas.

Who knows, some day Notre Dame may have an afternoon audience with the Pope and then take on the Rome Gladiators that night in the Colosseum. The original one, that is.

28

IS IT CBS OR IOU?

I couldn't believe my eyes. There it was in a 30-point bold headline on the sports page. "NCAA, CBS AGREE ON $1 BILLION CONTRACT."

The blockbuster deal in 1990 involved exclusive television rights to the Final Four basketball classic for seven years. In this age of sports megabucks, the size of the contract didn't surprise me. However, the fact that CBS was involved blew my mind.

In the 23 years I've published the *National Directory of College Athletics*, the company often referred to as "the Tiffany network" was the biggest "deadbeat" we had for paying its bills. Oh sure, the CBS sports people ordered healthy amounts of our publications annually, and we never failed to get paid. But, most of the time we had to wait nine or 10 months after delivery to get our money. Sometimes longer.

The later years were the worst. It got so bad that we wouldn't take new orders from CBS until we checked to see if the company that pays Dan Rather two million a year had a clean slate. I dug up some records for this chapter.

A Federal Express airbill dated August 23, 1988, indicates our company shipped 30 directories to Len DeLuca, CBS Sports, 30th Floor, 51 West 52nd Street, New York, NY. Attached to it is a note that reflects we were still making monthly calls as late as May 5, 1989, almost nine months later, trying to collect the overdue amount of $450.

In August 1990, the year of the billion dollar deal with NCAA, our office got a call from a person I had known a long time before she joined CBS Sports.

"We're having a big staff meeting in a couple days," she started, "and we need 60 of your directories overnight. Just send them Federal Express."

When I heard about this order, I had to call her right back.

"We appreciate the business from CBS," I explained, "but we can't do a thing until payment is received from last year."

"But we must have them immediately," she countered. "They're vital to our meeting."

"I'm sorry, but this isn't the first time we've been stiffed by CBS. Why does your business office treat us this way?"

"Oh, you're not the only one who has to wait for their money," she explained. "This happens all the time."

"Well, cut back on some of those big salaries you're paying Rather, Brent Musburger and the other hot-shots at CBS," I added, "and you might get caught up on the overdue bills."

We held our line and didn't ship the books until payment for the previous year's order was received. Then, as requested, we sent them Federal Express at an expense of more than $100.

What gives? Here's a company that's worth five billion dollars, or that's what Westinghouse paid for it not long ago, and it won't take care of its petty cash accounts. I was having trouble sorting our the logic behind all this. That is, until I read a late 1995 column by Andy Rooney in the Amarillo newspaper under the headline, "Laurence Tisch Sold Out CBS."

A long-time employee of CBS, the straight-shooting Rooney pointed out that erosion of the distinguished New York broadcasting giant started taking place in the mid-80s. That's when Tisch gained control, and about the same time we began having trouble with our collections.

"Those of us who have been here a long time," analyzed Rooney, "began to notice the carpets in the hallways were dirty. Spots where people had spilled coffee with milk and sugar were left uncleaned. Under President Frank Stanton, the CBS building had been hospital-clean and as tastefully decorated as an art gallery."

He added that "dirty carpets became an early warning signal of what was to happen to the whole CBS operation." Key people like Diane Sawyer and Charles Kuralt jumped ship. And CBS, once a consistent leader in the ratings game with ABC and NBC, slipped badly in that area. But the ultimate embarrassment came a couple years ago when upstart Fox Network outbid them for prestigious National Football League rights, stripping away the real plum of CBS Sports for years. CBS was the original network of the NFL.

Thanks, Andy, for filling in important pieces to this 10-year-old riddle. It all makes sense now.

While CBS consistently played the waiting game with accounts receivable, collections generally posed few problems for us at the

Publishing Ranch. Receiving weird letters requesting free directories was another story.

In a mail-order business, letters are the lifeline of the operation, making every day seem like Christmas morning. When our box is opened at the post office daily, it's pot luck time. Opening and sorting the mail always occupied much of the morning time of Shaine LeGrand and other secretaries of the past.

Off-the-wall letters were so commonplace that we started saving them and making a special file. I'd like to share some of them here, most of which deal with the business of hustling free books. The first one was addressed to "Ray Franks, Editor and Publisher-VERY PERSONAL":

> *My Dear Mr. Franks:*
>
> *You do not know me but I know of your fine achievements for college publications. I've been your admirer for quite a while, even before now when I lived in Amarillo. I've always been loyal to Texas teams in all categories.*
>
> *Sir, I beg for a big favor. Due to my long severe illness in the hospital since mid-December and humane Christian charity, please arrange free by mail your latest issue of the National Directory of College Athletics. When well, I could have afforded it.*
>
> *Please do not refuse my desperate need for this book during my illness.*
>
> *Your Fan, Bless Ever,*
>
> *R.B.*
> *Bronx, NY*
>
> *P.S.: Please do not phone. Too ill to speak. Thanks ever.*

In this hand-written letter, all the personal pronouns "I" appeared in small letters. Needless to say, we did not feel this was a genuine request worthy of a complimentary directory. The emotion, however, did stir the cockles of our heart, if only temporarily. And why would we want to phone, even if he had included a number?

✦ ✦ ✦ ✦ ✦

This second letter is self-explanatory. Read on.

Greetings:
> *I have always been a big sports fan of all sports, and I would like very*

much for you to send me an extra copy of the National Directory of College Athletics (women's edition only).

Please understand this letter. I am an inmate here at the State Prison and I hopefully hope that you will send me a free copy of your women's edition complete with names of women's coaches and addresses in college athletics. I know that this will help me a lot to get in touch with my favorite teams. I would appreciate your help and concern very much. It feels so good to help!

I am respectfully,

Teddy "Bear" B.
State Prison
Reidsville, GA 30499

My first thought was: "Is Teddy Bear a man or woman?" My second concern was: "If it's a man, why does he want names and addresses of women coaches?" And my third thought was: "I wonder what he's in prison for?" No, we didn't mail "Teddy Bear" a free book.

✦ ✦ ✦ ✦ ✦

From Brooklyn, New York, came this short and strange request.

To Whom It May Concern:

I would appreciate it if you can send me information on how I can obtain a Directory that has scholarship information for Hispanic women. I am on my school's varsity volleyball team.

Sincerely Yours,

A.T.A.
Brooklyn, NY

Even in this era of wacko multi-culturalism, I found this letter weird. How in the world could a directory be arranged to accommodate ethnic groups?

✦ ✦ ✦ ✦ ✦

Occasionally, we received unusual letters from overseas.

Dear Sirs:

I guess you don't receive many letters from here and this one should attract your attention. Or at least, I hope so.

I work as a sportswriter here in Italy and am much interested in

American sports. I would like one of your Directories, and maybe it will help me find a way to America.

Your consideration will be much appreciated.

Yours sincerely,

F.I.
Lucera, Italy

Our Directories did not come with maps, but I hope the young man made it.

✦ ✦ ✦ ✦ ✦

This next epistle came from overseas also, hand-written from a basketball player with high ideals.

Dear Sir:

I am a young boy of 17 years old and also a student in Nigeria. I have an average height of six feet, nine inches and a vertical jumping ability of about five feet, four inches. I am an outstanding basketball player and have represented my state in so many competitions.

At last year's sports festival, I led my state to victory and won my first gold medal in life. Also in many state competitions, I was voted MVP.

I would be grateful if you would consider my application for a Directory so I can find a college with a basketball scholarship. But the most important thing is the list of all colleges so I can write them for admission into their school.

I would be very glad if my application is properly taken care of. I really rely on you.

Best regards,

Olasunkammin Iakeye
Nigeria

Six foot-nine inches and still growing. Hmmm. I forwarded this letter on to Dale Brown, a good friend and basketball coach at LSU who recruits world-wide. I've been waiting to see Iakeye's name in basketball boxscores, but haven't yet.

✦ ✦ ✦ ✦ ✦

I've saved the best for last. You might want to read it twice.

Dear Sir,

I am the father of five children; three are in college now and the others are twin girls in high school. I am in prison and have been for 4½ years; likely, I will be for another year to year and a half.

Due to my situation, I am not able to do for my children what I would like to be able to do financially. However, I am active seeking opportunities for them, and my youngest are quite gifted athletically. They are especially good at soccer and basketball. As sophomores, they play on the varsity team in both sports.

I am working on seeking opportunities for them and starting early. However, my financial resources are really tough and I can't afford to spend much. I am interested in the book you have concerning female athletes entitled National Directory of College Athletics (Women's Edition). I wonder if you might have an out-dated edition that you could give me; I could put it to good use and I would certainly appreciate it. If you could do this, I'd be happy to pay the postage.

Your help would be appreciated; thanks for your consideration, in any case.

Sincerely,

D.R.R.
Summit House
Steilacoom, WA

Yes, we did honor this request. Not with an old, outdated directory, but with a new edition just off the press.

29

BLUNDER DOWN UNDER ... OR UNFAIR DINKUM?

The bags were barely unpacked from the Arctic Bowl when I first learned of a new venture called the "Australia Bowl". Unlike the football game played in Finland, which matched an American college team against a home country squad, this one would pit two Division I U.S. aggregations on foreign soil 10,000 miles from home.

Never having been to the South Pacific, I was licking my chops when Ted Livingston first contacted our office and extended an invitation to be in on another "intercollegiate first". At that time, Ted was assistant to the athletic director at University of Hawaii and had been contracted to be "game manager", and in general help the Aussies extend the scope of American-style football to still new horizons. Western Athletic Conference members Wyoming and Texas-El Paso had been booked as participants.

"We would like for you to come along and be a part of an exciting sports spectacle," said Livingston. "Complimentary, of course."

So, the first week in December, 1985, just five months after the Arctic Bowl, my wife and I headed for Melbourne, Australia, with notepad, camera and ten rolls of Kodak slide film.

And while the 10-day adventure to the bottom half of the world was an exhilarating escapade, the promotional side of the game had its problems. In fact, **it was a game that almost was not played**. Consider these zany events leading up to the main attraction.

Seventy-two hours before kickoff, the Wyoming and UTEP contingents of 250 players and officials, landed at Melbourne's International Airport and were greeted with the news:

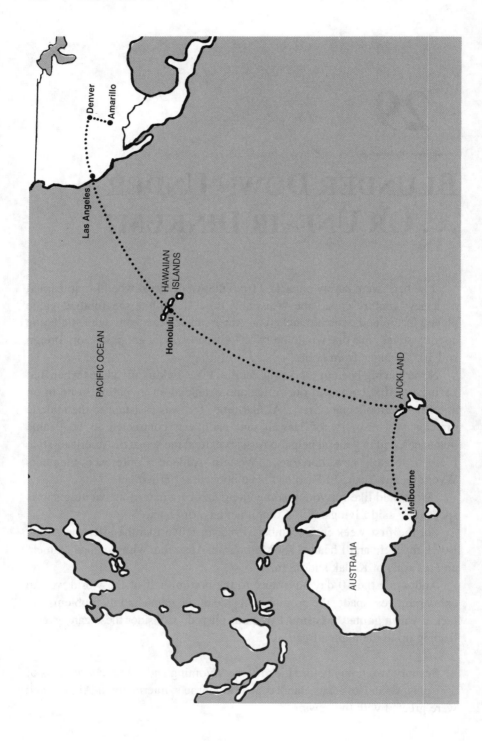

"The game's in trouble . . . it may not be played."

We arrived a day later, in the company of Western Athletic Conference officials, and heard the same discouraging news. We were told the Australian company promoting the international spectacular, Frontline Communications, had encountered serious financial problems and President Barry Shawyer had just collapsed under stress and was hospitalized. Earlier, the young bespectacled Shawyer had blamed the declining state of the Australian dollar for part of his headache, plus disappointing pre-game ticket sales. Costs were spiralling, too. What had started out as a liberal budget, including frills galore, now had escalated some half-million dollars above the projection.

There was real trouble in River City, and a plane-load of football players was faced with the possibility of making the 10,000-mile return trip to the U.S. without so much as one snap from center. Without question, the stakes in this overseas promotion were a lot higher than say, the Arctic Bowl.

Adversity often brings out the best in all of us and there was plenty to be concerned about at this stage. Representatives of both the Australian and American interests rallied together and started making modifications and adjustments.

Canceled were the welcoming banquet, a barbecue at the zoo, city sightseeing tours and air fare to Sydney, a scheduled bonus for all Yanks before leaving the flattest, smallest, oldest and driest continent in the world. Earlier, the appearance of University of Southern California's marching Trojan band had been axed in a move than had to be described as "ominous". That spared the budget a whopping $300,000. You see how these aggressive Aussie promoters were thinking in the beginning.

Uppermost in the minds of all concerned was "save the game". Around-the-clock meetings and work continued and 24 hours before scheduled kickoff, the project still hung in the balance. In-fighting among some Australian sponsors clouded the picture even more. They were being squeezed for additional funds beyond initial commitments. The state and national governments were solicited too.

Randy Upton, manager of the American Chamber of Commerce in Melbourne, visualized another problem. "Cancellation of this game could sour U.S. - Australian athletic relations in general," he feared.

American boosters accompanying the teams got into the act, too. They started passing the hat, and it was reported Mayor Jonathan Rogers of El Paso raised more than $1000 in two hours among UTEP supporters. Even Don McLean, the American singer who is big in Australia, agreed to perform at half-time for nothing. He too had been a casualty of last-minute budget slicing.

With fingers crossed and officials perspiring, the game unfolded as scheduled. On December 7 (a date that brought a nation together after disaster struck in 1941), Wyoming rallied in the final minutes to pull out a 23-21 squeaker before 25,000 confused but thoroughly entertained Aussies. Sports fans "down under" know little about American-style football, which they call "gridiron". Football to them means Australian rules football, rugby or soccer. Their only exposure to this fast-spreading U.S. fixation has been NFL delayed telecasts.

The historic game was carried live on national television, and the reports were excellent. However, that too surely contributed to the disappointing numbers in the stands.

While they were far from knowledgeable about the rules and mechanics of the American creation, the fans enjoyed the quality of the fast-paced, closely-played game that demanded their attention from beginning to end. It was not the contest you expected from two teams with a total sum of three wins between them.

A testimony to the game's artistic success, hundreds of fans spilled out of the stands and onto the playing surface at game's end. They wanted autographs and just an opportunity to talk with the Americans. Even game officials, who also had been flown in to call the contest, and cheerleaders from Wyoming and UTEP were stopped for signatures. They milled around for 30 minutes after the contest.

Another telltale sign of the game's success was the rush on souvenirs. Sweat shirts, buttons and banners had been slow movers before the game. However, after completion, stadium shops were inundated with clawing fans who wanted to buy anything with "Australia Bowl" emblazoned on it.

Sue Mott, Australian sports writer, described the game this way in The Australian newspaper: "The gargantuan gridiron troops, with their grossly exaggerated bodies and fiendishly complicated game plans, enraptured the VFL Park crowd who probably understood one-tenth of what was going on during the three-hour clash."

Fans who paid $10 (or $6.50 U.S. money) to see the game were vocal in their assessment of the happenings.

"It was terribly confusing to start with, but quite easy to pick up once I understood it," said Melbourne businessman Charles Chatfield. "It was great, especially the long-distance throws. That was really spectacular."

"Loved it . . . want it back again! . . . Having a great time," enthused a student.

"I enjoyed it but I would have liked to see more cheer squads," said a

The sign on the bus says it all. In an austerity move, we joined the players in riding a bus from Melbourne to Sydney, a blessing in disguise. (Bottom right) Ted Livingston, game manager of the Australia Bowl, pets a kangaroo at the local zoo.

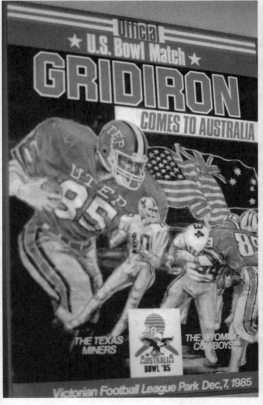

housewife. "I thought it was great value for the money, and I'd love to go again."

"I came because I was curious," offered a young executive. "Yes, I would come back. It was a worthwhile trip."

A teen-age male didn't like it as much as Australian-rules football. "The American game doesn't have the continuity of our sport. There's too much starting and stopping and too many huddles."

There was a mixed verdict in the press box, where I viewed the game. Most Aussie writers appeared confused in the beginning, but quickly figured out what was happening. They admitted it was "very exciting sport" and generally gave it a "thumbs up" in their accounts the following day.

Of course, there were exceptions. Melbourne sports reporter Greg Hobbs ridiculed the use of equipment. "We can't understand why you fellows wear all that padding and gear. And those helmets? My goodness, take it all off and I think these players are 3-foot-six and four stone (56 pounds)."

Hobbs pointed out that cricket still ranked No. 1 with Aussie fans. During the Australia Bowl event, promoters had a lot of competition. Australia met New Zealand in a big cricket encounter; Scotland and Australia tangled in soccer; a championship boxing match was staged; there was Saturday horse racing, and the finals of the Australian Tennis Open were winding down. Though staged in December, it was springtime "down under". Seasons flip flop above and below the Equator.

The positive commentary was vociferous and varied.

"The Australian people were just fantastic," surmised Dr. Joe Kearney, Commissioner of the Western Athletic Conference, who has since retired. "They were as warm and friendly as any people you want to meet. It was a tremendous educational and cultural experience for both teams."

Accolades flowed freely even though neither WAC team came close to receiving its original guarantee. Wyoming is believed to have come up $25,000 short of its promised share and UTEP, the home team, returned with more than $50,000 uncollected.

UTEP Coach Bill Yung, who along with Wyoming Coach Al Kincaid, had been fired before the trip, defended the promoters. "Nobody else was doing it. These guys had the vision and instead of knocking them we really need to recognize that and give them some credit."

"It was incredible . . . the people of Australia were so warm and friendly," commented Eric Cooper, the Miners' inside linebacker. "We felt like celebrities there, it was awesome."

Burt Reynolds starred in a movie about prison football called "The Longest Yard". The saga in Australia could have been labeled the "Longest Road Game" or the "Longest Home Game", as far as that goes. It was a regularly-scheduled home game for the Texas school before being switched to Melbourne . . . by mutual consent.

The logistics of such a trip are staggering. After a 140-mile bus ride from Laramie to Denver, Wyoming flew to Los Angeles on the first leg. After switching to a DC-10, it was on to Melbourne with refueling stops in Honolulu and Auckland, New Zealand. For the round trip, air time spanned 44 hours over 20,538 miles.

My wife and I enjoy travel immensely. You might call us "avid travelers". But this was the toughest for us to rebound from, even with stops in Denver, Los Angeles, Honolulu and Auckland. Few would dispute it was the longest road trip by U.S. footballers. About the only way it could be topped would be to convert the parking lot of the Taj Mahal into a playing field or book a floating iceberg at the South Pole.

In addition to 60 players, each college filled its 125-official party allotment with coaches, trainers, cheerleaders and school officials and wives. Both passports and visas were required for everyone.

The only incident resembling a problem in transportation occurred on the trip over at Auckland's Air Terminal. The jumbo jet full of wide-bodied football players was stuck there for three hours when a door on their plane first refused to open. And after it finally opened, it refused to close. The next day when we stopped at the same terminal on our way to Melbourne, we encountered Tina Turner and her entourage checking through the New Zealand customs. She had just completed a tour of Australia and New Zealand, and must have had 20 or 30 funky types following her like puppy dogs.

The game was the catalyst but few would overlook the side benefits of traveling half-way around the world and spending 10 days in another country.

The players marveled at the Aussie accent and picked up on it immediately. So impressed were UTEP players that they changed their chant at the end of team talk huddles. It used to be "win!" While in Australia, it was "g'day mate!"

The Americans were flattered to be the focal point of a downtown parade in Melbourne the day before the game. Even a light rain failed to dampen their spirits as they swaggered along in shorts and game jerseys to the applause of an appreciative crowd. For some, it was the highlight of the trip.

It was as if this sprawling city of three million was saying, "Hello, America, glad to have you with us." Aussies are friendly and gregarious people, and often would step into the street to shake hands with the Americans. The warmth emanating from our hosts was infectious. Also remember it was Christmas season down under. Despite summer-time temperatures, buildings and street lamps were decorated with red bells and glitzy garland and a festive fervor was in the air. Aussies are extroverts and don't need much of an excuse to have a good time.

Considered the financial center of Australia, Melbourne is located at the southern tip of the continent. The capital of Victoria, one of six states, it is characterized by wide boulevards, gracious gardens and public monuments. Lots of palm trees, too.

When the financial crunch canceled the official tours, John Adams of the Western Athletic Conference scheduled a bus for Americans staying at Old Melbourne Hotel. "I came too far to miss seeing the sights of Melbourne," he reasoned.

A photographer at heart, I thoroughly enjoyed the half-day tour. We quickly found that Aussies drive on the wrong side of the street, just as they do in England. Colorful mounted police and the appearance of royal crests on lampposts were other tell-tale signs that Australia still has ties with the mother country. Electric streetcars give a cosmopolitan look and marinas loaded with boats of all sizes remind that the Yarra River, Port Phillip Bay and the South Pacific Ocean are not far away.

Before leaving Melbourne, Ted and Beth Livingston took us to a local zoo, where we got to see kangaroos eyeball to eyeball. These strange animals look like over-size deformed rabbits who should be getting around with crutches. How could anyone make the marathon trip to Australia without snapping a kangaroo picture or buying a boomerang and sheepskin rug? We also got closeup views of the koala bear and emu, other unusual creatures indigenous to Aussieland. Hanging around in trees, the koala bears appear to be about the size of opossums and raccoons and reflect little resemblance to the grizzly or brown bear species found in North America. They more closely resemble stuffed teddy bears.

Our stay at Old Melbourne Hotel was memorable. More closely resembling a motel in style, it featured beautiful flower gardens, clinging ivy and decorative ornamental iron. Its tastefully-decorated outside patio was the site of many coffee and tea-sipping sessions with our new friends from Australia and the WAC Conference. Ted and Beth Livingston immediately impressed me as people of substance and we have maintained a light

Certainly one of the classic landmarks of the world is Sydney's Opera House. We got a close look on a harbor cruise.

So excited, the Aussie fans flooded the field after the first Australia Bowl. (Left) American football players were featured in a downtown parade despite a steady rain.

corresponding relationship with them. After retiring from University of Hawaii, Ted moved to Bellingham, Washington, where he still keeps his hand in sailing, an addictive avocation.

"Who wants to take the bus to Sydney?" came the question from WAC Commissioner Joe Kearney. When budget cuts were made earlier, bus travel was substituted for air fare on the post-game journey to Sydney, a bubbling metropolis of 3½ million. The Wyoming contingent decided to spend more time in Melbourne and leave directly for the States from there.

However, the UTEP party and WAC officials opted for the 600-mile, 12-hour bus ride across the south corner of the country. We also chose the latter plan and it was a true blessing in disguise. It was our only opportunity to see Australia's sprawling countryside.

It was with great excitement that we boarded our buses bright and early. Shortly after leaving the city limits of Melbourne, we discovered that this was "big sky" country reminiscent of West Texas. We found the rolling countryside well stocked with sheep, cattle and kangaroos.

In certain areas of America, it is not uncommon to encounter roadside signs labeled "deer crossing". Down under, the lightly traveled highways are dotted with square signs that warn: "Kangaroos—Next 25km". Complete with a silhouette of these strange-looking creatures. Not far from the highway, we would see these over-sized jackrabbits leaping out in the fields, completely oblivious of our presence.

Driving along the endless pastures, dotted with occasional hills and eucalyptus trees that look more like mesquite bushes, we soon discovered why Australia is labeled the world's driest continent. While some of the ranch land sported light green patches of grass, most of it was light brown and reflected the lack of adequate rainfall.

"Drought can drive grazing ranches into terrible debt or even off their land," we were told by Aussies making the motor coach excursion with us. "We lead the world in wool production by a wide margin, but synthetic fibers are posing a threat to this industry."

Shortly after passing from the state of Victoria into New South Wales, we pulled into the sleepy little town of Albury. After finding a lush green city park, we devoured a brown-bag lunch of a foot-long submarine sandwich, cookies, chips and a soft drink. Picnics in Australia are not that different from those in the States.

The balance of the long bus ride was more of the same, scenery wise, but what a contrast we would find in Sydney. Called the "San Francisco of Australia", this eastern seaport is the country's largest and liveliest city. Like its California sister, Sydney is punctuated with breath-taking bridges, colorful marinas, hilly streets and countless miles of coast for a playground.

We devoted the good part of one day to a harbor cruise that took us out to a neighborhood crowded with beautiful cliffside homes overlooking sandy beaches, some of them nude. The highlight of the experience was nudging up close to Sydney's famous Opera House and getting a long look at this high-profile landmark. It has to be one of the ten most visible addresses of the world and it was no disappointment up close.

Financed by a series of lotteries run by the state government, it was designed by Danish architect Jorn Utzon and completed in 1973. Actually, it was 14 years in construction at a place called Bennelong Point, a peninsula that juts out into the harbor. Offering entertainment from all the performing arts, it has a seating capacity of 5,200 and restaurants cater for those attending performances as well as the sightseeing public. A trip to Sydney would not be complete without a close-up of this fabulous structure. From the water, Sydney's skyline is breath-taking, certainly one of the most striking in the world.

The department stores are similar to those in the States, just the language has a peculiar twist. For example, Floy spotted a big red sign that said, "Shop the convenient way—Layby". Of course, in the U.S., it's called "lay-away". At a curbside eatery, instead of "fast food", the expression "take-away food" was advertised.

The only complaint I have about Sydney is we didn't have enough time to fully explore it. However, on our last evening in this bright light of the Pacific, we were treated to a special time. Floy and I were escorted to the Cruising Yacht Club on Rushcutter Bay by new friends Ted and Beth Livingston and WAC Commissioner Joe Kearney and wife Dory. There we savored a sumptuous seafood meal in the setting of a peaceful marina overlooking a picture of shimmering blue water. A nice finale to a great experience.

As we headed homeward the next morning, over the mammoth South Pacific Ocean, two observations came to mind. The first involved logistics. Australia is more sparse that I ever thought, and no wonder they continually offer incentive programs to attract more people to this great land of opportunity. The country is about the size of the U.S. in area, and has only 15 million residents. Nearly half of those are found in the two metropolises of Melbourne and Sydney.

The second thought related to the people. After traveling to most populated areas of the world, I genuinely believe Australians are more similar to Americans than any other people. Their personality is definitely outgoing and they possess the same pioneer spirit that was evident in the settling and development of the United States.

Australia Bowl '85 was not a picture perfect operation but Ted Livingston, who was loaned to the promoters because of his vast experience in U.S. collegiate athletics, had some astute observations.

In his post-game assessment, the soft-spoken sailing enthusiast told why he thought the event was a financial failure: (1) not enough time; (2) inexperience of the promoters; (3) difficulties of communication; (4) failure to follow the contract; (5) unanimous desire to see the project succeed.

Out of the rubble came these four plus factors, as Livingston saw it: (1) the quality of the people involved; (2) quality of the game itself; (3) quality of the fans and press; and (4) value of the entire experience to the participants.

And as Paul Harvey says: "Now for the rest of the story".

With the stigma of financial failure still fresh on their minds, officials said no to an Australia Bowl in 1986. But the following year, it was a different story. With a blue ribbon committee of key Australian leaders heading it up, American-style football returned in a new wrapper. The time, it was called the "Melbourne Bowl".

But new labels don't always guarantee success. "While the promotion in 1985 went bankrupt three days before the game, the one in '87 bellied up three days after it was over," updated my buddy Ted Livingston, who handled game operations both times. Livingston and Brigham Young Athletic Director Glen Tuckett barely got out of the country before creditors pounced down and started sifting through the rubble.

Here's what happened. Western Athletic Conference schools Brigham Young University and Colorado State were booked to meet in a regularly-scheduled game, just as the '85 game was formatted. However, officials decided to move it from VFL Park to Princess Park and portable bleachers were installed. That added to the expense level and tickets were hiked to $25, another mistake.

"About 13,000 showed up for the game," remembers Livingston, "and that was only half of what the first bowl venture attracted." Besides that, television revenue expected from U.S. sources never materialized. In America, the game was being aired at 10:30 on a Friday night and everybody knows that time belongs to high school football. Everyone but the Aussies.

This time, the American teams got their guarantee up front. But plenty of

Australian businesses got hurt badly, especially that hotel that housed both football teams. So what's the fate of American-style football in Australia? Who knows? But I'm not betting against its return. These Aussies are sporting and fun-loving people who root for the underdog. Which is little surprise from a country first settled by boat-loads of prisoners who got a second chance from overcrowded jails in England.

Dick Enberg and Brent Musburger probably never heard of them. John Madden could never have reached them by bus.

Nevertheless, the two little-known football bowl games I covered in 1985 afforded an interesting achievement. Not that the Guinness Record Book people would care, I was the only member of the media to cover both the Arctic and Australia Bowls, the northern-most and southern-most American-style football games played in the world. And in the same year.

Additionally fascinating, both games were played in the springtime, although six months apart. How can that be? The Arctic Bowl was staged in early June in Oulu, Finland, just 150 miles south of the Arctic Circle, and the Australia Bowl premiered December 7 in down-under Melbourne, about halfway between the Equator and Antarctica. Seasons flip-flop above and below the Equator.

While the achievement is of the "so what" category, my frequent flyer mileage chart was the biggest winner. The roundtrip excursion from Amarillo, Texas, to northern Finland netted 9,100 miles and the marathon journey to the land of boomerangs and kangaroos (by way of Hawaii and New Zealand) added another 20,538.

30

THE OL' COACH

It was in the mid-50's, when I was still on the West Texas State payroll, that a fictitious character called the "Ol' Coach" started to formulate in my mind.

I usually traveled with coaches in cars and on buses in those days for out-of-town football and basketball games. There was plenty of time for light-hearted kibitzing and joking. Long-time assistant football coach and PE instructor Hatcher Brown was the clown prince of the West Texas staff. He was quick to seize on any humorous situation and make the most of it.

"Look at that old coach out there," I remember hearing Hatcher say, spotting a wino wobbling down the streets of El Paso. "Man, that guy's seen a lot of kickoffs", he would laugh in his full, throaty manner.

Hardly anyone will argue that coaching is one of the most unique professions in the world. A coach's success is based solely on trying to get his or her counterpart fired. On top one day, a coach can be buried beneath the rubble the next. It's an emotional roller-coaster ride, at best.

The idea of creating a cartoon character to symbolize such a wacky and insecure profession seemed like a good one. In the back of my mind, I kept storing up thoughts and possibilities that seemed endless. After all, the coaching merry-go-round is a funny business, and at that time I was working in a cauldron of coaching characters.

Then, one day the idea became more vivid. One of the ten best cartoonists in the whole United States was renting office space at the Publishing Ranch, and when I broached my friend, Glenn Zulauf, he loved the idea. I would submit cartoon ideas and handle the promotion, and Glenn would perform the artwork. It was an instant partnership, and we had a blast doing it.

In all fairness, Zulauf, whom I first met while in the Air Force, also contributed mightily with ideas. At his peak, this brilliant artist, with anequally remarkable sense of humor, hit all the major magazine markets in the country with free-lance cartoons. The credits include Esquire, Life, Look, Playboy and Better Homes and Gardens. Many were the times on a cold wintry day that we sat around the office brainstorming ideas for our new "baby". Those were fun times and produced enough good stuff for 49 cartoons over a period of several years.

The Ol' Coach first saw the light of day in the fall of 1965. He emerged as a leathery-faced, battle-scarred, big-eared and pot-bellied character with an ever-present cap on his head and whistle around his neck. He is almost grotesque in style. One guy even wrote us and complained, "that he didn't represent the typical coach of today". He suggested we scrap the character.

"Lighten up", I thought, and threw the letter in the nearest waste basket.

Actually, the face for Ol' Coach is a likeness of a master sergeant both Zulauf and I knew quite well during our days at Amarillo Air Force Base. The first editor of the base newspaper on which Glenn and I were contributors, Sam Krieble was the typical grizzled career military man who spent more time sipping beer at the NCO Club than he did reading his Sunday School lesson. Even the hair that curled around his big ears was retained in the cartoon look-alike.

Designed to be ridiculous and funny, our new creation was an instant hit. The basic look never changed from the original cartoon, which consisted of a profile of a solemn Ol' Coach surrounded by 22 one-liner gags in the margins. Typical was a line that pointed to a towel on his right shoulder that said: "Towel for crying on or throwing in."

While the Ol' Coach was first limited to exposure in four or five cartoons annually in the Western and Southern state coaching directories, which Glenn and I published separately, he soon was to become a national celebrity. Early interest in this spokesman for the coaching industry soared, and we knew we had a winner.

The idea for the first of three Ol' Coach Jokebooks came along two years later, and that project gained the disheveled old jock instant national notoriety.

"A most felicitous brainstorm," wrote Herman Masin of Scholastic Coach magazine, the country's No. 1 monthly coaching periodical. "Several years ago the co-editors of this dandy little collection of coaches' anecdotes created a hugely amusing cartoon character called the 'Ol' Coach'. It achieved instant success wherever it appeared."

The review continued: "The Ol' Coach Jokebook contains 14 full-page Ol' Coach cartoons plus several hundred amusing anecdotes and one-liners.

The stories make very amusing reading as well as juicy fodder for public speaking chores. At three bucks for the lot, you can't go wrong."

Reviews also appeared in *Athletic Journal* and *Texas Coach* magazine, assuring its success. Five thousand copies were sold quickly, one to the late Paul "Bear" Bryant, then the legendary football coach at University of Alabama.

"Please send me one of those jokebooks I've been hearing so much about," he wrote. Enclosed was a personal check for three dollars, which was never cashed. It's still framed on my office wall.

Probably no coach in history has been the center of more humorous stories that the Bear, a hard-nosed, eccentric leader who produced winners at Kentucky, Texas A&M and Alabama. Mention his name at coaching conventions and somebody always has a new Bear joke to tell. At least eight or ten involving Bryant appear in our first jokebook.

Here's one of the funniest:

> *A mythical fishing expedition involves Coach Bear Bryant and his bitter rival at Auburn, Shug Jordan.*
>
> *The two men were in a small boat well out from shore when a storm blew up. The boat capsized. Bryant splashed around in the water frantically and finally had to be rescued by Jordan.*
>
> *"Listen, Shug," a water-logged and shame-faced Bryant said to his rival," I'd appreciate it if you wouldn't let it get out to my folks at home that I couldn't walk on water."*
>
> *"Okay, it's a deal," Jordan replied, "so long as you don't let my people know that I didn't let you drown."*

Bear Bryant portrayed that tough, hell-bent image in early years. Clark Jarnagin, former West Texas State football coach, told me about a time he was coaching under Bryant at North Carolina Pre-Flight School during World War II.

"Bear, myself and a couple other assistants went into a local restaurant for a bite to eat," remembered Clark. "Over in the corner, a jukebox was wailing away with a loud country and western tune that some customer had punched. Bear didn't like it, and told no one in particular 'to go pull the plug'! We all looked at each other. Finally, one of the assistants walked across the floor and snuffed out the raucous sound. Bear looked up with a wry grin, and continued reading the menu."

The legend of Bear Bryant lingers on long after his exploits on the sideline. Only recently it was announced a commemorative stamp

This cartoon started it all for the Ol' Coach.

portraying Bear will be part of a four-stamp series honoring collegiate and professional coaches. The stamp's final design will not be unveiled until 1997, but a preliminary version carries a head-and-shoulders profile of the Bear sporting his signature houndstooth hat. And being a coach who posted 323 wins and six national championships during his 37-year career, Bryant's head is ringed, halo-style, by a bright corona.

On the heels of success of the jokebooks came more new ventures. Glenn and I found an export company that made paper mache banks, and the Ol' Coach was developed into a seven-inch statue. There he stood with a clipboard in his hand, a whistle around his neck and a red cap on his head. Only one thing wrong, the banks were made in Japan and he wound up with squinty eyes. The coaching world loved them anyway and the order of 500 sold quickly. When we tried to get more, the price had skyrocketed and buying additional banks became prohibitive. Those who got in on the ground floor wound up with collectibles and we had to return orders and checks for several years.

And it didn't stop there. We took the Ol' Coach and developed new cartoons for large calendars that were sold to sporting goods companies. Names and phone numbers of the regional companies, along with a short advertising message, were imprinted on the wall calendars. They then were used for give-away promotions to school athletic departments.

Then along came Ol' Coach and Mrs. Ol' Coach stationery and 9x12 inch reprints of cartoons suitable for decorating office and den walls. After the run of 5,000 jokebooks was diminished, we got busy and put together a second edition in 1971. It was called the *New Ol' Coach Jokebook*. A third volume was produced ten years later, labeled the *Ol' Coach on the Banquet Circuit*. All new stories and all new cartoons, which reflects just how comedic this profession can be.

We took a little different approach on the first jokebook in 1967, as far as gathering material. We sent a letter to hundreds of coaches around the country asking for favorite stories. For each one submitted, we gave them a credit line at the bottom of the contribution and mailed them a free jokebook.

The response was impressive and many good stories ensued. One of my favorites came from Phil Woolpert, then basketball coach at U. of San Diego in California. I had met Phil, a gentle even-tempered man, back in 1955 when West Texas State played his undefeated national champion San Francisco Dons in the opening round of the NCAA Playoffs. His story involved one of the all-time greats on that team, 6-9 center Bill Russell. Here was his contribution:

In New York for the Holiday Festival several years ago, the U. of San Francisco basketball team decided to have a little Christmas celebration because the boys had missed Christmas at home.

At the conclusion of the dinner, Coach Phil Woolpert told the boys that each of them would receive a little gift in celebration of the holiday. With that, one of the guards raised his hand, and asked if the gift was going to be money.

Woolpert replied he wouldn't think of giving the team members "a gift as cold as money."

Quick as a flash, Bill Russell jumped up and exclaimed: "Freeze me, daddy, freeze me!"

After having been around for 30 years, the Ol' Coach is alive and well today and still a source of conversation in the athletic world. The response we have received over the years has been overwhelming and well diversified, to say the least. Copies of the third jokebook still enjoy steady sales. When Zulauf moved to Mena, Arkansas, a number of years ago, he sold his interest to me.

Long-time Philadelphia 76ers general manager Pat Williams, and now general manager of the Orlando Magic in the NBA, had this to say about the last compilation:

"I've been collecting good clean humor for 10 years. The third *Ol' Coach Jokebook* is one of the best sources I've ever read. It's must material for any serious humorist."

One of the most heart-warming testimonials came from Billy Sellers when he was at Randolph Southern School in Shellman, Georgia, a few years ago:

Dear Mr. Franks:

I have just finished reading your book, the Ol' Coach on the Banquet Circuit, and it would be an understatement to say I enjoyed it. Being a coach in a small Southwest Georgia farming community doesn't bring a lot of excitement, but this book that I received as a gift has made a long year seem almost worthwhile.

Several of the anecdotes mentioned in this book have occurred either to me or some of my coaching friends in the area. It's amazing to realize that what seems to be the worst of times, really, if one reflects on them, turns out to be comical.

Now there's a guy after my own heart. He accepted the exaggerated cartoon character in the right spirit, unlike the guy who thought it was "too grotesque". With all the peculiarities of the coaching business - pleasing alumni, spoon-feeding spoiled athletes and mollifying administration - how can anyone keep his or her sanity without light moments? It takes a special breed to handle all this pressure, and the Ol' Coach was designed to be someone who's the embodiment of all these characteristics.

One of my favorite cartoons penned by the master southpaw, Zulauf, has the Ol' Coach propped up in a hospital bed with his right leg in a cast and hanging from a ceiling pulley. His arms are also in casts and he has a depressed look on his face. The nurse is standing nearby reading a get-well card that says:

"It's from the athletic council . . . they wish you a speedy recovery, by a vote of 4 to 3."

One of the jokebooks got all the way to Bogota, Columbia, in the hands of an old high school friend, Earl Hanks, who has a travel agency there.

"I enjoyed reading your *Ol' Coach Jokebook* very much," wrote Earl. "And as I do a great deal of public speaking, I plan on blatantly plagiarizing your material without, of course, giving you any sort of credit at all."

Not all users of the Ol' Coach and his products have been as honest as Earl. Images of the Ol' Coach and specific cartoons have appeared in a number of places and on numerous products without permission. A few years ago when I attended the Texas High School Coaches Convention, the largest such conclave in the world, I saw a youngster coming toward me with a decal of the Ol' Coach on his white T-shirt. And while no court action has ever been initiated for improper use of a copyrighted product, it has been contemplated on more than one occasion.

On the other hand, most people are aware that the grand old jock of the sports world is a protected species. Only a couple months ago, I had a call from Bridget Sandquist, president of the Iowa Coaches Wives Association, requesting permission to use a cartoon of Mrs. Ol' Coach in their quarterly newsletter. The Ol' Coach's counterpart came onto the scene a year after her husband's classic premier cartoon. Like Ol' Coach, she is wearing a disheveled look on her face and a worn-out letter-sweater surrounded by 15 one-liners. Designed to portray the typical coach's wife, a critter of immense loyalty and endurance, the cartoon has for one prop a big black pot of beans with the following comment:

"Bottomless pot of beans . . . for that unpredictable meal and unexpected guests."

Yes, the Ol' Coach has been around the block a few times and has appeared in the best of neighborhoods. But I tend to think he might have

from the athletic council. . .they wish you a speedy recovery, by a vote of 4 to 3"

"Ya know, I still like to look, but I can't remember why"

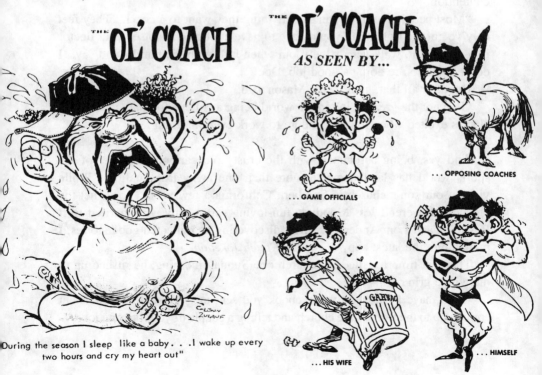

During the season I sleep like a baby. . . .I wake up every two hours and cry my heart out"

reached the zenith of public acclaim several years ago at the retirement roast of legendary football coach "Cactus Jack" Curtice. One of those characters who never lost his sense of humor, Curtice was a winner at West Texas State, U. of Utah, Stanford and UC-Santa Barbara.

One of the organizers of this testimonial dinner was Jim Campbell of All-American Sporting Goods in Santa Barbara, CA. Jim had seen a massive eight-foot square oil-cloth painting of the Ol' Coach at our booth at the National Sporting Goods Convention in Chicago, and asked for permission to borrow it.

"Jack is winding up 40 years of coaching," explained Campbell, "and I can't think of anyone who exemplifies your cartoon friend any better."

When we received newspaper clippings of the event, we were startled and delighted. There in the presence of such legendary sports figures as Lynn "Pappy" Waldorf of Northwestern, Clark Shaughnessy of Stanford and the Chicago Bears, Duffy Daugherty of Michigan State, Milt Bruhn of Wisconsin, John Ralston of Stanford and Paul Zimmerman of the Los Angeles Times appeared the Ol' Coach. His solemn puss, with cap, whistle and beady eyes, was placed on a curtain just behind the speaker's podium. He was the centerpiece of the affair, no doubt about it.

That coaching is a zany way of life is not questionable. Only recently, I read some quotes from Kansas football coach Glen Mason that verifies this contention.

"Most people feel they can say anything they want to a coach. They feel they've got the right. But you'd have to have a lot of guts to see your doctor in a restaurant, walk across the room when he's with his family, and say: I don't think you're doing a good job, Doc."

But after all that, guess what Mason said:

"I've got the greatest job in the world being a college football coach. I'm always excited when I get up and go to work every morning."

And yes, being associated with the crusty old cartoon character of the sports world has landed me in more than one awkward situation. While visiting our son's church in Southern California a few years ago, I met the preacher, Reverend Jess Moody, a fun-loving sort of guy who married Burt Reynolds and Loni Anderson. After discovering he collected good stories, I mailed him the latest copy of the *Ol' Coach Jokebook*.

The next time I visited his church one Sunday morning, he rushed up to me with a grin on his face.

"Man, have I enjoyed that jokebook you sent me," he said. "How about coming up to the front of the church and telling a couple of your favorite jokes?"

He was dead serious, and I was stunned. Sure, mini-skirts, short-shorts and tank tops are perfectly acceptable in church in wacky California, but I couldn't figure out any way to make Ol' Coach jokes compatible with the strains of "How Great Thou Art".

31

BASKETBALL FUN
IN THE SUN

"We would like to make you an offer you can't refuse," wrote Duane "Moose" Woltzen in June of 1989. "Let this memo serve as your official invitation to visit with us at the 4th annual Bahamas Goombay Shootout Basketball Tourney in Nassau, Jan. 1-8, 1990."

It took me about a New York minute to make a decision of acceptance. When I told my trusty traveling partner, wife Floy, she was half-packed when I got home for lunch. Several years earlier, we had taken a three-day mini-cruise to Freeport on Grand Bahama Island in the Caribbean. But this would be our first excursion to Nassau, the sleepy seaside resort 190 miles southeast of Miami and only 200 miles north of communist-infested Cuba.

The letter was my first personal contact with Woltzen in 16 years. This is the same guy who was knocked dizzy by a crazed Cuban basketballer wielding a folding chair during the U.S. - Cuban brawl at the 1973 World University Games in Moscow, Russia. At that time, Moose was athletic director and basketball coach at Lakeland College in Sheboygan, Wisconsin. In Russia, he was serving as team manager for the men's basketball team.

Now Moose was out of coaching and co-owner with another former coach, Lee Frederick, of Sport Tours International in Milwaukee.

"When you consider that a large majority of your listings in the *National Directory of College Athletics* are Division III and NAIA schools, covering this event for your yearly pictorial might make a lot of sense," wrote Woltzen. His reasoning was sound, so much so that we did feature this unique athletic event in the ensuing 1990-91 Directory. So what if Blackbeard, the pirate, and James Bond had been there before us.

With my Minolta SRT camera and a bag full of film, we left Amarillo for

Miami on New Year's Day. Giving up the football bowl games would be a small sacrifice for a week on an island paradise that attracts four million tourists yearly.

When we approached BahamasAir in Miami for our connecting flight to Nassau, we quickly found out it was going to be a different kind of week. Lester, the clerk on duty, took our ticket coupons but didn't offer boarding passes in return.

"You don't need a boarding pass," he explained, and pointing directly toward me added:

"You will be 2-B and your wife 2-C." That was it, verbal boarding passes. We later learned a favorite expression around travel agencies goes like this:

"If you have time to spare, fly BahamasAir!"

With that kind of start, who could argue that a week in balmy Nassau would be one of the most laid-back times in our life. Coaches, players, relatives and fans all fell into a slow-motion pattern too when they congregated on New Providence Island for the fourth annual Goombay Shootout the first week of the new decade.

"Don't get in a hurry," warned tournament officials at the opening meeting. "This is the most on-time we'll be the entire week."

As the week progressed, the prediction proved to be an astute one. Schedules weren't worth the paper they were printed on but as mainland visitors started enjoying the 85-degree tropical climate and blending into the relaxed lifestyle of the Caribbean, no one really cared. They call it a basketball tournament but it's more like a happening. Oh sure, they keep scorebooks, assemble statistics and declare champions, but all that seems almost incidental to the total picture.

At this particular tournament, Sports Tours co-owner Lee Frederick told the 150 players at the initial briefing:

"We will play 24 games in six days, and you will be sunning on the beaches, para-sailing on Paradise Beach, skin diving in the Caribbean, sightseeing the island, gambling in the casinos, dancing at Peanut Taylors, and maybe . . . just maybe you might make some new friends."

He added that 13 visiting teams had come to Nassau, but by the third day there would be only one. "This is a great atmosphere for making friends, and in all probability will be the greatest week of your life."

Frederick, a tall, handsome ex-jock, went so far as to label it "the best basketball tournament in the world." It's the only competition that stages both men's and women's play simultaneously in the same gymnasium, a strong attribute.

Here's how it works. In the 1990 classic, six women's teams and seven men's squads from 10 U.S. states and Canada joined clubs from the Bahamas to make up two eight-team fields. Four games a day were played for an entire week until champions were crowned, leaving adequate time to discover the diversified attractions that make the Bahamas a special vacation spot for world travelers.

The names of the participating teams aren't likely to turn many heads. You won't find Bobby Knight, Dean Smith and high profile colleges like Indiana and North Carolina at this tournament. Despite the lustre of a tropical island setting, it attracts the lesser-knowns like DePauw, Dubuque, Holy Family, Judson, Defiance and Doane for a very good reason. They must pay their own way.

That's right. Airfare, meals, hotel everything. In an age where college athletics is considered big business and athletes are spoon-fed, (and many want to be paid like professionals), it seems incredulous that players will foot their own costs while playing for good ol' Columbia Union.

Not only that but four of the teams were NCAA Division III and offer no scholarship aid to players. The balance belong to the NAIA, where some help is available at most membership schools. Interestingly, it was two scholarship schools—Oklahoma Baptist and Simon Fraser—that won the men's and women's championships.

The need for travel funds seems to stir the creative juices of most teams. University of Dubuque, who along with Oklahoma Baptist brought both their men's and women's teams, conducted raffles, painted houses, cut lawns and staged pizza parties. Those who sold raffle tickets were given a free ride and those who didn't had to come up with $150. Total cost of the trip for each member of the Dubuque contingent was $800.

Oklahoma Baptist sponsored a school-wide golf tournament to help raise money but surely the most unique plan was formulated at little Judson College, the Elgin, Illinois, school with only 600 enrollment. Prior to the Fourth of July, Coach JoDee Rigel and four other players drove several hundred miles to a small town in Tennessee, where for 10 days they sold firecrackers. It was necessary for them to stay in a tent 24 hours a day, sleeping there after closing for business. The Judson men's team was there also trying to raise money, and all of them rented one hotel room, where they took turns showering and changing clothes. "An ordeal," sighed one of the players, but the effort netted about $3,000.

Why would 13 college basketball teams give up eight days post-Christmas vacation and pay their own way to play in a tournament?

"The greatest education in the world," believes Dubuque men's coach Jon

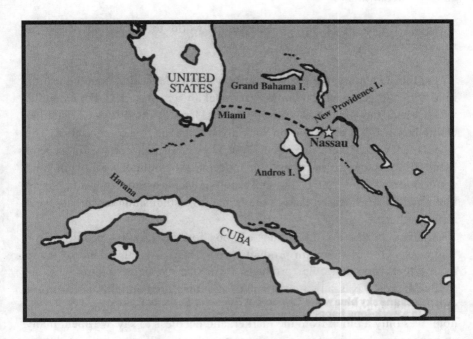

Only a short plane ride from Miami, Nassau is a favorite stop for cruise ships from all over the world. At the Goombay, collegians took advantage of the many water activities.

Davison. "I've long been a believer in world travel and its values in broadening young people."

On this adventure, the Franks family was afforded a first-hand education in history and geography, a bonus that travel always provides. For example, we learned the Bahamas were the first land sighted by Christopher Columbus in 1492, and it was on San Salvador that he first came ashore. The islands, of which there are about 700, were a British colony for several hundred years before becoming an independent commonwealth not long ago. During World War II, the Duke of Windsor was governor and during that time, the U.S. leased land in the Bahamas, establishing naval bases and airfields there.

Tourism is the No. 1 supplier of jobs for the 150,000 people in the Bahamas. One of the main products grown here is sisal, a kind of hemp from which rope and other products are made. Which explains why the Straw Market is Nassau's most popular shopping area and the first stop for tourists pouring off the steady stream of cruise ships docking nearby. Our hotel was only a block from the market, and needless to say, we spent many an hour there shopping for souvenirs to take back to Texas. An incredulous sight was watching native men and women balancing huge baskets of fruit and produce on their heads as they weaved their way along the market paths.

Also at the Straw Market, native girl hairdressers set up shop with a chair, mirror and a comb. We found out braided hair was "in" among college students and several of the female basketballers got the treatment. The going price was $2 a braid, which sounded cheap to me considering the time involved.

While the Franks twosome was content to lounge around the beach and watch the cruise ships come and go, the American basketballers used the inviting facilities for a Fort Lauderdale experience in the Caribbean. Nearly every waking minute, except for their time in the gym, was spent on the beach fronting the British Colonial Hotel, a Nassau landmark that served as our home away from home.

Because of the many attractions and distractions in and around the island, coaches were liberal with curfews and training rules. Coral World, Botanic Gardens, Straw Market, Bay Street, snorkeling and skin diving all got some of the action but the No. 1 scene for hanging out was the private white-sand beach of our hotel.

Nassau abounds in historical lore and the stately old British Colonial is located on the exact spot where much of it transpired. Fort Nassau, built in

1697 as headquarters for British colonial troops, once stood on the present site of the seaside hotel. The tropical atmosphere of the Bahamas also appealed to swashbuckling pirates between assaults on Spanish galleons carrying gold and silver from the New World to Spain. The most famous of them all, Edward "Blackbeard" Teach, took old Fort Nassau as his residence in the 1700s. When the fort later fell in disrepair, it was torn down and the first "Hotel Colonial" was constructed in 1899. Fire destroyed it in 1921 and the current facility was built back a year later.

Many tales are spun about the cutthroat pirates, treasure-laden ships, the American Revolutionary War and prohibition. And yes, the hotel and surrounding locations of New Providence Island provided a romantic setting for a James Bond movie. At the pier in back of the hotel is an encased one-sheet poster telling the world that the 1983 movie, "Never Say Never Again", was shot on location there. That landmark served as a backdrop for a lot of picture-taking for the 150 U.S. college athletes.

"Sean Connery, Kim Basinger and the entire crew stayed at the hotel," related sales manager Andre Newbold, himself a former middle distance runner at TCU. "Many scenes were shot on the beach, at the pier and on nearby Bay Street. I believe all the underwater scenes were filmed in the area."

Taking full advantage of its romantic past, the hotel has named one of its restaurants "Blackbeard's Forge" and one of its lounges "Never Say Never Again Gazebo Bar."

Working closely with Sport Tours are the Bahamas Amateur Basketball Association and the Bahamas Ministry of Tourism. The basketball group sells all-tournament tickets for $15 and all the proceeds benefit the country's entire basketball program, one of the Bahamas' most popular activities for all ages.

The '90 tournament brought to Nassau nearly 400 people, including coaches, players, referees, relatives and fans. At the opening reception New Year's night, a member of the tourism committee remarked: "Aren't you glad you're in Nassau tonight where it's 72 degrees. I just checked and it's 22 in Chicago and 28 in Milwaukee at this very minute."

"What a great excuse to visit Nassau in January," opined a mother of one of the Holy Family players who was retreating from the mid-winter chills of Philadelphia.

The Shootout reflected a definite international flavor. The Bahamians, who are strong in international competition, furnished three local teams and Canada sent a powerful women's team from Simon Fraser University of the

British Columbia province. At the get-acquainted party, three national anthems were sung, representing the U.S., Bahamas and Canada.

Of the 13 visiting teams, Simon Fraser had the distinction of making the longest trip. Traveling almost 4,000 miles and nearly 24 hours, the clan drove from Burnaby, B.C. to Seattle, then flew to Nassau by way of Atlanta.

The chief honcho of the tournament, Lee Frederick, would appear to have an enviable job during times like these. But it's not all fun and games. For example, Lee and three other staff members arrived in Nassau four days prior to the start of the event, spending most of that time cleaning the modest D.W. Davis High School gym, repairing leaks and handling last-minute details. During the tournament, Frederick and co-workers even took turns wiping perspiration spots off the floor and mopping between games.

A typical problem occurred during the men's semi-final game involving Catawba and Oklahoma Baptist. With 15 minutes remaining in a tight ball games, a bank of lights went out on the OBU end of the court. When it was determined they couldn't be repaired immediately, a similar group of lights was cut off at the other end, and play continued. Leaking roofs have been a common problem in the past but there was no rain this time.

While sitting on the hotel's back patio sipping ice tea one afternoon, Lee shared some of the interesting experiences of past promotions.

"Once in Dominique," grinned Lee, "we were sponsoring a college all-star game on an outdoor court. It just got underway when rain started pelting down. It kept getting harder and harder and I kept thinking officials would stop the game at any time. Even Prime Minister Eugenia Charles was on hand and the place was packed. Players were getting soaked, fans were drenched but the game continued until the very end."

One of the island's sports leaders approached Frederick. "One of the greatest games we've ever had here," he effused while wiping the accumulated moisture from his brow.

Another humorous incident happened in Jamaica, again on an outdoor court. Two U.S. all-star teams had been warned to bring an adequate supply of basketballs but only one was on the court when warm-ups started. Both teams proceeded to practice with the one ball before a backboard shot hit a protruding nail and just stuck. It was flat in seconds and a good two hours were exhausted before another ball was found and play resumed. Jamaica, like many other Caribbean islands, is scarce in basic athletic equipment and welcomes visiting Americans who often leave shoes and balls behind when they return home.

Players, coaches and officials all gather on the beach for this classic group picture.

Actually, the Goombay Shootout—one of Sport Tours International's best Caribbean promotions—is an accident. It's the outgrowth of a tournament that had been played in Curacao, an island in the Netherland Antilles near Venezuela. Eastern Airlines was involved as the main carrier to the tiny island until its financial nosedive threw storm clouds over the event. There were other factors too.

Officials started looking elsewhere and stumbled upon Nassau. It was a good marriage from the beginning, giving the sponsors a profitable bread-and-butter promotion and bringing thousands of tourist dollars annually to the Bahamas. "They're great people, friendly and accommodating," say Sport Tours representatives.

Likewise, the formation of Sport Tours is something of a freak. As basketball coaches in the college ranks—Frederick at Oakland University in Michigan and Woltzen at Lakeland in Wisconsin—they frequently took teams on trips out of the country.

"Hey, how do you go about doing that?" was a frequent question from fellow coaches. It was then that Frederick and Woltzen realized a need existed for sports travel managers. They opened for business in '84, and they're still going strong, including the annual Goombay Shootout every January.

After a week in paradise, some 150 collegians reluctantly prepared for the return home, suntanned and relaxed despite having played three games in seven days. "A tournament like this brings teams and players together in an unusual way," remarked Kim Bishop, a member of the Oklahoma Baptist women's squad. "We played and beat DePauw in the opening round game. The very next day all the players from both teams were running around together."

Long after the scores of the games and the names of the tournament champions have faded into obscurity, fond memories of the Bahamas linger on. Who can soon forget the pulsating sounds of the disco music wafting long into the night, the pungent smell of fried conch and the lapping, gentle waves on pristine white beaches?

Oh yes, the tournament. Oklahoma Baptist defeated Defiance College, 85-66, for the men's title, and Simon Fraser easily handled the OBU women's squad, 77-46, in the other championship battle.

As if anyone really cared.

32

UNCONVENTIONAL CONVENTIONS

Many of them former coaches, college athletic directors represent an exceptional group of people. Then it comes as no surprise that they know how to stage exceptional conventions.

From the time we linked up with NACDA, those of us at the Publishing Ranch were treated as family. And that included being invited to their two big conventions yearly—the main event in June and a spring affair called the "Facilities and Fund-Raising Clinic." Smart opportunists, the AD's for years staged the latter conclave concurrently with NCAA's Final Four basketball tournament. We rarely missed either event.

It's easy to see why. While a heavy schedule of business and educational programs is conducted at the granddaddy affair, athletic directors choose their sites carefully. For years they have been alternating between Florida (usually marvelous Marco Island) and West Coast resorts, making sure golf courses and tennis courts are close by. Then consider almost every meal at the four-day affair is complimentary, thanks to businesses trying to get the attention of the people who control athletic department purse strings.

And the speakers. My goodness, it's like a Who's Who of the sports world. A former Michigan football star better known for his career in politics, then U.S. Representative Gerald Ford addressed the first convention in 1967. I later heard President Ford speak at a Holiday Bowl luncheon in San Diego, and he delivered a Bob Hope joke that's worth repeating. For years, the president and Hope were golfing buddies around Palm Springs.

"You know the president had a good golf game the other day," Hope told a national audience on his Tonight Show. "He had an eagle, a birdie, an elk, a moose and finally a Mason."

Son Randy and I attended the next NACDA event in Cleveland, where we got to meet the great Jesse Owens, star of the 1936 Olympics and at that time head of a public relations firm. Of all the photo opportunities I've blown, this might have been the biggest.

Then along came such luminaries as Pete Rozelle, commissioner of the NFL; Bud Wilkinson, ex-Oklahoma University coach; Roone Arledge, president of ABC Sports; and a slew of famous sportscasters, including Bob Costas, Frank Gifford, Keith Jackson, Curt Gowdy, Jim Simpson and Charlie Jones.

Peter Ueberroth offered a different touch. Unknown as a travel agency executive until 1984, he's the guy who exercised daring entrepreneurial techniques to make a silk purse out of a sow's ear at the Los Angeles Olympics. Naturally, I perked up my business ears when he moved toward the podium.

When prolific and best-selling author James Michener addressed the athletic directors in 1981, I turned to Floy and asked: "What's this guy doing at a sports convention?"

"There's not a bigger sports fan in America than James Michener," said the tall, elderly legend of the writing world. When I approached the speaker's dais after his address, he revealed he was once a sportswriter and still follows today's sports events in the morning newspaper. "I loved writing sports," he explained, "but writing books pays just a little bit better."

But my favorite convention speaker in more than two decades was a most unlikely individual. Most of us entered the grand ballroom of Marco Island's Marriott Hotel hoping the meal would be sufficient to make up for a boring speaker. After all, maverick New York Yankee owner George Steinbrenner had done little to stir my interest.

What a surprise, and his 20-minute speech was a gem. Talking off the cuff and mixing choice stories with serious material, Steinbrenner said all the right things.

"When they called me several months ago about this," he related, "I was asked if I believe in free speech."

"Certainly," he answered.

"Then, you're going to make one in Florida at the NACDA meeting," said Pete Carlesimo, former college AD and Executive Director of the NIT.

His burning desire for winning was touched. "Winning isn't everything to me . . . it's second to breathing."

Then he got serious. "With all this country's great resources and technology, do you know what our greatest asset is?" he asked. "Our young people! Forget about the crumby two percent that get all the headlines.

Conventions bring out all the celebrities.
David with announcer Curt Gowdy.

I met Kareem Abdul Jabbar at a sporting goods
convention in the Astrodome.

And yes, O.J. Simpson poses for a picture long before he became the center of newscasts. People
always ask "who's the guy on the left?" I have no idea.

Let's back the 98 percent who will be tomorrow's leaders."

His pep talk was infectious, and athletic directors who had hung up their whistles years ago were bursting out of the room with renewed enthusiasm.

Before catching a plane back to New York to minister to the floundering Yankees, Steinbrenner passed a bulletin board jammed with announcements relative to the convention. Penned in large felt-tip lettering for all to see was:

"George S . . . Call Yogi!"

I mentioned earlier that our family was treated as NACDA family.

Laid-back Executive Director Mike Cleary, who normally locked himself in a hotel suite and orchestrated the convention with the expertise of a talented conductor, made sure we had table top space or a booth in the exhibit area. From that vantage point, we could gather advertising and late coaching changes.

In the early days, always reliable Marion Bier and Marge Fieber, on loan from the NCAA, helped us learn the ropes. Better friends we could not have found. Then later, it was Tim Gleason, Alice Belt and Dorothy Sikkila who came along to help make the conventions run like clockwork.

I didn't see Cleary much in our 23-year relationship with NACDA. Our dealings were mainly long-distance, impersonal but effective. The same was true at conventions.

"Sorry we didn't have more time to visit at the convention," he told me once. "I thought ours was a good marriage from the beginning, and nothing has happened to change my mind."

As with most conventions, renewing acquaintances with old friends is one of the more delightful side benefits. In 23 years, we met a lot of special people among college athletic directors and exhibiting advertisers, but one family stands out above all.

"Hey, hey, let me help you carry in that display," was a booming cynical comment I would hear coming from across the room as we arrived in the exhibit area of NACDA conventions. Because of the nature of our business, I would usually be carrying a briefcase filled with advertising brochures and a rolled-up sign under my arm. Ours was a simple exhibit.

The voice always belonged to Roald Sorensen, a stocky, middle-aged North Carolinian with a dry sense of humor. He kidded me about our skimpy exhibit because it required hours of huffing and puffing to get his heavy, cumbersome basketball equipment set up in his booth. Roald took a couple of basketball-related inventions, developed them and created a world-wide business. First it was a rebounding practice product, called "McCall's

The Chicago Cubs' great Ernie Banks visits with the Directory publisher.

Friends Roald and Lowrey (his daughter) Sorensen chat with Floy at NACDA convention.

It's not what you think. My wife did sing at Caesars Palace in Las Vegas, but at a breakfast for Fellowship of Christian Athletes.

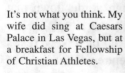

Rebounder", a staple item in every junior high, high school and college program. Then he came along with "Hydra-Rib", the first hydraulic basketball goal that now is found in all major arenas in America and the world. Entrepreneurship at its best!

Also a former college public relations director and state directory publisher, Roald and I hit it off from the start. With wife Maurine and children Drew and Lowrey, they regularly took the Franks family on side excursions at the close of conventions. We flew to the shows and the Sorensens necessarily drove a van to handle their bulky equipment. That was another source of good-natured kidding.

The social excursions involving our two families never lacked for excitement. After one Miami convention, they wanted to show us the Florida Keys. We had never been there, and the 150-mile drive down Highway One, flanked on one side by the Atlantic Ocean and the other by the Gulf of Mexico, was awesome. After touring Ernest Hemingway's home in Key West and getting our first taste of Key lime pie, we had a near catastrophe on the return. Never much of a clock-watcher, Roald was told the Franks had only 40 minutes to catch a plane at Miami International Airport. We were 30 miles away. He floor-boarded that van, launching the wives into near-hysteria, and pulled up to our terminal with five minutes to spare.

On another occasion, the Sorensens pulled a Hydra-Rib on a flat-bed trailer cross country all the way from Raleigh, North Carolina, to a convention in San Diego, California. Crossing the wide-open spaces of New Mexico, a dirt devil caught the van blind-side, flipping it over into the grassy median—trailer, Hydra-Rib and all.

Undaunted by the accident, Roald insisted we borrow chairs from our motel rooms, load them into the banged-up van and make a side trip to nearby Tijuana, Mexico, at the close of the convention. A fearless driver, Roald got us lost in the back alleys looking for a pottery store. We hit pot holes big enough to bury a 747, winding up in parts of the rough border town that should have been off limits to Americanos. And probably were.

After a long bout with a rare respiratory disease, Roald died New Year's Day, 1996. But the legacy of a dear friend and daring entrepreneur lives on as long as those "Hydra-Rib" logos keep popping up on close-up backboard shots during televised basketball games.

33

FINAL FOUR ECSTASY

Conservative sportscaster Brent Musburger refers to it as "March Madness". Dick Vitale tags it "the big dance, baby". I call it pure ecstasy.

I'm speaking of the Final Four, the label that's been attached to the NCAA Division I Basketball Championship, and the premier sporting event in the world. At least, in my opinion.

In addition to their premier convention each June, members of the college athletic directors association stage smaller specialized clinics. For years, one called the Facilities and Fund-Raising Clinic was held concurrently with the Final Four, and for obvious reasons.

Maybe the toughest ticket in all of sports, the tournament made tickets available (for face value) to members of NACDA. And since the Franks had the same opportunity, we took in eight of them.

Television does a superb job covering sports today, but there's an element at the Final Four that can't be captured by the camera lens. Maybe it's the pre-game activity outside the arena or the excitement that abounds in hotel lobbies. Whatever it is, the charisma has been building ever since Larry Bird, Magic Johnson and Michael Jordan came onto the scene in the late 70s.

"The Final Four symbolizes the Great American Dream," long-time NCAA Executive Director Walter Byers once uttered. Amarillo News Sports Editor Jon Mark Beilue summed it up this way:

"March Madness embodies just about everything that makes sports so fascinating. You like drama, it's there. You like the underdog overcoming the odds, it's there. You like controversy, it's there. You like a quick conclusion to the playoffs—it begins and ends before you know it."

A rebel at heart, I find myself pulling for almost every underdog when the 64-team bracket starts competition in early March. Who in the world would give unknown Eastern Michigan a chance against perennial power

Duke or Ivy Leaguer Princeton a reasonable shot at defending champion UCLA? And what about little Drexel, a college that sounds more like a drugstore, in its game with mighty Memphis State. Of course, you know what happened. Every one of those underdogs sprung the big upset in 1996's opening round, just as the Davids of college basketball have been doing for years.

The first Final Four I was privileged to see was at all places, the Houston Astrodome. It was 1971 and the first time for NCAA officials to venture into one of those spacious covered complexes that are common-place hosts these days. Unlike today, tickets were not that tough to come by so five friends and I made the trip as a group.

"It was a spectacular setting," remembers lawyer friend George Dowlen, "but I felt like I was a mile away from the action. Another thing that comes to mind was the outstanding play of that Villanova player who dominated against a team that's produced the likes of Bill Walton, Lew Alcindor, Sidney Wicks and Walt Hazard." Incidentally, a home-grown Texan with a slow drawl, George later was the presiding judge of the famous and controversial Cullen Davis murder trial that was moved from Fort Worth to Amarillo in 1977.

I had seen baseball played in the Astrodome prior to this trip, and it struck me as being better suited to the configuration of the world's first dome. The trend is leaning toward more and more dome settings for this premium sports event, obviously to give more people an opportunity to attend and increase gross receipts. But after packing in 20,000 around the playing area, I find those additional seats not to my liking. Even with binoculars, it's a stretch.

In this history-making setting, 45,000 spectators showed up to see Johnny Wooden—coached UCLA win its seventh title in eight years. The Bruins defeated a feisty Villanova team suited out in black shoes, 68-62. Villanova's second-place finish was later dotted with an asterisk in the record books when the tournament's most valuable player, Howard Porter, was deemed ineligible.

The next Final Four I attended was 1983 when the famous basketball fraternity of Phi Slama Jama was reaping most of the sports page headlines. The doctors of dunk from University of Houston, featuring the great Nigerian, Akeem Olajuwon, were odds-on favorites to take it all in Albuquerque's Pit. Tickets were hard to find but NACDA's simultaneous Facilities Clinic in the Duke city made it possible for me to come up with four tickets. Daughter Debbie and son-in-law Tim Sharp, who live in the beautiful New Mexico metropolis, were delighted.

Fans who were there and those who witnessed on television will never forget the finish, the most repeated highlight in NCAA basketball history. Sure you remember. In the second half, Coach Guy Lewis put a governor on Houston's run-and-gun game, trying to run off some clock. But the strategy back-fired. Out-manned North Carolina State got the ball for a last shot with the score tied at 52. With only a few seconds left, Dereck Whittenberg let fly an off-balance shot that fell short of the basket. Just as everyone was anticipating overtime, sophomore Lorenzo Charles of the Wolfpack grabbed the errant air ball and stuffed it home at the buzzer. The 18,000 fans jammed in the Pit went bonkers, but not nearly as wild as State coach Jim Valvano, who jumped around the floor like a kangaroo with a craw full of hot picante sauce.

Having been around sports all my adult life, memorable moments have been plentiful. However, I can't remember any that tops this one.

Everyone gave Albuquerque high marks for hosting a great tournament but local officials knew it would be its first and last Final Four. While the Pit was a perfect setting for the tournament, with its close-up seating arrangement, escalating interest in the Final Four proved to be a crunch for a city of 400,000. Some visitors had to commute to Grants, New Mexico, 70 miles away, to find motel facilities.

The next Final Four, two years later, is one I'll never forget. It may not go down in history with Roy Riegels' wrong-way run in the 1929 Rose Bowl, but I made a catastrophic decision on April Fool's Day, 1985.

Here I was in Lexington, Kentucky, with the wife and two tickets to the NCAA championship basketball game between Villanova and Georgetown. The question was: "To go or not to go?"

We had been among the 23,135 fans who jammed Rupp Arena for Saturday's semi-final round. The following day we exhibited at NACDA's Southeast Facility and Fund-Raising Clinic at the Continental Inn.

"The two best teams met Saturday, when Georgetown easily handled St. John's 77-59," I reasoned. "What chance does a team like Villanova with a 24-10 record have against Pat Ewing and his big bullies in the finals?"

The decision was made to leave Lexington early Monday morning and get a head-start back to Texas. Thirteen hours later it was time to pull into the Holiday Inn at Russellville, Arkansas; open a bag of mustard Whoppers, french fries and Dr. Pepper; and watch the championship "mismatch" on television.

The rest is history. Not only did we miss witnessing in person one of the most dramatic upsets in college history but Coach Rollie Massimino masterminded a near-perfect game plan. It took equally brilliant execution by the Wildcats to pull off the 66-64 upset.

There's another way of looking at the big blunder, though. By watching the game on TV, we were part of the biggest audience ever to see a college basketball game on CBS.

A year later, I stayed for the finals and saw Denny Crum and his Louisville Cardinals edge out Duke, 72-69, in a thriller at Dallas' Reunion Arena. In 1988, it was time to celebrate the NCAA's 50th anniversary tournament on the association's home turf, Kansas City. It was an unusual finale as Kansas, led by Danny Manning, notched Oklahoma, 83-79, in all-Big Eight title game. Emblazoned across a fan's back at the tournament was a bumper sticker that read: "64-62=Big Eight". In case you forgot, there were 64 teams that started the tourney.

It was on to Seattle and the Kingdome in '89. I remember watching Dick Vitale draw huge crowds in a downtown mall with his periodic remotes for ESPN right up until game time. "Shoot the rock, diaper dandies" and all that Vitale jargon could be heard as he entertained thousands. No doubt, the basketball talkaholic loves his work and fans come out in droves wherever he appears.

This tournament had its strange twist too. Big Ten champion Michigan was getting a lot of attention because it was being coached by all people, an assistant by the name of Steve Fisher. It happened this way. After guiding the Wolverines to the conference crown, head coach Bill Frieder announced he was moving west to take the job at Arizona State. No doubt he assumed he would be allowed to guide his team in tournament play.

"That's it," announced disgruntled Michigan athletic director Bo Schembechler, who's a smoldering volcano even when things are going well. "We want a Michigan man coaching a Michigan team," he said and tossed the ball to Frieder's quiet and unassuming assistant, Fisher. With little time to get nervous, Fisher and his team waded through four opponents and made it to Seattle. Then, with a torrential rainstorm raging outside, the amazing Wolverines pulled a heart-stopping 80-79 overtime victory against P.J. Carlesimo's talented Seton Hall Pirates. What a Cinderella story.

We had heard so much about the sights around Seattle, and a previous convention visit didn't allow for free time. However, after scheduling a boat trip to Vancouver and a day in British Columbia, it had to be scrubbed. This was spring in the Northwest, and it rained from the day we arrived until we left.

In Denver, a year later, there were no surprises. For years at odds with the NCAA, grizzled Jerry Tarkanian led his Nevada-Las Vegas team to an easy

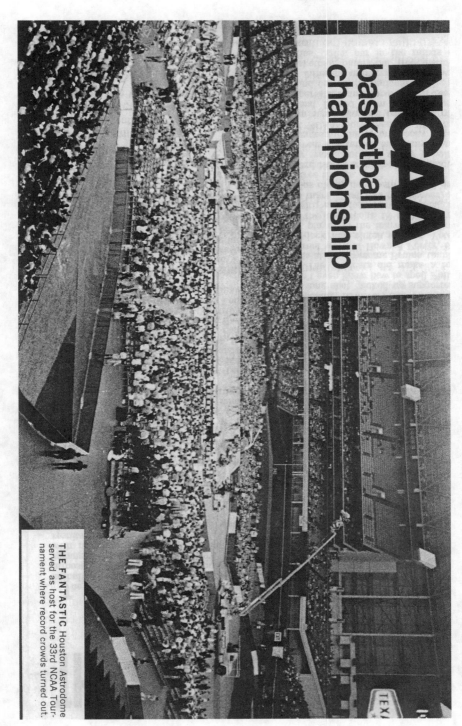

NCAA basketball championship

THE FANTASTIC Houston Astrodome served as host for the 33rd NCAA Tournament where record crowds turned out.

103-73 win over Duke. It was the activity outside 17,000-seat McNichols Arena that created the most excitement.

Because of the size of the arena, ticket scalping was at an all-time high. Of the eight Final Fours I've attended, this was the toughest ticket. Scalping is illegal in Colorado but that didn't stop the action. As we walked through the parking lot for the semi-final games Saturday afternoon, son David and his friend, Byron Beall, were approached by a Denver businessman and an out-of-town acquaintance.

"Boys, you interested in selling your tickets?" queried one of the men. Even though they knew scalping wasn't kosher, these guys wanted tickets so badly they pulled out 20 one-hundred-dollar bills in broad daylight. They offered it to the boys for two tournament tickets.

"I've never seen that many hundred dollar bills in my life," said bug-eyed Byron. For a couple of young married guys who always need an extra buck, $2000 in cash was tempting.

My last Final Four was Indianapolis in 1991. Even though the big domes will be used exclusively in the future, tickets are getting more scarce for groups. It was inevitable that NACDA's annual allotment for attendees to its Facilities Clinic would dry up. When that happened, the yearly convention was moved to another time and another place. With it went my opportunity to get tickets to the greatest show on earth.

While Duke defeated Kansas, 72-65, in an uneventful finale, the fireworks came in the semi-final round on Saturday. Normally cool, even-tempered Dean Smith, long-time successful coach at North Carolina, got tossed out of his team's semi-final game with Kansas. The Tarheels were not performing well and he picked up his first technical midway of the second half. After a spirited exchange, he got the second "T", which translates to automatic expulsion in the college game.

34

ALL-TIME HERO— SARAH THOMPSON

They say there aren't as many heroes today for young people to idolize. With big bucks spoiling many professional athletes and our country wallowing in moral decay, that's probably true.

However, I've found one. Her story will make the hair stand up on the back of your neck. I heard it from Joe Dean, personable and energetic athletic director at LSU, the same guy who introduced the term "string music" to listeners of his radio basketball broadcasts. I heard it at a Fellowship of Christian Athletes breakfast at a college athletic directors convention a few years ago.

Looking for a way to show our appreciation to college ADs for being loyal purchasers of the National Directory of College Athletics, our company sponsored the FCA breakfast at annual NACDA conventions for six years. We tried to find speakers who would inspire the 150 to 200 college officials who showed up each year.

One time it was Bill Curry, current football coach at Kentucky. Then I remember Jim Garner, former athletic director at Appalachian State and Oklahoma State, delivering a stirring spiritual message. And who could ever forget that personal testimony of Archie Griffin, two-time Heisman Trophy winner at Ohio State. At 5-7 and 180 pounds, he overcame great odds to reach the zenith of college football, all the time remaining levelheaded, resisting temptation and maintaining a strong Christian witness.

But Joe Dean's message was a zinger, almost unbelievable.

The story involves Sarah Thompson, a loyal LSU fan who lives in Shreveport. "She's about 14 now," Joe told me recently. "She's beginning to wear a little lipstick."

About six years ago, when she was eight, Sarah wanted to learn how toswim. I mean really badly. She got out there most every day, working hard and applying all the principles she'd been taught.

With her parents watching and encouraging, she stayed with it. But it was hard for her, really difficult. It seemed at times she was making progress, then at times nothing. No doubt at some point, she would liked to have thrown in the towel. But, you see, that would have been impossible. Sarah has no arms. And only one leg.

"She's a remarkable young lady with a wonderful Christian spirit," said Joe. "She stayed with it and learned how to swim, living out one of the gutsiest stories I've ever heard. A pretty girl with a wonderful mind, she was born with an abnormal amount of deformities. Her arms never came out of their sockets."

Sarah and her family are huge LSU fans. "I invited her to come and sit in my box at one of the football games," related Joe, "but she prefers to be down in the handicap area. Down there she's closer to the players when they come out on the field."

Better watch out, Joe. Spunky Sarah, who has endured 23 surgeries so far, may be trying to get out there on the field and kick field goals with that one leg.

35

MEETING THE PRESIDENT ... WELL, ALMOST

The story of our long and amiable relationship with Fellowship of Christian Athletes wouldn't be complete without telling you about a wacky weekend in the summer of 1990.

"Will you join me and several top FCA supporters at a special Rose Garden meeting with President Bush on Friday, June 3?" This eye-popping paragraph was the start of a letter we received from Dick Abel, President of FCA, two months earlier.

We started looking at the calendar and the timing was perfect. We were scheduled to be at the annual convention of college athletic directors in Florida on the 10th, and this would be a nice stopover on the way down there. Besides that, how many times do you have a chance to meet the President of the United States?

For a donation to FCA, a fine organization with an outstanding track record, a star-studded weekend had been lined up for 300 supporters. Included were accommodations at the quaint and elegant Mayflower Hotel, just a stone's throw from the White House.

"In addition to our meeting with the President and other senior administrative officials, you'll also enjoy a private tour of the White House," continued the juicy details in Dick's invitation. "Then on Saturday morning, you will be guests at a brunch and tennis exhibition at the home of Vice President Dan Quayle." It was getting better all the time.

Combined with other special dinners and programs, topped off with worship services at recently renovated Washington National Cathedral on Sunday, it had all the ingredients of a dream weekend. Our letter of acceptance was in the mail pronto and my wife dashed out the front door to get her a new wardrobe of clothes.

On June 4, three days before leaving for Washington, came the first hint that there was trouble in River City, and maybe the special weekend might get watered down.

"Due to last minute changes, President will not be present at White House briefing," reported a Western Union mailgram from Dick Abel. "White House has invited us to arrival ceremony on South Lawn when President returns Sunday afternoon at 3 p.m."

We changed our plans to be on the South Lawn for the delayed meeting with President Bush, and at the briefing Friday morning, Vice President Quayle filled the gap. However, it was in the briefing room of the Old Executive Office Building, not on the White House lawn.

Oh yes, another gentleman appeared at the Friday briefing who later would be in the center of everyone's newscasts, a guy by the name of Kenneth Starr. At that time, the current independent investigator of the Whitewater scandal was a member of the Office of the Solicitor General in the U.S. Department of Justice.

Saturday morning came and our private tour of the White House was canceled. No reason was offered. Then two hours later, the scheduled brunch at the Vice President and Mrs. Quayle's home was axed. No explanation again.

The dinner program that evening featuring Jeannette Clift George did proceed on schedule and the bus ride to Washington National Cathedral Sunday morning was fulfilled.

Just when it appeared the original schedule might mean something, we got word that the revamped Sunday afternoon meeting with the President also had been scrubbed. Some of us had adjusted plane schedules to accommodate the earlier change in plans, only to see them go up in flames. For some, it was the last straw.

I met two old friends from the coaching fraternity, and they were miffed like the rest of us. We rode on the bus to church Sunday morning with Ken Hayes, whom I had met when he coached basketball at New Mexico State. Then on the first day, we bumped into David Kent, former tennis coach at Amarillo High School, West Texas State and Texas A&M.

"Due to poor planning on the part of the White House, our group was not informed until we arrived in Washington that none of the White House activities would take place as planned," wrote David, and wife Eileen, in a letter to President Bush. "Our local newspaper had interviewed us before we left and the excitement was all over our city about this wonderful event."

I don't know if David ever got a reply from the White House. We never learned how much FCA was at fault, if at all, but that organization did offer to return anyone's contribution.

Washington, D.C., has long worn the label of "a wild and wacky town", and it did little to change that image in the summer of 1990.

36

AMARILLO BY MORNING, NOON OR NIGHT

About once a month driving around town I see a bumper sticker that reads: "I wasn't born in Amarillo, Texas, but I got here as fast as I could."

If you're going to have a business called the "Publishing Ranch," then Amarillo, Texas, is the perfect place for it. And while the western flavor of our company's name is little more than a gimmick, this quiet laid-back city of 170,000 in the heart of cowboy country is the real thing. It's pure western, complete with far-flung ranches, working cowboys, horses, cattle and chewing tobacco.

Shoot, you can't miss the image. Entering Amarillo from the east on Interstate 40, you'll pass by the Big Texan, a well-advertised restaurant that offers a free 72-ounce steak if eaten in an hour. You'll even see a cowboy on horseback waving from the parking lot.

Then coming in from the west, you pass by Cadillac Ranch, a collection of old Cadillac cars half-buried in a nearby field. This attraction, equally well-advertised by the national media, is the art-form of Texan Stanley Marsh, whom some feel isn't playing with a full deck. About 20 miles west of the city, there's a huge cattle feedlot, whose pungent aroma leaves little doubt you're entering cowboy country.

Near the center of downtown Amarillo, also on heavily-traveled I-40, is the international headquarters of the American Quarter Horse Association. With more than two million horses registered to almost a million owners living in all corners of the world, it is the largest breed of equine on record. A brand new museum, resplendent with a life-size bronze horse out front, is next door.

And if you just happen to be wearing blinders while driving through the city, you'll most likely hear western singer George Strait belt out that popular hit, "Amarillo By Morning," on your car radio. It extolls the trials and tribulations of a rodeo itinerant and has produced priceless world-wide exposure for the city.

More than 40 years ago when I first moved to West Texas, I found the big orange-colored sky and boundless panorama of distant horizons almost more than I could comprehend. I still do. Interestingly, at the time I checked in at Amarillo Air Force Base in 1951, "Orange Colored Sky" by Nat King Cole was the hottest thing on the jukebox. A couple years ago, Hollywood came to the Panhandle to shoot its closing scene of a brilliant sunset for the movie, "Indiana Jones, The Last Crusade."

I'm not alone in this love affair with one of the last outposts of the Old West. The list of avowed fans sharing this passion, as varied as it is long, includes legendary artist Georgia O'Keeffe. Then add the names of famous television sportscaster Lesley Visser and baseball great Doug Rader.

Called by many the leading American artist of the 20th century, O'Keeffe came to Amarillo as a 24-year-old school teacher in 1912. She lived in the area four of the next six years.

"I couldn't believe Texas was real," she said on her arrival from Wisconsin. "When I got there, there wasn't a blade of green grass or a leaf to be seen, but I was absolutely crazy about it."

The eccentric teacher-artist, who lived out her golden years in nearby New Mexico, quickly found extreme beauty in a land where many see only barrenness. "The plains, the wonderful great big sky, makes me want to breathe so deep that I'll break," O'Keeffe was quoted in various research pieces. Rising before dawn to watch the sunrise and taking long walks every evening to view the brilliant sunsets, she created some of her finest works during this period. Even years later, she produced many abstract water colors and oils that reflected her love affair with space, skies and emptiness. She died at age 98 in 1986.

Columnist Andy Rooney did a piece on names of cities, proclaiming most of them to be dull. Not so Amarillo. Meaning "yellow" in Spanish, it was thought to have been named after a colored cast that appeared on Wild Horse Lake, site of the first railroad workers' camp that later became the heart of early Amarillo.

But it's the lilting ring of the name that gets your attention. It fits well in songs and song titles, as well as movies. It was George Strait's long-running hit, "Amarillo By Morning," that caused television sports announcer Lesley

Visser to become enamored with the city.

I first discovered this fact in the fall of 1993. My son, David, a videotape director-producer in Dallas, was moonlighting for CBS Sports at the Cowboys-Eagles game. David and Visser were in the production truck watching the monitor when another Amarilloan, William Thomas, made an outstanding play for the Eagles.

"He's from Amarillo, Texas, and that's my favorite town," said Visser, who resides in New York City.

David couldn't believe his ears. "That's where I'm from," he turned with a quizzical look.

"You're kidding!" she exclaimed. "I've never been there, but it became my favorite town because of that song, Amarillo By Morning. In fact, that's why I started wearing cowboy boots."

With that, David told me, she kicked out a shapely leg and proudly showed off genuine black ostrich cowboy boots.

After hearing this story, I mailed her a packet of Amarillo Chamber of Commerce material. A following note from her included these comments:

"I am so honored and thrilled to be considered an honorary Amarilloan. In my next life, I'm going to grow up in the Lone Star state and join the rodeo. Meanwhile, thanks for all the goodies, and your son is a doll."

George Strait's 1983 hit was not the first song to bring attention to the "queen city of the Texas Panhandle". In 1973, Wichita Falls crooner Don Cherry recorded "When You Leave Amarillo, Turn Out The Lights," and two years later, bluegrass warbler Emmylou Harris turned out a nonsensical song simply named "Amarillo."

There was something about the 70s. In 1977, popular songwriter and recording artist Neal Sedaka produced his version of "Amarillo" that told about his "Sweet Maria." It enjoyed moderate success, enough to be remembered by a German waitress in Dachau, near Munich, eight years later. After learning our hometown, she sang the song straight through without missing a word or beat.

Finally, I found one titled "Amarillo USA" by Randy King, a Texas swing toe-tapper with bad geography. One line goes "my heart lies in old Amarillo, down where the bluebonnets grow." He must have been thinking about Austin.

Then there's the movie connection. Long been linked with the romantic Old West, the city's name appears in three Class B westerns produced in the late 1940s. The best known of the bunch is Roy Rogers and Trigger in the 1948 release, "In Old Amarillo." "Marshall of Amarillo" featured Rocky Lane, and Charles Starrett played the good guy in "The Kid From

One of three western movies filmed with Amarillo in the title.

Amarillo." No Academy Awards here but plenty of national exposure. I have old posters of all three movies in my Amarillo memorabilia collection.

While Lesley Visser proclaimed a passion for a Texas town she'd never visited, a different type of testimony comes from Doug Rader, long-time major league baseball player, coach and manager. An outstanding third baseman, Doug came to the Panhandle when it was fielding a team in the Class AA Texas League, a farm club of the Texas Rangers.

"I would love to play in Amarillo the rest of my career," Doug often told the media, "if only it had a major league team." Originally from Illinois, he attributed his fondness for the area to the friendly people and cool summer nights. He eventually moved on to the Rangers, carving out an outstanding career as a major leaguer. He also had a shot at managing the club, along with a string of many, before heading out to other pastures.

To some, the city's changeable weather is its most famous trademark. I find it charming. You can sunburn in February as quickly as you can freeze.

We can have four inches of snow one day and play golf the next. It's a fact Amarillo has more winter sunshine days than Miami, Florida. At 3,700 feet altitude, we experience high dry weather that produces pleasant summer nights and little humidity. To me, that's idyllic. Yet, outsiders think we live with one foot on the North Pole and the other in the frying pan.

In the spring of '95, the phone rang and a down-state niece, Shelly Caramanian, was asking excitedly: "Are you guys okay? We just heard on the weather that Amarillo was being wrecked by a tornado."

Truth of the matter we were experiencing near perfect weather. Twelve hours earlier, a windstorm had blown over a house trailer and killed a man, giving base for the totally inaccurate and exaggerated report on the late news. Just another example of old images being perpetuated by weather forecasters interested in juicing facts.

Then there's the matter of the flat, pancake-like terrain of Amarillo and the surrounding Panhandle. Some call it ugly and boring; I find it beautiful and thrilling. Whatever the assessment, let me explain how it all came about. The following fable, one of my favorites, is attributed to George Autry, long-time printer and early proprietor:

It was one of those days when God was creating the Earth. He was working on Texas as darkness fell at the end of the day, and had to quit.

He gave the Great Plains of West Texas a smoothing stroke and said to Himself, "In the morning, I'll come back and make it pretty like the rest of the world, with lakes and streams and mountains and trees."

But next morning when He returned, it had hardened like concrete overnight. As He thought about having to tear it all out and make it over, He had a happy thought. "I know what I'll do," He said, "I'll just make some people who like it this way."

And He did!

37

LABOR OF LOVE

The Amarillo story wouldn't be complete without relating a project that I call a "labor of love". It involves Amarillo's 100th anniversary in 1987, and it was one of the few journalistic endeavors I've attempted unrelated to sports.

A year earlier, friend Jay Ketelle reminded that our favorite city was approaching an important historical milestone.

"I have more than 200 old Amarillo postcards," revealed Jay, who like me migrated to Texas by way of the Air Force and chose to stay. "Would you be interested in taking them and producing a commemorative book for the anniversary?"

The challenge struck a responsive chord and we formed a partnership on the spot. I spent six delightful months in research, dividing my time between Central Library and elderly pioneers who gave me vital first-hand information on the cards.

The hard-back, four-color, coffee table book, titled *Amarillo, Texas-The First 100 Years*, was an instant hit. At $19.87 a pop, a price we selected to fall under $20 and one that coincided with the anniversary year, 5,000 copies were sold the first year. Local bookstores couldn't keep them stocked, and there it was on display stands in the same company with James Michener's big hit, *Texas*, and other best-sellers. My first project to have retail bookstore appeal, I found myself standing around Hastings and B. Dalton stores watching to see if anyone would pick it up and buy it.

"Will there be a second edition?" we were asked. After thinking Jay had cornered every worthwhile postcard ever printed about Amarillo, we learned differently. People who bought the first volume brought us never-before-seen cards from family albums and closet shoe boxes. Filled almost completely with "loaners", a second postcard volume was produced a year later.

"I don't know when I've had so much fun learning history," commented Pattilou Dawkins, Amarillo Centennial Committee co-chairman. "You have not only provided Amarillo with an excellent social commentary but also a marvelous pictorial format of our heritage."

Pattilou hit the nail on the head. It was a different approach to history, one that reminded people of places where they had eaten a grilled cheese sandwich and sipped a Coke or took in a movie almost every weekend.

Typical cards included Polk Street scenes dating back to 1900, famous homes of wealthy cattlemen and historical landmarks. One such card portrayed a picture of the lobby of old Amarillo Hotel, the city's first and a favorite meeting place for cattlemen. Research revealed that was the very place Will Rogers entered one afternoon and secured his first job as a cowboy. Having just completed his studies at Kemper Military Academy in Missouri, he was looking for adventure on a Texas ranch.

A relative of Lela Finklea mailed her a copy in California for a Christmas present. A member of an early Amarillo jewelry store family, Mrs. Finklea pored over the book for several hours and then became so enthused she called over and shared the nostalgia with her daughter, movie star Cyd Charisse.

"We stayed up almost all night devouring the book and recalling special memories," Mrs. Finklea later related. Of course, Cyd is easily Amarillo's most important export to the entertainment industry, starring in more than 25 feature movies. Her famous dance routine with Gene Kelly in "Singing in the Rain" and later roles opposite Fred Astaire will long be remembered by buffs of the silver screen.

Her aunt in Amarillo, Tula VanShaw, was one of those early residents who contributed reams of valuable information to the postcard books. She also put me in touch with her famous niece, a relationship that resulted in meeting her personally.

It was the summer of 1994, and son David asked Floy and me to come to Dallas for the weekend. They had a surprise for us.

"Of all the people in show business, who would you rather see in person?" asked David. I was stumped, but Floy threw out the name, "Cyd Charisse".

"You're in luck," he said. "we have four tickets to see her at Casa Manana Theater in Fort Worth. She's performing there in the stage play, Grand Hotel."

Previous correspondence with the long-time MGM leading lady who started her dancing career at 14 with the Ballet Russe gave us the confidence to try getting backstage. We had seen her perform in "Charlie Girl" at

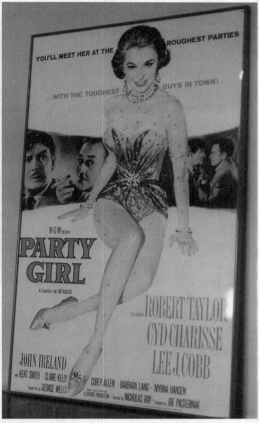

Amarillo's Ron Ely, one of several to play Tarzan in the movies, returned to the old hometown and signed a movie poster. (Right) A movie poster featuring Amarillo's Cyd Charisse 40 years before she met with the Franks after a show in Fort Worth. David and Sandy, far right, arranged for the surprise meeting.

London's Victoria Palace Theater a few years previous, sending a program backstage to be signed.

"You really should have stopped by my dressing room in London," she later wrote. "Amarillo is always welcome." Before leaving for Casa Manana, we typed out a short note, reminding the venerable star of the Amarillo postcard books and her earlier remark about the London experience. We handed it to the theater manager, and shortly were informed to be back in the green room after the performance. We were bubbling with excitement.

Cyd was marvelous in the role of Elizaveta Grushinskaya, an older ballerina who falls in love with a young baron. At 72, her dancing was limited to a few warm-up exercises, but it was exciting to see her up there still performing. And she looked great for any age.

"Are you the Franks family?" asked a portly man after we had waited in the entry area about five minutes. He then led us to her dressing room and opened the door for us. There she was dressed in casual cream slacks and loose-fitting blue denim shirt, a stark contrast to the elegant gowns and gorgeous furs she wore in the show. She extended her hand and a smile creased her still attractive face. During the course of the 10-minute visit, Cyd was gracious, warm and almost shy.

"Do you still live in Amarillo?" she asked with genuine interest. Then she proceeded to tell us about her Aunt Tula and four cousins coming over from Amarillo a week earlier. She agreed to pictures with our family (wife Floy, son David, his wife Sandy and myself) before signing our playbills. She was in no hurry, even though others were waiting to get autographs.

Besides Charisse, Amarillo has produced two other movie stars of importance. Carolyn Jones, who attended Amarillo High School with my wife, co-starred in a number of Hollywood productions and later appeared on a TV hit series, the "Addams Family." A serious drama student in school, she headed West shortly after graduation, studied hard and did quite well for herself. At one time she was married to Aaron Spelling, noted producer.

"She was not particularly popular in high school," remembers Floy, "and some place along the way she got a nose job."

Former Amarillo High School football player Ron Ely also made the grade in Hollywood, becoming best known for his role as Tarzan in the late 60s.

"My early interest in the movie industry was sparked by a job I had at the old Rex Theater," he told a Friends of the Library audience on a recent return to the old hometown. "I worked picking up papers, changing the marquee and other chores that I was too young to be doing."

After his talk, was I surprised when Head Librarian Mary Kay Snell presented Ely with copies of the Amarillo postcard books.

38

TO RUSSIA, WITH FOOTBALL

After spending two weeks in Moscow, Russia, covering the World University Games in 1973, I told Garet Von Netzer of the Amarillo Daily News sports department:

"It was an experience all right, but not one I would want to repeat."

They say time has a way of making you forget the unpleasant things of life. Nineteen years after that adventure, I changed my mind and agreed to return to the country Winston Churchill characterized as "a riddle in a mystery inside an enigma." The invitation from Deborah Dunston, president of International Sports Connection, was much too attractive to refuse.

"I would like to personally invite you to accompany the Western Maryland Green Terrors when they make history as the first collegiate football team to travel to Moscow and play a Russian team," she wrote. "If you are interested, you would travel as the guest of ISC."

After having been involved in pioneering football experiences in Japan, Finland and Australia, how could I resist this opportunity?

If I had been the superstitious type, I probably would not have left on Friday, the 13th, to join 47 football players and another two dozen coaches, fans and officials on what was still another step in the globalization of American-style football. It was March, 1992, and the timing couldn't have been better for an eight-day, 14,000-mile trip to this land of intrigue, mystique and rebellion.

A political firecracker was exploding in the old Soviet Union now labeled the Commonwealth of Independent States. A 75-year-old yolk called communism had been cast aside only six months previous, and a faint resemblance of democracy was marching in. In essence, we were being afforded front row seats to one of history's greatest reformations, political and economic changes that would have been considered incomprehensible in our lifetime.

It didn't take long to detect a different climate. In 1973, just before reaching the Moscow airport, we were briefed on what we could and could not do in the strict police state, the country many labeled "the evil empire." We were warned to leave all religious material on the plane, keep our distance from the Russian people and take no pictures of the airport, bridges or anything else that might compromise security. This time, not a peep.

Even getting through customs was easier. Drably-dressed uniformed agents did little more than glance at our passports and visas and whisked us through in record time. I even detected an occasional smile from Russian officials when gregarious Americans would accost them with a hearty "hello, how are you?" More of the same when we checked in at our hotel, the Red Star, a better than average facility that only recently housed high-ranking communist military officials.

The marathon journey that had taken us from Washington, D.C. to Paris and then on to Moscow had left us ravenous. And the first meal in reforming Moscow was a surprise. Grilled beefsteak, cold cuts, shredded carrots and beets, rice, rye and white bread, fresh fruit, coconut ice cream and Pepsi hit the spot. Most players gave it a "two thumbs up" with one exception. The cola was hot and flat, as it was the remainder of our Russian odyssey. Despite hints from American officials, the Russian waiters insisted on opening soft drinks and placing them on the table hours before mealtime.

In general, I thought the selection and quality of food was better than had been expected, especially at a time when supplies in this vast country were strained. We were told that fresh oranges and bananas, delicacies in the land of the big bear, were flown in from Israel, no doubt as a special favor to visiting American athletes. While some items were in short supply, carrots, beets and cabbage were not.

"It must have been a banner year for carrots and beets," commented one burly lineman after having them served nearly every meal, even sometimes for breakfast. Although the entree was varied with ample portions of chicken, fish and steak, those same vegetables were always there. We had been warned to bring plenty of peanut butter and crackers, but I rarely touched mine.

Before leaving the dining room that first night, we got a thorough briefing. Coach Dale Sprague reminded his Western Maryland players of "this wonderful opportunity to see history in the making." Kent Dunston, vice-president of the sponsoring sports travel and marketing firm from Gadsden, Alabama, explained the monetary situation.

"The U.S. dollar rules Moscow," he said. "But be careful where you exchange your money, and only exchange what you plan to spend. On the return, you'll get little for left-over rubles." He explained that because the Russian economy was in total chaos, the ruble is devalued almost daily.

Then Vladimir Gomelski, International Sports Connection's Moscow representative, whetted our appetite for the sights and sounds of his city of eight million. He reminded that the whirlwind schedule would include the famous religious complex at Zagorsk, the Moscow Circus, Red Square, Arbat Street, the Kremlin (and its inner treasures) and McDonald's. Yes, McDonald's Restaurant, at that time the largest in all the world. And, of course, the football game.

"It may be the most exciting five days of your life," added the bearded Dunston. Nineteen years ago, there was little time, or freedom, for sight-seeing. My adventure juices were flowing and I could hardly wait until next morning.

On our first full day in Russia, a Sunday, we boarded two buses for a two-hour, 45-mile trip to Zagorsk, an experience that was well-documented at the beginning of this book. Getting separated from my group and having to find my way back to Moscow without a single ruble in my pocket is an adventure that will not soon be forgotten. Later in the day, the Western Maryland football team had its problems too. They spent two hours finding a football practice facility for their first workout.

Monday was earmarked for more sight-seeing, this time at one of the most recognizable landmarks in the world. Coming up on Red Square, called Russia's guardian of the past, is a breath-taking experience, no matter how many times you've been there. We parked near St. Basil's Cathedral, the multi-colored, onion-domed edifice that stands out like Disneyland in the Sahara Desert. Nineteen years after having first visited Red Square, little had changed.

"Isn't this something?" expressed Dale Sprague, the Western Maryland coach, upon seeing the magnificent structure for the first time. "There's no way you can measure the value of this trip. It's absolutely priceless." Besides that, the trip was scheduled during spring break so no classroom time would be missed.

Walking around this 600-year-old landmark, we entered the storied brick-paved courtyard that appears regularly on world-wide newscasts. It's about the size of 20 football fields and even more impressive in person. Red Square is Russia. With Lenin's Tomb and the huge GUM government-owned department store rimming the area, and the Kremlin lurking behind a 30-foot wall, photo opportunities were plentiful. On this day, Lenin's mausoleum

"James Bond" came to mind when I first met Russian friends Vladimir and Larissa Gomelski, our guides in Moscow. (Right) Former Denver Bronco coach John Ralston and wife Patty on Red Square, in front of the Kremlin.

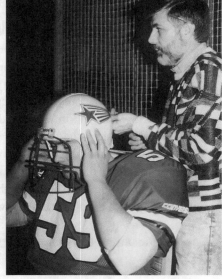

Kent Dunston, ISC's tour director, custom fits Russian football players with new headgear from America. A new Rolex watch wouldn't have made them happier.

was closed to the public with two guards standing at the entrance. Later in the week, however, I would return and accomplish what thousands of Russians used to do daily.

Monday afternoon was reserved for a stiff workout, and then the Green Terrors joined the Russian team, called the Euro-Asian All-Stars, for a combined clinic. It was one of four such inter-action seminars, designed to teach basic fundamentals and technique to the hosts. "This might be the most important time for the Russian athletes," observed Coach Sprague, who was impressed with many of their physical characteristics.

It's Tuesday, and it's game day! After a rigorous sight-seeing schedule, the American athletes welcomed the opportunity to sleep in and eat a mid-morning brunch. Most of the day was reserved for rest before the hour-long ride to the game site. Russian television has little to offer, except newscasts in Russian. However, one of the six channels on my set was CNN, our only contact with the outside world for nearly a week.

The game was played before 4,000 curious fans in a twilight setting at the Central Sports Club of the Red Army (CSKA), an enclosed soccer facility with low ceilings and no hash marks on the field. When punts and kickoffs occasionally hit the ceiling, action was stopped and the down replayed. Surprisingly though, the stadium, and other practice facilities, sported modern synthetic turf.

Western Maryland, an NCAA Division III non-scholarship school, scored on its first three possessions. The larger Russians got their only touchdown in the last minute of play, an event that evoked uproarious applause from the crowd. The final count could have been more lopsided than 47-7, but everyone went home happy. Fans cheered for both teams when an exciting play warranted it.

Russian fans paid 20 rubles to see the international sports attraction. While that's the equivalent of only 25 cents in U.S. currency, it was a considerable outlay at a time when prices of food and other staples were escalating at a rapid pace. Twenty teams had been playing American-style football in Moscow only three years. And while the fledgling league staged its first "Super Bowl" in 1991, and attracted 12,000 fans in a rainstorm, few locals really understand the game.

Arkady Semyonov, a Muscovite interpreter who accompanied the Americans three days, was witnessing his first football contest. "I didn't understand a thing," he said. "All those guys were yelling and running around on the field and all of a sudden it was 47-0."

On the day of the game and at the exact starting time of the exhibition, an anti-Boris Yeltsin rally was staged by several thousand old-line communists near Red Square, not far from the soccer stadium. We drove by on the way to the game, and I wanted to jump out and get a close-up picture.

"Oh no, you must stay in the car," warned our interpreter. "These people are real trouble-makers and could cause real harm." Isn't it interesting that what was for 75 years the majority is now the minority in a country torn by strife and hardship for hundreds of years.

"The Russians are great athletes and eager to learn," commented John Ralston, former Stanford and Denver Bronco coach, who was their mentor for this game. He was in Moscow a week before we arrived, his fourth trip to the land of vodka and caviar, in a advisory capacity.

"When they first got serious about American football here, they started looking for just the best athletes," recalled Ralston, who brings wife Patty with him and makes a vacation out of it too. They had the best track stars, the fastest runners and the highest jumpers. They even recruited a javelin thrower for quarterback.

"It didn't take them long," added the genial Ralston, "to know they needed more beef and strength. That's when they went to bobsledders and wrestlers."

What the Russians possess in physical stature, they lack in technique. "They need a lot of coaching and especially a lot of help on basics," surmised WMC's Coach Sprague. "And that's what this week was all about in a large sense, teaching them American expertise in a game we invented. Right now they have 25-year-old bodies with 12-year-old skills."

Andre Gromov, a 300-pound Russian noseguard, was asked how he like American football. "It is very difficult," he said in surprisingly good English, "but I like it much better than bobsledding." Gromov also expressed his fascination with the gladiator look of football equipment and likes the "hitting" the sport offers. The Russians are professionals and their only job is playing sports. They have been elevated to hero status by their people and receive twice the salary of regular government employees.

Gromov and his teammates get little coaching when Ralston isn't around, and that's most of the time. And when he's there, handicaps are numerous. An interpreter, usually a Russian college girl, is required to communicate fully with his players. Emotion and inflection are usually lost when coaching instruction is translated, and sometimes there are even greater problems. On one occasion, Ralston was trying to illustrate tackling technique.

"Wrap em up, wrap em up," he shouted, extending his arms outward. The interpreter, a college girl, paused for a second, extended her arms and repeated "wrap em up, wrap em up" in English. The Russian footballers offered puzzled looks and it was then Ralston realized some American expressions are not translatable.

Getting to know Ralston, who at the time was in the process of helping organize a corporate-owned football league for non-college athletes in the U.S., was a real bonus of the trip. A genuinely nice guy, he told me he had been involved in teaching Russians football for three reasons.

"First, I have a real compassion for the Russian people," he said. "They have endured so much hardship through the years." The 66-year-old veteran added that he likes to keep his hand in coaching and also "wants to help globalize our wonderful sport of football." He later was lured out of retirement and currently is head coach at San Jose State.

The Western Maryland contingent quickly learned that Russian people genuinely like Americans and attempt to emulate them in many ways. During the lavish pre-game and half-time festivities, young Muscovites danced and sang American songs with authority, ranging from country and western to rock and roll. One rock group performed a song that translated, "American Boy, I Will Go With You To America." It was No. 1 on their hit parade.

On day five, the morning after the game, we were treated to an experience that was impossible in 1973. For years, few Russians had the opportunity to go inside the Kremlin walls and view the priceless wealth of the Armory Museum. We were taken to this area as a group and carefully screened at the door. "No pictures, please," we were told.

The sight was stunning and confusing. As we viewed room after room of heavily jeweled carriages, gold, silver, platinum and emerald-studded crowns, goblets, platters, crosses, candlesticks and armor, I was reminded of the country's current poverty status. Why not cash in some of these treasures and start reducing the debt? Then, visions of Ivan the Terrible, Peter the Great and Catherine the Great welled up in my head. These are proud people, and to destroy their past, even though it was wicked for the most part, would be the ultimate blow to their legacy. I've visited many museums the world over but this one represented the greatest display of raw wealth.

Some of Moscow's most striking onion-domed mosques also reside in the Kremlin. If they weren't painted with a bright array of colors, they were covered with gold leaf. You have to see it to believe it.

That night, we were treated to Moscow's famous one-ring circus, featuring what else—big brown bears—before having free time most of

Thursday. Everyone was pulling out the shopping lists and taking care of back-home requests.

While capitalism might have been taboo in the past, the Americans found individual entrepreneurship running rampant during their short visit. On the second full day in Moscow, boys and young men swarmed them with souvenirs on Red Square. The Americans were up to the challenge, though, swapping golf caps, shirts and chocolate bars for Russian hand-made products in a raw display of free enterprise.

"Hey, mister, how about a designer fur hat?" I heard from my backside. I turned around and saw this young Russian boy trying to wheel and deal with Glenn Johnson, a 240-pound tackle who came prepared. He whipped out a Green Terror T-shirt and swapped it even-steven for a black rabbit fur hat. Comrade Lenin must have been squirming in his open casket in the famous mausoleum only a few yards away.

Later in the trip, the Americans were treated to a shopping fantasy on Arbat Street, a mile-long boulevard roped off from traffic and bearing hundreds of tables and individual dealers. Looking very much like an American weekend flea market, the bigger selection included hand-made table cloths, flags, painted eggs, military uniforms and samovars. Still the favorite, though, were the fascinating matroyska nest dolls that ranged from small sets of three to the giant size of 21. After choosing several different styles for the wife, my choice was the "political" set. The largest hand-painted doll was the likeness of Boris Yeltsin (smaller carvings of Gorbachev, Kruschev, Stalin and Lenin, in that order, were nestled inside). The young dealers told us English was required in school, and most handled the language like pros. They knew the value of the American dollar also.

We found the currency exchange about 85 rubles for one U.S. dollar, affording good bargains in the shopping experience. A can of caviar cost the equivalent of 50 cents and popular rabbit fur hats sold for ten dollars. Mink hats brought 35 dollars and ermine was the most expensive at $200.

Little wonder free enterprise was everywhere. Most Russians have to moonlight to make ends meet. In 1992, common laborers were earning about $8 a month, an engineer $12 and a doctor around $20. Officially, Boris Yeltsin, the president, was being paid only 5,500 rubles monthly, which translates to about 65 U.S. dollars. It's a wonder he wasn't on Red Square, selling and signing his look-alike wooden dolls.

It was the third day in Moscow before the footballers convinced Coach Sprague they should visit one of the newest landmarks, the city's one and only McDonald's. While the Red Star Hotel restaurant had furnished bountiful amounts of adequate food, the young tourists started yearning for a "fast food fix."

Devaluation of the ruble really came into play at Moscow's golden arch, about the size of a football field and capable of seating 700. Big Macs sold for 35 rubles, or about 40 cents, and that after a big hike in prices the first of the year. One homesick player bought 20 hamburgers, eating a few on the premises and taking the rest back to his room for snack food. Along with fries and a milk shake, total cost was less than four dollars.

Most agreed that taste was the same 5,000 miles from Maryland but the selection shorter. No quarter-pounders, fish fillets or breakfast items. Milk shakes are big hits in the old Soviet Union. They come in vanilla, strawberry and chocolate flavors and are much more popular than soft drinks.

As much as the food itself, Russians seem to clamor to McDonald's and wait in long lines for the atmosphere. It offers a slice of America just around the block from their crowded apartments and economic headaches.

"We come here a lot to see the foreigners," revealed a friendly Russian schoolboy sitting next to us nursing a cheeseburger and vanilla shake. "Sometimes, my friends and I spend an hour here enjoying the scenery."

About the similarity to taste back in the states, the McDonald people take no chances. Careful attention is paid to minute details. From the time the small calf is weaned from its mother in a Russian feed-lot, its diet is closely monitored until it grows up to become a "Big Mac." On the day we were there, I glanced behind the long counter and must have seen 200 Russian young people scurrying around taking and filling orders. I spotted one paper placemat that included an application for work. All information was printed in Russian except the high-profile "McDonald's" logo, which appeared in English.

Across the street on Central Tverskaya Avenue, the country's only Pizza Hut was selling take-out slices for 16 rubles, or about 20 cents. However, they haven't begun to approach the popularity of McDonald's, where lines often stretch a block long even before getting inside.

When players made subsequent trips to McDonald's by taxi, they found monetary confusion and "gouging" in the country's ever-changing economy. Predatory cabbies often would ask 1,000 rubles for a 20-minute trip from the hotel and then accept 200 (about $2.50) if challenged. Many cab drivers are moonlighters, supplementing their average monthly salary of about $8.

In addition to a changing economy, Americans found a new stance on religion. Some visitors freely distributed religious material on Red Square and in the hotel, and locals were seen attending services in the onion-domed cathedrals and churches without fear of retaliation. Only recently, my preacher, Gil Lain, my former pastor Shad Rue and 200 people from the Texas Panhandle visited Russia, openly leading evangelistic services in the evening and handing out literature and witnessing on the streets in daytime hours. In many ways, a country that only recently espoused belief in no god has fewer restrictions on spreading the gospel than the United States, a land founded by God-fearing, Bible-believing people. A strange paradox, one I don't understand.

Another sign of the times on this visit, we saw the demise of *Pravda*, the official newspaper of Russia's communist party for 80 years. "It is being suspended on Friday for lack of funds," reported its editor in the International Herald Tribune. The word "Pravda" means "truth" in Russian and once commanded circulation of 11.1 million. That figure had slipped to a mere 111,000 when the paper bit the dust.

Long before the U.S. government offered economic aid to the new Confederation of Independent States, American sporting goods manufacturers were helping equip them for football. Mike May, Director of Communications for SGMA (Sporting Goods Manufacturers Association), accompanied the small Maryland school to Moscow and helped in the distribution of much-needed equipment. The Riddell Company sent some 50 modern air helmets and H.G. Peake, Wilson, Spalding and Zubaz all chipped in with gear, in addition to an SGMA grant from the Super Show.

"When they first started playing football," reminded ISC's Dunston, "the Russians often wore motorcycle helmets and street shoes. It's the best they had."

The new helmets, gaily decorated with a red and blue shooting star that replaced the outdated hammer and sickle logo, brought big smiles to the Russian gladiators, but also provoked a two-man brawl. Dunston did the fitting of the prized headgear at one of the joint practice sessions and was almost finished when it happened.

The supply of medium-sized helmets was diminished when one lineman realized he wasn't going to get a good fit. He walked over to the already-sized helmets, ripped a teammate's name from one and took it to Dunston for fitting. The original owner saw what was happening and when he tried to retrieve his new prize, a fistfight ensued.

"That's one reason I believe the Russians will excel at football," noted Dunston, "because they are proud and aggressive people and very competitive. Look how they have succeeded with another American game— basketball—after only 30 years of experience."

Americans Mike and Toni May visit Arbat Street, Moscow's answer to the weekend fleat market in the U.S. (Below) Western Maryland football players become "great fur traders".

Long lines formerly gathered at Lenin's Tomb on Red Square. That wasn't the case on this trip.

The long lines that are no more at Lenin's Tomb can be found at McDonald's not far away. That's a Big Mac off a Russian menu (lower left), and hundreds of Russian teenagers man the counters (lower right).

Прия

«Биг Мак»

2 рубленых бифштекса из натуральной цельной говядины, нарезанные листики салата латука, ломтик сыра, кусочки маринованного огурца, лук, сложенные в разрезанную булочку, посыпанную семечками кунжута

A key person in the execution of Western Maryland's big adventure was Vladmir Gomelski, ISC's associate in Russia and an important sports broadcaster in the RTR (Russian Television and Radio) Network. He's the son of Alexander Gomelski, a veteran coach of the old USSR's national basketball team who now lives in America. Besides being our man Friday in Russia, chain-smoking Vladimir had other duties during the international game. The creator of the NBA basketball game of the week on Russian TV, he was the play-by-play announcer for Western Maryland's overseas event that reached 70 million households countrywide. The contest was edited and shown shortly after it was played, then telecast again five days later.

When I first met Vladimir and wife Larissa, I said to myself, "James Bond." Handsome Vladimir, in his black leather coat, and beautiful Larissa, always draped in a sumptuous, full-length black fox fur coat with hat to match, certainly fit the mold of Hollywood KGB agents. Besides looking the part, both speak fluent English and effuse continental mystique. Come to think of it, I never did ask what both were doing when communism went into the dumpster.

We take for granted in America many things that are delicacies in Russia. For example, Vladimir craves fresh fruit, something that is in short supply even among the most influential Russians. Another American food favorite of his is shrimp cocktail, a dish he eats with both hands on his occasional trips to the States.

Sightseeing opportunities abounded while traveling with the football team, but some of the most memorable times came with new friends Mike and wife Toni May. On occasion when coaches and players were headed out to a practice session, group leader Kent Dunston would flip us some keys and say: "Take the rented car, our driver and interpreter, and have some fun."

Equally interested in antiques, the Mays joined me scouring shops all over massive Moscow while catching glimpses of landmarks along the way. Our driver, Alexander, and Arkady, the translator, provided insightful commentary as we passed along the Moscow River, KGB Headquarters, Pushkin Museum, Gorky Park and a 300-foot high statue of Yuri Gargarian, first man in space.

"I wonder if the tomb is open today?" I mumbled as we neared Red Square one morning. "Let's take a look," agreed Mike and Toni. The driver floor-boarded the Russian-made Volga and in no time we were at the brick-lined entrance of the mammoth courtyard near police headquarters.

From a distance, we saw no lines and assumed it was still off base to tourists and countrymen alike. But as we approached the entrance that bears his name in the strange-looking Cyrillic alphabet, the big granite doors appeared to be open. I couldn't believe my eyes. I had witnessed loyal Russian comrades standing four abreast in half-mile long lines in 1973. Some spent a good part of a day playing the waiting game, a favorite pastime in this part of the world. Funny thing, the long lines that formerly waited to see Lenin can now be found only a few blocks away at McDonald's.

"What a difference a purge makes," I told our interpreter. He advised that Vladimir Ilich Lenin, and all his symbols, had quickly fallen from grace with the demise of communism. Stories of atrocities and much evil-doing are being linked to his regime. The country's second biggest city to the north, Leningrad, had only recently been renamed, taking its original label of "St. Petersburg." Slowly but surely, the stigma of a fallen hero is bringing down statues and all references to the architect of the old USSR.

Only a handful of people preceded the four of us as we moved up the three granite steps to the entrance. A sober guard stood nearby making sure no cameras were taken inside. It was an eerie feeling. We were about to enter the world's best publicized mausoleum, one that Russian leaders stand on each spring to view the May Day shenanigans. After getting inside, we turned to the left and descended two short flights of stairs. Our eyes moved past rigid military guards, armed with guns, and there he was as big as Dallas, characterized by that famous receding hairline, goatee and mustache.

Bright lights were focused on the head of one of the world's most famous political revolutionaries as he lay in something that resembled a casket. A glass case covered his entire body. It was situated squarely in the middle of the large room while velvet ropes and a half-dozen soldiers kept viewers at a reasonable distance. His face, which looked more like a character out of a wax museum, had few lines and appeared youthful. Of course, he was only 57 when he died in 1924, seven years after toppling the last Russian czar, Nicholas II.

There were no more than a dozen of us in the cool, dark mausoleum when a Russian woman blurted out something from the other side of the room.

"She was speaking to Lenin," revealed our interpreter, "something about being sorry that the job didn't get completed."

Arkady told us the older woman, wearing a black scarf, would have been in big trouble only a few months ago. It would have been considered irreverent and intolerable, deserving of major punishment. "Now," he said, "the guards just turn away and pretend they don't hear it."

What's more, we were told by local officials the tomb may be dismantled and removed, along with Lenin's corpse. That's Russia all right, king of the hill one day and at the bottom of the heap the next.

We had been warned of the escalating crime rate, the result of fewer uniformed people on the streets and infiltration of the Mafia. I found out first hand one day while leaving a cab at Arbat Street.

The Mays and I had just finished a noontime snack at McDonald's and planned some more shopping at the country's biggest outdoor arts and crafts fair. Mike and Toni left the taxi first and started up the street while I finished paying the fare. Just as I turned around, I saw this swarm of maybe a dozen dark-skinned children, in the 8-10 age group.

When they circled me and first started reaching into my trench coat pockets, I thought they were only begging for gum or candy. This is commonplace at Red Square. But when they began pulling at my camera bag hanging around my neck and reaching for my pants pockets, a light went on. I had seen a segment on 60 Minutes some time ago about bands of gypsy children who roam Europe preying on tourists and isolated individuals. I then realized these little devils were planning to rob me in broad daylight.

"Get away before I have to knock you away," I yelled, knowing full well they didn't understand English.

Lucky I had the camera bag. Grabbing the strap with both hands, I started flailing away from one side to the other. One and then two fell back, but the others kept boring in closer and had already ripped one button off my coat. Little arms and hands were coming at me from all directions, much like tentacles on an octopus.

About this time, Mike and Toni heard the commotion behind them and turned to see the attempted pick-pocket robbery in progress. While nearby Russians only stood and watched, my friends hustled back to give me a hand. At this point, the little would-be thieves scattered like a covey of quail.

There was nothing of value in my coat pockets. And because my coat was buttoned and the belt buckled, they were unable to reach my trouser pockets, where I had my money, passport and credit cards. Final score: Franks 1; Gypsies 0.

Our leader from International Sports Connection, Kent Dunston, also became a statistic in the crime wave that has been increasing at the rate of 30% a year. When visiting a big flea market on the outskirts of Moscow, he reached into his pocket and came up with some bills to pay for a purchase.

While he was trying to select the right one, a teenage boy zipped by, grabbed all the money from his hands and fled into the crowd.

"We located a policeman right away," said Kent, "but we searched the place over to no avail." While I only lost a button, Kent wasn't as fortunate. The young thief got away with four twenty-dollar bills, U.S. currency. That represents a lot of buying power in this economically-strapped country.

And what did the U.S. collegians think about their Moscow adventure, the first overseas trip for all but five?

"We were treated royally by the people on the streets," recalled defensive lineman Chris Edie. "The Russian women dress much better than I expected and we didn't see all the poverty we expected."

Butch Schaffer, a freshman wingback, had pictured tanks and military everywhere. He thought general living conditions would be worse than he saw. All-time senior rushing leader Eric Frees, who scored two touchdowns in limited action, termed it "a chance of a lifetime." He said he had been "terribly excited" from the time he first heard about the trip, his first outside the country.

Studying Russian history in college came in handy for quarterback Paul McCord. He spent most of one evening with his Russian counterpart at the signal-calling position, Paul Chernyavskii. He was able to ask some insightful questions.

"Earlier, I was a communist for personal gain," related Chernyavskii, "and we were told that capitalism was wicked." He related to McCord that what's happening now is more confusing to the Russians than to the rest of the world. "No one knows what's really going on!"

In an undertaking designed to move 72 people halfway around the world and back, there are bound to be some glitches. Though minimal, one involved the man charged with the logistics of the entire trip. Fred Asbell was checking in his group with Air France on the first leg of the return trip from Moscow to Paris.

"The plane is overbooked and one or two of your people will have to stay behind and take the next available flight," Asbell was told. The American frowned. "Look, we came over as a group and we're leaving as a group," he responded with firmness.

Air France officials quickly huddled, scratched their heads and checked their passenger lists over and over. After considerable time, they found a solution. Asbell was offered a jump seat in the cockpit, which he readily accepted. As it turned out, after all the worry and confusion, an empty seatwas found just before takeoff.

Another innovative procedure was invoked to solve a problem during the game. Sophomore fullback Mo Klotz suffered a leg injury in the fourth quarter that called for an ice pack. Ice is more scarce than hen's teeth in most European countries but Bob Duvall, alumni physical therapist, had an idea. He dashed out a side door to the nearest snow bank and filled a plastic trash bag. It worked just fine as a knee wrap.

With the Russian economy in disarray, tour officials were greeted with "surprises" on arrival in Moscow. First, they were slapped with a new 28% sales tax on all expenditures incurred in Russia, including hotel expenses and meals. Then they found out that Olympic Arena, where the game had been scheduled, couldn't be utilized unless the facility's administrator was paid one thousand U.S. dollars, under the table. Blackmail and bribes are part of the ball-game today in a troubled Russia, but American officials chose to say "nyet." They moved from a stadium that holds 38,000 to one that has a 7,000 seat capacity. But it was more than adequate for the 4,000 people who showed up.

All basic costs of the trip were the responsibility of the players themselves. A portion of the $1,800 per person fee was covered by campus fund-raisers such as pizza parties. This arrangement is typical at schools without scholarships and large athletic budgets.

Another surprise came at the farewell dinner when a high Russian official, Stanislav Kramamenko, joined them at the hotel. He spoke in sober terms. Through an interpreter, he said:

"You are brave to come to our country in these troubled times. I know this type of athletic competition will help bring together our great countries, the two most important in the world." Kramamenko, General Secretary of the Trade Unions of the Commonwealth, was a major figure in rebuffing the attempted coup in late '91. In other words, he was considered to be the modern day Patrick Henry of his country.

John Ralston, Russia's interim coach and a keen observer of what's been happening the past few years, had these perceptions:

"In football, the Russians need American coaches to teach them technique more than anything else. In the big picture, the Russian people could use American know-how more than anything else. More than money, food and medicine, they need to learn the definition of two words, incentive and pride.

"These words are unimportant in a communistic or socialistic state. If some retired Americans, and we have many who have taken early retirement, could come over here and live for a year, teaching technique in all aspects of life, it would do wonders."

39

MILWAUKEE, NOT MAYO'S

"St. Mary's Hospital," I instructed the cab driver at American Airlines terminal in Milwaukee.

The ruddy-faced man wearing a Brewers baseball cap turned around, looked at his two passengers and asked: "Which one of you is getting your ticker fixed?"

It was June, 1992, and I was facing the biggest medical challenge of my life—a second open-heart by-pass operation. And only three months after the exhausting journey to Russia with the Western Maryland football team.

"But why Milwaukee?" was a question I was being asked by my friends and relatives in Texas. "Hey," they would say, "have you checked out Houston where Denton Cooley and Michael DeBakey have made that city the cardiac capital of the world?"

"Is the Mayo Clinic in Milwaukee?" was another often asked question I had to field. Friends scratched their heads with a perplexed look when I told them that the famous Mayo Clinic was in Rochester, Minnesota, not Milwaukee, and I had no intention of going there.

Others insisted that Phoenix had a highly-respected heart clinic, and yes, Amarillo is doing good work in the field of by-pass surgery. My first such operation was performed in the old hometown in 1977, with no complaints.

So why Milwaukee? After the first by-pass surgery, I read everything I could find on the delicate procedure. The basics I knew. After a 12-inch incision is made in the middle of the chest, the rib cage is parted with a saw. The patient is hooked up to an artificial heart pump, and veins, usually taken from the leg, are sewed into place, routing new blood flow around clogged arteries.

The names of Dr. Dudley Johnson and St. Mary's Hospital first came to my attention in the late 1980s. Jerry Nelson, the son of good friend Denzil

Nelson, went there after being told by Amarillo surgeons that "he was inoperable". He too had experienced by-pass surgery several years previous.

"A first-class facility in every way," is the way Denzil explained the Milwaukee hospital after returning to Texas with a glowing report. "They come in there from all over the world," he added, "and most of them are needing difficult heart procedures. About half of their patents have had previous open-heart surgeries."

Knowing full well that a second by-pass operation carries more risks, I promptly started a file on Dr. Johnson, who heads up a team of three cardiovascular and thoracic surgeons called Milwaukee Heart Surgery Associates. But I guess the one thing that really attracted my attention was the fact that this remarkable group performs a little-known procedure called a "coronary endarterectomy".

This technique, little used by most surgeons because it requires enormous skill and is very time-consuming, takes the word "inoperable" out of Dr. Johnson's vocabulary. In this procedure, surgeons actually slit an existing artery, scrape out the cholesterol and then reconstruct it using a vein. Doing just one endarterectomy may take as long as two to three hours.

"If these doctors are this meticulous, then this is where I want to be in case I need a second by-pass operation," I told my wife. Forget Houston and Phoenix, Milwaukee was No. 1 on my list.

Five years after first hearing about this "wonder team" and 15 years after my first by-pass operation, I was entering St. Mary's Hospital, located on the shores of Lake Michigan. My cardiologist in Amarillo, Dr. Pedro Hernandez, had determined from a catherization that I was in bad shape. Tightness across my back had restricted my exercise regimen for a couple years, and I knew this day was forthcoming. It was just a matter of when.

From the time the smiling Carolyn greeted us in Admitting, I knew we had made the right decision. We arrived at the hospital about noon after the morning flight from Amarillo. Tests of all kinds were executed smoothly after the paperwork. By 5 p.m. I was in my room and Dr. Saed Saedi was at my bedside.

"I will be your surgeon and we will get in there first thing tomorrow morning," said the olive-skinned man with a thick Middle-Eastern accent. From the time I had called Milwaukee for an operation schedule, I knew Dr. Saedi would be my head surgeon, not Dr. Johnson. Members of the three-doctor team work closely together and to get Dr. Johnson as the lead-man would have meant another two months of waiting. I didn't have the time.

Besides, research had told me that Dr. Johnson personally trains his associates, and often assists in their operations. I felt completely at ease as Dr. Saedi spent 10 minutes reviewing the procedure and fielding my questions. Business-like but still extremely personable. Of course, knowing I had fellow Christian prayer-warriors remembering me back in Texas lessened my apprehension.

An evening meal consisted of small portions of fish, carrots, potatoes, skim milk and an orange. After watching a 20-minute pre-op film, Floy and I walked around the cardiac wing. We found a pleasant surprise. Nurses had told us "another man from your city is in the hospital," and sure enough, when we looked in a room at the end of the hall, there were Art and Dottie Khoury. A long-time importer of oriental rugs in the Texas Panhandle, Art had just undergone his third by-pass operation, his first in Milwaukee.

A sleeping pill ensured a good night's rest, eventually quieting the antics of a disturbed roommate who kept trying to get dressed and leave the hospital. I think they had Sam on the wrong floor, he should have been in the psychiatric pavilion.

It was Tuesday morning, June 30, and the day started with a shower scrubdown with a special cleansing liquid at 5:30. Then came the anesthesiologist at 6 for a short chat, followed by my wife. Floy was staying at the Astor Hotel, a quaint little place decorated with antiques only a few minutes from the hospital. St. Mary's has a special arrangement to shuttle spouses to and from the hotel, another nice touch that makes hospital visits more palatable for relatives.

I was wheeled into the pre-operation area at 7, where the anesthetic was started. Right at 8 the operation began, where four by-passes and one endarterectomy were negotiated in six hours. I was in recovery for about an hour and then wheeled into ICU. My life had been put on hold a second time thanks to a heart-lung machine, and now the process of reactivating my life-sustaining organs was underway.

Wednesday, the day after surgery, was not a good day. Undoubtedly, the worst. My first remembrances were the words of Floy.

"You're doing great, you're doing just great," she exclaimed in a manner that was convincing. And then came the scolding from a nurse to not bite so hard on that blooming tube in my mouth. That tube, and about a hundred other attachments, stayed with me for that first walk down the hall 24 hours after surgery. In fact, the tubes, wires and monitoring apparatus didn't start coming off until they moved me into a regular room, number 562, the next day. The calls from friends and loved ones were music to my ears, and I now knew that I was over the hump.

Hallelujah and thank you, God!

I had dodged another bullet, and I knew I had been under the care of the very best cardiac medical team in the world with the finest technology and facilities. What a great feeling!

The first meal Thursday was soft diet stuff, but real food was brought in Friday. Roast beef, boiled potatoes, broccoli and a pudding of unknown origin. It was the third of July and that night, the sounds of SummerFest could be heard from the shores of Lake Michigan not far away. My room overlooked the big body of water, but I was in no condition to enjoy it. On the other hand, Floy and other spouses of heart patients were treated to a birdseye view of the fireworks extravaganza from the rooftop of the Astor Hotel. Snacks and beverages were provided, making for still another nice public relations move.

Saturday, the Fourth of July, was a wonderful day. The last monitoring apparatus was taken away, and I felt like leaping out of bed and singing a couple verses of "Yankee Doodle Dandy". My doctors and nurses were assuring me "it was a picture perfect operation" and healing was ahead of schedule. Like no other hospital I've been in, St. Mary's trains nurses to make you feel special, like you're the only patient in the cardiac wing. Individualized attention, it's called.

Then we received another bonus. Later that day, a hospital nutritionist appeared in our room. She sat down and visited for maybe 30 minutes, leaving behind a specially-prepared cookbook for healthy eating. Four years later, Floy still uses a wonderful safflower oil salad dressing straight out of the book. On weekdays, patients and spouses are invited to nutrition classes in a nearby conference room, and long after returning home, I received follow-up questionnaires so the surgical team could keep track of my progress. Few medical people are that thorough.

On Sunday morning, I told Dr. Kenneth Bortin, my Milwaukee cardiologist, that I thought I could sleep better in my bed back in Texas. He smiled and said he would check with the other doctors.

"Hospitals are for sick people," he said in an afternoon visit, "and we've decided to send you back to Texas. We normally keep out-of-state patients around for two weeks, but you're way ahead of most of them. Get those bags packed."

Monday morning at 7:30 Dr. Bortin gave me a token stress test and we were in a cab on our way to the airport by 10. We were boarding a plane back to Amarillo exactly one week after arriving in Milwaukee and only six days after the second by-pass operation. Whew!

The trip home was uneventful, except for a cute episode involving food. After changing planes in Chicago, we were served a small turkey and cheese half-sandwich, a bag of potato chips and a chocolate chip cookie. While the hospital food was first-class, I couldn't wait to get something different in my mouth. Something with a little salt and grease. I must have inhaled that tiny sandwich in two or three bites.

Across the aisle from me sat a young boy who didn't touch his main course but ate the chocolate chip cookie. After eyeing his uneaten delicacy for a few moments, I leaned over and whispered:

"Son, are you going to eat your sandwich? And if not, I'll trade you my cookie for it."

A bit startled, he replied, "Oh no, no you can have it. And I don't really want another cookie."

A chapter related to health wouldn't be complete without commentary about a remarkable man, Dr. Jay Wooten, my dentist since 1954. Without a history of heart disease in my family, I'm convinced my problems have stemmed from self-imposed stress. Specialists put that ingredient near the top of contributing causes of heart-related problems.

Well, Jay Wooten addressed that factor early in life. Ever since I've been going down the highway 15 miles to see the Canyon, Texas, dentist, he has maintained a commitment to an unusual regimen. Knowing full well the life of a dentist is filled with stress, Jay shows up at his office three weeks of every month and goes fishing the fourth. Something a lot of people would like to do, but few have the guts to actually put into practice.

In the early days, his biggest problem was finding buddies who could take off a week at a time. Sometimes, he and his friends would stay close to home; other times he would explore the wiles of Canada or the best fishing holes of Mexico. Occasionally, when the fishing expeditions don't materialize, he'll just stick around the house all week.

Always ready with a good story or joke that keeps him and his patients cackling, he relates one adventure that didn't end on a happy note. On a jaunt to Mexico, Jay loaded up his $28,000 motor home with food and friends and headed south of the border.

"We paid a Mexican boy to watch the vehicle while we fished," remembers Jay. "But after having been there two days, some bandidos came down out of the mountains, strong-armed our guard, hot-wired the RV and drove off with it."

The robbery was reported to Mexican police, who only shook their heads in consolation. They explained that these were "very mean bandidos" and to go after them would be extremely risky. About par for the course in Mexico. Jay never saw that RV again, and hometown friends had to make the long drive to Mexico to retrieve the red-faced dentist, his buddies and their boat-trailer.

While Jay might be suspect in his choice of fishing spots, he has my vote for the person who best knows how to manipulate his time and keep stress to a minimum.

40

MOSCOW, ONE MORE TIME

Moscow, Russia, in the dead of winter on my 40th wedding anniversary. With my wife and 25 attractive college girls. No way.

That was exactly the situation I found myself in as the world was saying goodbye to 1992 and hello to 1993. It was only nine months after accompanying Western Maryland's football team to a country whose political and economic climate was changing faster that the weather in West Texas.

Actually, it was a combined business-pleasure trip, a win-win situation for everyone. My wife got her first look at a land draped in intrigue and mystery and I had the opportunity to cover the first appearance of an American high-kick college dance team in the former Soviet Union.

A casual phone conversation with John Ralston, the former Stanford and Denver Bronco football coach, during the summer of '92 triggered the whole thing. John, who tutored the Russian all-star team against Western Maryland and one of the nicest guys in the whole world, said he had been in contact with the International Sports Connection people in Alabama.

"I believe they're lining up a Russian trip for a junior college dance team down in Texas," he related. "You might want to check it out."

That comment perked up my ears and a quick call to Deborah Dunston, ISC's president, confirmed John's thoughts. "We'd love to have you along to cover Trinity Valley's experience," said the gracious Mrs. Dunston. "It's our treat."

Equally excited, the National Junior College Association wanted coverage for its monthly magazine, the Juco Review. "We'll use everything you send us," offered Executive Director George Killian, a long-time friend I first met at the World University Games in Moscow in 1973.

But why chapters on three separate trips to the same country in this book? A valid question. In my opinion, few cultures would warrant this much

Red Square will never be the same after a visit from the Cardettes of Texas.

attention, but Russia is an exception. A major player on the world stage for centuries, it is a land that has always fascinated me and been important to the United States. Sometimes as an ally, and often as a foe. And just maybe those action-packed James Bond movies have contributed heavily to the mystique that is Russia.

Each trip has afforded a different look and hopefully, a different story. When I was first there in 1973, the ruthless communists were in solid control and involved in a white-hot cold war with the U.S. The peaceful revolution had been in place only six months on the second journey in early 1992, and we were to witness changes of another kind less than a year later. Besides, this trip was allowing me to see Russia in the wintertime, a season I thoroughly enjoy and most closely associate with the world's largest producer of fur hats and fur coats.

It didn't take long to find out the Russians were experiencing an unusually bad winter. Leaving Athens, Texas, a stone's throw from Dallas, three days after Christmas, the Lone Star contingent arrived in Moscow in the middle of a snowstorm. Shades of "Dr. Zhivago".

"We're 20,000 feet over the heart of Moscow but we can't land yet," advised the Delta Airlines pilot on the intercom. "The airport's closed so the snow can be scraped from the runways. When this is accomplished, we'll be able to land in about 25 minutes."

Vladimir Gomelski, the sports announcer I got to know on the previous trip, and his pretty wife, Larissa, decked out in her ever-present, full-length black fox fur coat, were there to meet us. While tour director Kent Dunston, the 25 Cardette dancers and a support group of 17 rode the bus, Vladimir and Larissa drove Floy and myself to our hotel in their Russian-made Volga sedan.

"How's old Boris doing these days?" I asked, referring to Russia's new president, Boris Yeltsin.

"Times are worsening," Vladimir shook his head, substantiating what most of the world was seeing on newscasts every night. "Our people are experiencing a difficult time just having enough to eat with our new economy," he added, referring to Boris Yeltsin's plan to scrap the communistic system and invoke capitalistic ideas. It didn't get any better during the hour-long drive to Ismailovo Hotel, hearing that the ruble had inflated from 85-1 to 440-1 with the U.S. dollar in just nine months.

Despite the bitter, cold weather and fresh blanket of new snow, the Cardettes hit the ground running in their flashy red and black warm-ups. You can imagine the attention they evoked when I lined up 16 of these attractive, fresh-faced college girls on Red Square for a picture in front of majestic St. Basil's Cathedral. Surely, the ghost of Ivan the Terrible managed a grin and old Vladimir Lenin must have blinked once or twice from his mausoleum only a short distance away.

Even though they were experiencing tumultuous economical and political times, the Russians were flashing signs of the holiday season with gaily-decorated banners. While Christmas is celebrated January 7 in the former Soviet Union, we were told that the street signs heralded the New Year in that crazy-looking Cyrillic alphabet. Santa Claus is an unknown here, but a similar character dressed in red and known as "Father Frost" thrills the Muscovite youngsters. Even employees threw some red paper bells and tinsel rope on a scraggly evergreen tree in front of our hotel.

Good thing it was Christmas season. Director Jean Baker and the Cardettes had to settle for a performance at a children's holiday party in a basketball gymnasium. Originally, the Cardettes, who previously have danced in France, Switzerland, the Bahamas and in most high-profile American parades, were scheduled to be featured at the Granatkin Memorial Soccer Tournament in Moscow. But as with many plans in Russia these days, the tourney was cancelled at the last minute, thanks to a worsening economy that spurred cuts in sports budgets.

Embarrassed Russian promoters and Kent Dunston of ISC put their heads together and came up with the alternative plan. Decked out in white boots, short skirts and red cowgirl hats, the Cardettes wowed hundreds of children and parents with a flawless, singing-dancing, 15-minute routine that closed with the strains of "Deep in The Heart of Texas."

"At least we performed in a gymnasium," remarked one of the girls, who normally dance at basketball and football games back in Texas. Regardless of the occasion, the Russians loved it. One Muscovite mother approached me and wanted to know where else they would be appearing on the trip. She wanted to see more. Also performing in the show, members of the famous Moscow Circus troupe were extremely complimentary as they watched from backstage. So much so the boys tried to secure phone numbers.

But that was par for the course. Decked out in thermal underwear, heavy coats, mittens and ear muffs, the bevy of smiling beauties stopped traffic wherever they went. Be it Red Square, the Moscow Circus or McDonald's, they were closely scrutinized by the local gentry, normally a collection of drably-dressed, solemn-faced people.

Oh sure, this trip had its similarities to the one with the football team less than a year ago. After all, how many sight-seeing attractions are there in a

A long way from home over the holidays, the Cardettes find a scrawny evergreen tree decorated with paper items in front of our hotel.

Father Frost, Russia's answer to Santa Claus, wouldn't allow me to take his picture. He normally charges a fee and uses his own photographer. (Lower right), wearing her silver fox fur hat, Floy doesn't appear pleased with the Russian menu. That's Director Jean Baker at the table.

bankrupt country that's 50 years behind the rest of the world? But one event made it different, I mean really distinguishable.

An evening at the world-famous Bolshoi Ballet was a dream come true for a dance troupe from America. Not huge fans of ballet (the Nutcracker is our speed), Floy and I nevertheless could hardly wait until Sunday evening when our group donned our finest threads and headed for downtown Moscow. After a three-block walk from our hotel, we descended two long flights of stairs and boarded the city's celebrated subway.

As we neared the storied 207-year-old Bolshoi Theater, we felt a special treat was awaiting. Nine huge Georgian-style white columns in front give the building a distinguished appearance. Then, as we stepped inside we were overwhelmed by rich marble, deep red velvet and glistening crystal chandeliers. Wow, what a thrill.

As we headed toward our seats to see the classic, "Giselle", I imagined how many dignitaries from all over the world had walked this same path. Political leaders, movie stars, business magnates. Our box seats were quite good, in the second balcony with a head-on view of the stage.

It was a cold evening, as were all of them on this adventure, and Floy and I carried our topcoats to our seats. Well, almost. As we pulled back a red velvet curtain to enter our box, a huge hand resembling a meat hook came from out of the blue and clutched Floy's red wool coat with authority.

"Nyet, nyet!" warned a burly, stern-faced Russian woman who could play fullback for the Dallas Cowboys. She pointed a finger at us and started tugging at Floy's wrap.

"What's going on here?" exclaimed a surprised Floy, digging in with both feet and trying to retain possession of the coat.

Now picture this. Here we are in the setting of one of the most elegant and most distinguished theaters of the world, one that has spawned Mikhail Baryshnikov, Rudolf Nureyev and many other greats of ballet, and two women who can't understand each other are playing tug of war. Then, we realized what was happening. Apparently, protocol at the Bolshoi calls for checking all coats once you enter the building. We had upset tradition in a big way, and the elderly Russian woman was in a position to demonstrate authority for maybe the only time in her life. We relented, and went with the flow.

Our group departed Moscow three days before Christmas (remember, it's celebrated January 7 in that part of the world), but we were there for New Year's Eve. The party in our hotel's grand ballroom started with dinner. Then came a number of variety acts, including a routine by a trademark Cossack dance group. This too was a special treat for a fellow dance team from Texas.

The evening was a time for the beleaguered Russians to forget their myriad of problems and look hopefully to the future. They mixed and danced with the college girls from America and other foreign visitors as language and cultural differences seemed not to matter. Of course, the Russian, French and Italian women were no match for the Cardettes, flashing their best cutesy, southern belle personalities.

"The face of Moscow is changing almost daily," observed Kent Dunston, our leader with International Sports Connection and a regular visitor to the former Soviet Union. In just nine months, I noticed a decided difference on Red Square. Non-existent in my two previous visits, beggars were everywhere. Russians are proud people, and we learned that most of those involved in panhandling were part of an organized racket.

As we started to board our bus and leave Red Square, a woman carrying a small child draped in a light blanket approached us with her hand out. She pointed to the young boy and grunted something, implying he was ill and needed medicine. Floy and I were both touched but our Russian interpreter waved them off.

"Don't be fooled by these people," she said. "These gypsies work the streets of Moscow and are part of the Russian Mafia. It is one big scam." Further indication of mob infiltration, numerous "Casino" signs could be spotted flashing in gaudy neon against a backdrop of nothingness. Yes, since the fall of communism, open gambling, along with prostitution and street crime, has proliferated on the Moscow scene.

Another drastic contrast on this trip was the quality of food. Whether worsening times had anything to do with it or merely the change in hotels, it was bad stuff.

Cardette director Baker, a stern taskmaster with the discipline of a drill sergeant, required her girls to show up at the dining room for every meal. Few ate more than a couple bites; most of them just stirred the fare around and faked ingestion.

Try as they did, adjusting to foreign food was perhaps the toughest part of the collegians' overseas adventure. They had never encountered green peas, cole slaw and smoked fish for breakfast back in Texas. And if the food wasn't eaten at one meal, it would usually show up again the next day. Fortunately, before leaving America, the girls had packed an adequate supply of peanut butter, salsa and corn chips.

A journey such as this wouldn't be complete without adequate time for shopping, especially when the group is composed almost entirely of women. And while the food at Izmailovo Hotel was horrendous, there was one advantage to staying at this property on the outskirts of the city. The famous Izmailovo weekend flea market was only a 10-minute walk down the street. We had heard bizarre stories of Russians bringing valuable family heirlooms to this market, just trying to stave off the ravages of poverty.

Despite sub-freezing temperatures and intermittent wet snow in an early January setting, dealers started setting up shortly after dawn on Saturday. By mid-morning, there must have been 300 capitalistic entrepreneurs ready for business. Floy and I had prepared for this moment, being the consummate junkers back home. We awakened early, got into our thermal underwear and heavy clothing, then headed down the snow-packed road to the market.

Drooling at the prospect of finding priceless treasures, I especially was on the lookout for antique clocks. A collector since 1979, I have never seen more than two or three Russian clocks in my life. The first day was a disappointment. Yes, there were fur hats, matroyshka dolls, table cloths, painted eggs, flags and a few incidental antiques. But no clocks. Floy, who is a real trouper when it comes to shopping but barely able to withstand the bitter cold, bought a beautiful rag doll from the Russian woman who made it. I purchased five rabbit fur hats for friends back home.

"I've never been so cold in my life," muttered Floy after traipsing up and down the rows of frozen tundra in a light snowstorm for half a day. It was a real test of our loyalty to a hobby we both have enjoyed for years. We even considered skipping the scene the next day although we had visited less than half of the booths.

But we didn't. After a good night's rest and locating some hand warmers, we returned to the scene of the crime with fresh enthusiasm. It was not any more productive until we were about ready to leave the snow-packed premises, and call it quits.

"This looks interesting," alerted Floy, pointing to an old alarm clock nestled among a number of tools on a crude wooden table. On closer inspection, I found it to be a German Gustav Becker nickel-plated alarm with bell on top. The Gustav Becker name is found on quality grandfather and wall clocks, but I had never seen its label on an alarm. I bought it for 10 U.S. dollars, having absolutely no idea of its true value. I still don't.

It wasn't what I had come all the way to Russia for but only a few tables down the row I spotted an interesting-looking wall clock propped up against the leg of a card table. Specks of snow rested on top, giving it a frosted look.

Near Red Square we found beggars posing as gypsies with sick children. See woman carrying young child in right of picture. We were told they were aligned with the Mafia. (Right) Cardettes ready to enter the 30-foot high Kremlin walls. (Lower left) I found a Russian clock at a weekend flea market.

"What kind of clock?" I asked the bearded, fur-hatted gentleman who was trying to keep warm shifting from one foot to the other.

"Russian", he said.

"Old or new?" I asked.

"About 50 or 60 years old," he answered in remarkably good English. It was Art Deco, about the 30s or 40s. A "plain Jane" in style, the light tan veneer wall clock had a clean brass pendulum and beveled glass at the bottom. Even the original key was there. The name of the Russian manufacturer appeared just below the keyhole and I later found out it translates to "Yantar" in English. The word means "amber" in Russian.

Next to the clock resting on the packed snow was a crude cardboard sign with the price scribbled in pencil: "2,000 Rubles."

"I'll take it," I said, counting out 20 100-ruble denominations. The Russian seemed pleased with his sale, and I had another unique clock for my collection. I was surprised no one had snapped it up earlier.

"How much is that in American dollars?" asked my wife as we headed back to the hotel. I really didn't know at first. But after putting a pencil to the numbers and figuring a ratio of 450 rubles to one dollar (the exchange rate on that day), it came to $4.44. I was not trying to take advantage of the Russian man; just paying the price he was asking.

Actually, these two clocks were the second and third Russian time-pieces I had in my collection. On the trip nine months earlier to Moscow with Western Maryland's football team, I had found a beauty, the most valuable of the three. Here's how it happened.

I was strolling along Arbat Street, Moscow's downtown flea market with Americans Mike and Toni May, when I spotted a sign that was easy to read in any language. "Antiquities" loomed brightly against a gray sky and had an arrow pointing to a building off the beaten path, half a block away.

We hurried up the brick-paved street and found the antique shop. When we entered, we discovered American capitalism practices had already preceded us. The store was a mini antique mall; five rooms, five different Russian dealers. And this only six months after the fall of communism.

I saw little that interested me until we reached the last room.

"Look," exclaimed Toni, grabbing my arm and pointing to a wall clock just inside the left entry. Standing out like St. Basil's Cathedral against a pale blue sky on Red Square, this honey-oak beauty had a curved top and bottom, beveled leaded glass and just enough carving to make it distinctive. As I got nearer, I noticed it had an over-sized 10-inch silver dial with the name of the

Russian maker on a separate metal panel just below 12 o'clock.

It appeared in the strange Russian Cyrillic alphabet, and I found out later it translates to "Pavel Burye." The store owner, a bearded man in his mid-50s, told me Burye was a well-known 19th century Russian clock-maker. But my eyes were attracted to a symbol between the man's first and last names, and therein lies an interesting story. It was an etching of a two-headed eagle, with frills, and represents the imperial czarist seal of the ruler in power at the time the clock was manufactured. Much like the royal seal in Great Britain.

The spring-wound movement, made by a German company that once had a factory in Russia, dates it to about 1870. That would put it in the reign of Alexander III, father of the last Russian czar, Nicholas II, who was overthrown in the 1917 Revolution. Documentation is important to clock collectors the world over.

There was little haggling over price since I knew it was an exceptional piece and the dealer liked the looks of American currency. Because it is forbidden to accept foreign currency in the former Soviet Union, except in hard-currency stores, he looked around and locked his door before completing the transaction.

Because this clock was a legitimate antique (anything at least 100 years old), getting it out of Russia posed some problems. Religious icons are on the forbidden list and other antiques can be removed, but only after mounds of paperwork are negotiated. And if you get the right customs agent.

In this case, I was living right. After submitting my receipt of purchase and declaring the clock on my customs slip, the Russian agent hesitated only a moment and then waved me on. Being with a large group and having our Russian friend, Vladimir, nearby didn't hurt anything.

At the metal detector stand, however, it was a different story. When the movement, packed in a separate carry-on bag, went through x-ray, it got the attention of a number of Russian inspectors. It was more like a fireworks display on the Fourth of July. They relegated me to the sidelines and meticulously checked every part of the metal works. Then, after determining it wasn't some kind of strange bomb, they waved me through.

Just when I thought I was home free, I faced still another obstacle. Starting to board our Air France plane that would take us from Moscow to Paris, I was stopped by a male steward with a cute little mustache.

"I'm sorry," he put up his hand, "but you can't bring that big package on the plane," referring to the clock case which was carefully wrapped in brown butcher paper and twine. "We have a full flight and the big carry-onitems will have to be checked with the luggage."

My heart sputtered for a moment. "But," I pleaded, "this is a valuable antique wood and glass clock and it will be in a hundred pieces if it's checked with the luggage." I wasn't about to let go of my prize, and the uniformed Frenchman must have sensed it.

"Well," he relented, "you'll have to keep it in the rack above you." Which is what I had in mind all the time. The movement, safely ensconced in my small carry-on bag, was placed on the floor under the seat in front of me. Safely in my sight.

It was a piece of cake rest of the way, even though we changed planes in Paris, Washington and Dallas before arriving in Amarillo, Texas, 20 hours later.

The fancy-carved oak clock now hangs in the eating area of our kitchen, and serves as a daily reminder of my experiences in the former Soviet Union. However, it's the plain, blonde veneer timepiece, the one I discovered in the snow at the flea market and is now at home in our reading room, that best reflects what Russia has been about for hundreds of years. It's simplicity reminds me of Vladimir, Larissa, Svetlana and Natasha, new Russian friends who have lived humbly under communistic oppression since birth but now have a glimmer of hope for freedom and a better way of life.

41

RETIREMENT, ROY AND NEWT

When an old football coach retired, a friend asked his wife what she thought about it. She frowned and said:

"Now I have twice as much husband and half as much income."

That could be the story of my retirement. I started thinking about it in the early 90s, especially after our children made comments like:

"Dad, the stress of publishing the Directories seems to be getting to you. Why don't you consider retiring and just take it easy?"

When none of our three children showed any interest in taking over the publishing business, we were inundated with inquiries from potential buyers. They came from friends, friends of friends and complete strangers from all walks of life.

After screening about a dozen legitimate prospects, we sold the two editions of the National Directory of College Athletics to a bright young investor from Cleveland, Ohio.

Jim Skoch had made it big in recycled aluminum, but he brought with him Kevin Cleary, an enthusiastic young man with varied experience in sports. With the addition of Kevin, the son of NACDA Executive Director Mike Cleary, the new ownership would retain close ties with the college athletic directors group. That was important in our final decision, making the transition with as few disruptions as possible.

We retained control of the name, "Publishing Ranch", kept the building and still continue marketing other publications already in print. However, the Directories constituted about 99% of the company's revenue and work load. The extra time we now enjoy finds my wife and I zipping around the country, ferreting out antiques and spending more time with the children, grandchildren and great grandchildren. Most certainly, the pace hasn't been any slower.

Take for example the fall of 1994. In the span of three weeks, I met two of my all-time heroes—Roy Rogers and Newt Gingrich. As different as two people can be, both are great Americans who have contributed mightily to their country.

On several occasions, my wife and I had passed by the Roy Rogers and Dale Evans Museum in Victorville, California, while traveling I-40 to the West Coast. Not until mid-October of '94 did we feel we had adequate time to stop and explore the premises. Once we had made the decision to visit, I could hardly wait to learn more about the King of the Cowboys and the Queen of the West, two people who entertained and inspired so many on the movie screen.

We were in the gift shop purchasing their new book, Happy Trails, when a woman tapped me on the shoulder and exclaimed excitedly:

"He's here, he just came in."

I turned around and there in the lobby bigger than life was Roy Rogers, dressed in a black cowboy outfit, white hat and cowboy boots. My heart started pounding. From a distance, he looked just like he did 50 years ago on the big movie screen despite the fact he was only three weeks away from being 83 years old. He looked great.

"I come here almost every morning to meet my friends and fans," said Roy, who still radiates the energy and enthusiasm of an All-American boy. Sipping on a cup of coffee, the man who was born Leonard Slye in Duck Run, Ohio, admitted he wasn't feeling good on this particular Friday morning.

"I wish I had the energy I once had; I get tired just walking around the house any more."

Even with his boots on, Roy appeared to be no taller than 5-9, my height, and was far trimmer. "I can still wear some of those fancy custom outfits Nudie Cohn made for me at Republic," he grinned, patting his flat stomach at the same time. When Roy grins, his eyes almost disappear, a characteristic that almost kept him out of the movies.

Standing in the middle of the Museum lobby with eight tourists around him, the cowboy legend revealed a little about what it was like in those early days. "After coming out here from Ohio looking for a better life, I soon found a spot with a Western band," he told us. "We played for nothing in the beginning and were starving to death. I mean it was tough in the 30s."

After landing a job with the Sons of the Pioneers, he was then summoned

I call this my "Roy and Floy" picture. We met the legendary cowboy star at his museum in California.

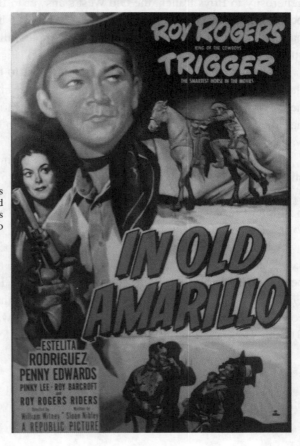

One of the many B westerns he made was called "In Old Amarillo". He said he was hospitalized in Amarillo during World War II.

to do a screen test when Republic Studios was looking for a leading singing cowboy.

"They didn't like me at first," he smiled. "They said my eyes were too squinty for a leading man. I got those from my dad."

After overcoming that handicap, Roy signed with Republic in 1937 and made 88 full-length movies with Trigger. When television came along, he and his golden palomino turned out another 104 episodes.

"You from Amarillo?" echoed the durable legend, after asking the members of the small group about their hometowns.

"I was in the hospital once in Amarillo," he recalled. "It was during World War II and I believe Amarillo Air Base was our last stop on the USO tour. I had a bad cold when I got there and it then developed into a bad case of the flu. They were afraid it might turn into pneumonia, and I spent two days out there in the hospital."

Roy and Dale are best remembered in the Texas Panhandle for their generosity to Boys Ranch, the Old West's answer to Boys Town. On several occasions, they gave cowboy boots to every boy at Christmas time, and once paid all expenses to take them out West to Apple Valley by train for a really special yuletide season.

"Where's Dale today?" asked the woman next to me. "Oh, she's over at the house writing a book or composing a song," he related. "She comes over here every once in a while. You know she had a heart attack a year ago, and has to take it easy." Then he revealed the two of them live in a house in Apple Valley, about 25 miles south of Victorville.

"We still have a ranch over there, but I sold all my horses. Of course, I still have my favorite right here in the museum. I go in and see Ol' Trigger every time I come out here. After he died, we had him mounted in his favorite position of raring up on his hind-legs. Everybody who comes in here wants to see Trigger. He's our best attraction."

A tourist noticed an unusual solid gold ring shaped like a small Western saddle on Roy's finger. He said it was his favorite, a piece of jewelry he'd been wearing for years. "The guy who made all of Trigger's fancy saddles, Ed Bohlin, designed and made this ring," informed the world's most famous cowboy. "When I asked him the price, I thought it would be something like $1,500. Boy, was I surprised when he sold it to me for $150."

There was a slight pause in the conversation.

"My wife and I saw you and Dale on the Trinity Broadcasting Network the other night," I remarked. "We certainly appreciate your Christian witness."

Roy's eyes lit up and he said: "I believe that's the only reason I'm still around." He too has endured two open heart operations.

"What do you like to do when you're not over here?" asked another visitor.

"I put on my Reeboks, baseball cap and jeans, and hit the flea markets," he answered, revealing that he's about as American as apple pie despite all his success and honors.

He said he collects about everything, and puts a lot of it in the Victorville museum.

"When I'm over here and involved in public functions, I wear my cowboy clothes. I believe my fans expect if of me."

Because they represent genuineness and integrity at a time when our country seems to be sinking deeper and deeper into moral decay, Roy and Dale remain heroes to many Americans. "God has been good to us," said the pleasant and almost shy-like Roy. "He's given us nine children, 26 grandchildren and 28 great grandchildren. Some day, I'm going to get them all together and tell them what's causing all this." Then he winked.

After some 45 minutes of holding court with his eight fans in a relaxed atmosphere more like someone's living room, the King of the Cowboys kindly announced there would be "no autographs." He explained he quit that practice a few years ago because he was spending all his time writing and not being able to visit with people, which is one of his most favorite things in all the world.

But photographs, sure! I pulled out our Minolta instant camera and started snapping away. Two visitors were caught empty-handed and I agreed to take pictures of them with Roy, later mailing them copies. My favorite was of the famous cowboy hugging my wife. I had it enlarged to a 20x30 inch poster for our game room and call it our "Roy and Floy" picture.

After the photo session, Roy informed us "he needed to go to work." Staying in place, he made a 360-degree turn, winked and said: "Guess that's about it. Think I'll go home."

Newt Gingrich is no movie idol but he's very much a hero in my books.

In November of '94, only five days before the momentous election that gave Conservative America control of Congress for the first time in 40 years, the stocky Georgian came to Amarillo to help bolster the campaign of U.S. Representative candidate Mac Thornberry. The breakfast was scheduled at the last minute and the Franks had planned to be out of town.

"Newt Gingrich is coming to town," Mac's wife Sally told Floy on the phone, "and we'd like for you and Mr. Franks to sit at the head table with us." Thornberry's bubbly and enthusiastic mate explained they had been appreciative of my letter-writing support in the Amarillo newspaper and thought I would like to meet the fire-ball Congressman who had been serving the Republican party well in the House of Representatives.

"You bet I would," I told my wife and we delayed a trip to Dallas for this once-in-a-lifetime opportunity. Little did we know just how important Mr. Newt would become in American politics, in only a few days.

The 200 people had about finished their breakfast of scrambled eggs, bacon, hash browns and biscuits when the 50-year-old Georgian with the full shock of salt and pepper hair walked through the doorway. There are some people who instantly make heads turn when they enter a room. Newt Gingrich is one of those people.

After spending several minutes shaking hands of supporters on the floor, he approached the speaker's table where a plate of cold breakfast victuals awaited. Sporting a pleasant smile, he shook hands with the six at the head table, calling each by his or her first name. Then he took a seat two chairs to my right. Only Sally Thornberry separated us.

It was about time for him to be introduced and he only played with his food. I saw him take a couple bites of crisp bacon, and that was about it. He was a man on a mission, making a whirlwind tour in a last-minute effort to help conservative Republicans "take back America." I had hoped to enter into some small-talk before he walked up to the podium but time just didn't permit.

I consider Ronald Reagan and Charlton Heston great communicators, but Newt is in their class. The former college professor with a doctorate in history stood up and espoused a brilliant 30-minute speech without a teleprompter or a single note. It was all off the cuff and rapid-fire, as is his style. In April of '95 when he delivered his "Contract With America" victory speech on national television, I noticed his pace was a lot slower. No doubt advisers had suggested the change for television.

It was in his Amarillo speech that I first heard the famous quote about the problems of America. "You know your country is in trouble when 12-year-olds are having babies, 15-year-olds are shooting each other and 18-year-olds are getting diplomas they can't read," he said.

Another quote that struck a chord with me went like this:

"This great land must turn toward God; after all, that's where all our power emanates. Every one of our founding fathers believed in the Creator."

This was less than a week before the November 6 election, and I doubt that even Newt really thought conservatives would take control of the House, let alone the Senate. "If the people in this country who favor a balanced budget amendment, line-item veto, term limits and an effective death penalty will turn out and vote, we might see a stunning upset next week," he predicted. Little did he know his wildest expectation would be exceeded.

"I heard him say at a later date that he first thought Republicans might gain control of the House when he was visiting Amarillo," related Sally Thornberry at a picnic in '96. "He called his wife that night and told her of his good vibrations."

We were in his presence less than an hour, hardly enough time to form an intelligent opinion. But if I had to select one word to describe the dynamic Speaker of the House, it would be "confidence". I dearly enjoy watching him flick away liberal television reporters trying to stump him with hardball questions. They come off as mere gnats in the presence of an intellectual giant, Sam Donaldson included.

Floy and I had hoped to get a picture with Gingrich after his speech. Floy had the camera in her purse, but officials whisked him away to a nearby room for a brief press conference.

Then, like Superman, he disappeared in a cloud of dust, on his way to a luncheon in Dallas 400 miles away. Believe me, folks, this guy is no ordinary mortal. He truly *is* a super man.

After being involved in sports for 50 years as a writer, editor, publicist and publisher, I have formed some definite opinions on how the arena has changed.

Believe me, there have been many but here are a few that come to mind:

MOST DISGUSTING—The hot-dogging of individual players is a fairly new development that is totally out of place in team sports. It makes me sick at my stomach. I remember Billy "White Shoes" Johnson of the Houston Oilers as the first to showboat after scoring a touchdown. Of course, it wasn't long until the flaunting and taunting filtered on down to the college and high school levels. I remember when Doak Walker and Kyle Rote scored touchdowns and laid the ball down on the turf as if it were another day at the office. That was class.

MOST OPPOSED TO—There's a lot of talk today about paying college athletes to play athletics. I say they're getting paid already. It's called a "scholarship". There are strong feelings on both sides of this issue and who knows what's going to happen. "The original concept of college athletics will be lost if we go to that," said David Ward, U. of Wisconsin chancellor."At that point, college will be no more than a farm team for the pros."

MOST SURPRISING DEVELOPMENT—Whoever thought someone would bottle water and actually get people to buy it at sports events? It's no longer just a two-way war between Coke and Pepsi in the sports marketing business. These are strange and bizarre times.

Famous people often are asked what they would like inscribed on their headstone. I'm sure that's something I won't have to address, but if it did happen, here's what I would want. With an apology to Bob Hope, I would like for it to read:

"FRANKS FOR THE MEMORIES!"